Dear Larry
What a gift that our [illegible]
paths have crossed [illegible]
again. I am blessed [illegible] this journey [illegible] you. Enjoy the [illegible]
Esther

LOST AND FOUND

AN ADOPTEE'S ASTONISHING SEARCH FOR THE TRUTH

Esther M Shapiro

Lost and Found
An Adoptee's Astonishing Search for the Truth

ISBN 978-1-7339419-0-7

Disclaimers:

All trademarks mentioned in this book are the property of their respective owners.

Some names and identifying details have been changed to protect the privacy of certain individuals.

I have tried to recreate events, locales and conversations from my memories of them. Others recollections of events or conversations may differ.

CONTENTS

PART ONE

The Hard Stuff

It's September 1972, Long Beach, New York, a small island on the south shore of Long Island. The trees are turning gold, red, and yellow like magic before my eyes. I'm eight and a half now. I just began third grade, and I'm especially excited to attend East School because this is the year I will learn to play the recorder, my very first instrument, as well as enjoy the amazing super dome playground. There is a sense of excitement and wonder and anticipation in the air.

Little did I know that my world was about to explode. I missed the first week of school because my parents took me on a cruise to Bermuda. It was the first cruise any of us had been on, and it was time away specifically to help me heal from the loss of my favorite aunt, Sylvia (my father's sister in-law), who I was closest to out of all my relatives. Oddly enough, my aunt Sylvia shares my mom's first name.

My parents didn't tell me about my aunt's passing until the day after the funeral. I was heartbroken, as I would have wanted to go, even needed to. Mom said I was too young to understand. Dad generally went along with her to keep the peace. I didn't realize at the time that I understood death more than she did.

My mother had never seen a dead body; she was terrified of death. My mother was terrified of a lot of things, and her daughter (me) would be the person who showed her what fear of the truth and lying to another could result in. In her mind, on one hand, I was too young to understand some things, and on the other hand, I was expected to already be an adult.

One of my mother's favorite stories about me was from that cruise:

Each evening the captain would have a group of guests at the captain's table for dinner. On the fifth evening, my parents were invited to his table, but I was not, as children weren't allowed at the captain's table. Our dining room table was a small, square table that seated four, but it was always just the three of us. At that meal, my parents went to the captain's table without me. I sat at our usual table, alone, with people staring and whispering all around me. I felt lonely, uncomfortable, isolated, and abandoned. I occasionally looked over at my parents. My father would wave and send a smile over (he was never really far from me, but it certainly felt that way); my mother never glanced at me. Yet I sat there, ordering my dinner and eating alone. That dinner may have been an hour in length, but when you're eight, it's an eternity, and it felt horrible.

My mother loved the story because she was so proud of how mature I was, saying, "You were such a big girl!" She was proud, and I was heartbroken. This wasn't the first time in my life I'd felt completely isolated and alone, nor would it be my last.

I'm enjoying third grade right from the very start. Every day in homeroom, the teacher picks a topic that we discuss and study, and when I get home, my mother asks how my day was and what the topic of discussion was. Today is no different. I arrive home in the afternoon as usual. My mother is upstairs in her bed, nursing another of her all-too-frequent headaches. She asks her routine questions. On this particular day, my response is "The topic today was adoption. Mom, am I adopted?" I ask the question that likely every kid asked their parents that day. Her response wasn't what one would expect.

My mother immediately began to cry, loudly and dramatically. My father came rushing up the stairs and asked me loudly, "What did you do to your mother?" I felt immediate guilt and remorse on one level, but on another level, even at eight years old, I knew I'd done nothing wrong. I simply asked a question. That was the moment that my entire life changed.

I'm standing there for what feels like an eternity, waiting for some explanation of this wailing she is doing. It seems ridiculously dramatic to me, as a simple yes or no would suffice.

She calms down a bit and tells my father what the topic was at school. They look at each other, communicating with their eyes, what looks like terror in both of them, and they proceed to share with me that I am, in fact, adopted.

I instantly am feeling a whirlwind of emotions—happy, curious, afraid, confused, excited, wondering. My mother tells me the only reason she's telling me now is because she's afraid my great aunt Ida, the family yenta, will slip and tell me the truth, and they don't want it to come from her. We rarely see Aunt Ida, so this makes no sense to me at all. I know that's a lie. I don't know how I know, but I know.

Mom told me that "she" (my birth mother) never wanted to be found, that I came from a Jewish background, and that was all they really knew about my birth family. My father didn't speak. Mom did all the talking and told me that she wasn't able to get pregnant. They started to argue and blame each other for the situation as I sat there on the edge of their bed, listening, stunned, confused, and in disbelief.

In this moment, I couldn't have cared less why they couldn't have a child of their own. I want to know who I am, my heritage, where I come from, if I have sisters or brothers, and why they're lying to me and haven't said anything until now. I felt as if I've been swept up by a tidal wave. Mom said that one day in 1963 her doctor called her up, saying that someone wanted to give up a child. Adoption agencies rejected them because they were in their forties and married late, so when this opportunity arose, after five years on adoption agency lists, they jumped on it. That was all the information I got that day.

It was a very surreal yet exciting moment for me. I was thinking about how lucky I was. I wanted to shout out to the world that I was like Annie from the Broadway show, but that desire was immediately squashed when my mother told me I was never to tell anyone, for any reason no matter what.

I felt a heavy, dark cloud descend up on me, and I hung my head down, feeling defeated and suffocated by my own truth.

Over the next five years, my mom told me six other stories, each different, often with new details that didn't match up with the previous stories, and Dad continued his silence anytime the subject came up.

One version was that my birth father was a doctor, another he was a businessman, and in another, there was no known birth father. I was first told there were lawyers involved. Then it was just the doctor. When there was a father in the story, I was always told he was Jewish. I was told it was a secret, yet my mom's sister, my aunt Mary, knew, because I was told she was the one who had picked me up at the hospital.

It seemed very important to my mother that I be Caucasian and Jewish (they were Jewish) because she said she would not have adopted any other type of child. She said that "she," my birth mother, went into the hospital assuming her (my adopted mom's) name and that I came home when I was one day old and that it was my aunt Mary who had picked me up at the hospital and brought me home.

The two parts of the story that remained consistent were that my birth mother assumed my adopted mother's name when she went into the hospital and that the father was Jewish, so she said I was Jewish. This only added to my confusion because I had been taught that it was the mother's lineage that determined if a child was Jewish, not the father. But for some reason, my case was "different," so she said.

None of this sat well with me, as I had no idea what was true or what was false. Like all children, we see our parents as God. We're to trust them as a source of unconditional love, honestly, guidance and wisdom. Yet when she shared anything, my stomach automatically turned, I could feel my blood rush to my head, and I wanted to scream with frustration. I just knew something wasn't right. By the time I was thirteen, I stopped believing anything she said. My father remained silent about the subject, and I had grown a very large mistrust for my mother. I finally stopped asking questions, even though my hunger for the truth was insatiable.

My father was truly my saving grace as a child. Those who knew my dad would tell you he was funny, generous, and would do whatever he could to make a woman smile. If he saw a woman, whether in infant diapers, adult diapers, or anything in between, his job was to make her feel good about herself. It was his mastery, and he did it well. The friends of mine he got to know loved and adored him. My adopted family called him Crazy Lary, because he was a bit crazy, quirkier really, but in a good and kind way. It was even part of why he only used one *R* in his name—he enjoyed being different. He never really hurt anyone unless he felt hurt first, but he sure could make you a bit crazy along with him.

Dad drove a taxi in Manhattan when I was a child, and at times in Long Beach, where we lived. He quit doing that when I was five when he purchased a small distribution route for Coca-Cola. He did very well and grew the route quickly, getting major locations in Manhattan. The business left him more time to be home in the evenings and weekends, and I felt much more safe and protected with him being around.

As long as I could remember, I had been terrified of my mother, even as an infant, toddler, and young child. I never felt safe with her. She often had a frightening look in her eyes. She would manhandle me when she took care of my physical needs, for example, pulling the knots in my hair with a brush and not gripping my hair, pulling my head in different directions to the point of tears. When she braided my hair, it also caused tears. She pulled my hair so tight that I had headaches all day. She called me weak or a baby if I complained in any way, so I just shut up and suffered through it. I remember her embrace being stiff and cold when and if she held me. She simply wasn't a warm person.

Aside from the adoption issue, my elementary school years were fairly average, I would say. I loved school because it got me away from my mother. I was happy to go to Hebrew school as well. Though I didn't know at that point about being adopted, in my heart, I somehow knew I wasn't Jewish. I spent as little time with her as possible, and I clung to my father as much as I could. Even though he wouldn't speak of the adoption, he also wasn't being cruel by lying to me with different stories and making things worse that way.

I started my period in the summer of 1976 when I was twelve and a half years old. I had no idea what was happening when I found blood on the back of my panties. I thought I was sick, or dying, but certain something was very wrong. I was scared. When I ran downstairs to tell my mom, she once again immediately started wailing, covered her face with her hands, and said, "Oh, my baby is not a baby anymore." What the heck did that mean? I was bleeding!

This was my introduction to the dreaded sex conversation, which she didn't explain very well at all and I wouldn't understand why until decades later. She had me use these monster-sized pads with an elastic belt and clips to hold it up that she had gotten from the hospital when she'd had her hysterectomy seven years prior. It was horrid trying to do anything with those things on, so my dad finally manned up and went to the store and bought me tampons.

I immediately took myself to the library and read everything I could about menstruating and reproduction, very little of it lining up with what my mother had told me. Growing up simply wasn't easy for me.

Thirteen was a powerful age for me in some ways. I was a bat mitzvah (Jewish coming of age ritual for girls), which was actually a wonderful experience for me. I had been in Hebrew school since I'd been five years old. I loved singing in Hebrew and often led the teen Shabbat services. The cantor and teachers were so loving and overall fun to be with. My parents never came to see me lead the services, not once, which always disappointed me, as I was raised being told that I had to marry Jewish, be Jewish, and follow all the traditions, none of which they observed, except when other family was involved. They themselves never went to Shabbat services or did any traditions at home. It was very much "do as we say, not as we do" in my home. But the bat mitzvah was a day of joy for us all. I sang my haftorah perfectly, and the celebration after was tremendous fun.

But there was one particular occurrence in my thirteenth year that awakened me to something I didn't understand for many years. On a frequent basis, I took the public bus to Oceanside or to Roosevelt Field and shopped with friends—typical young teenagers. I will only briefly mention that I still don't understand how my parents allowed a thirteen-year-old to travel alone like that or to have a 1:00 a.m. curfew, letting me ride my bike home alone at that hour. But as a teenager, I appreciated the freedom because it allowed me to be out of the house and away from my mother, a lot. But on this one particular day, I experienced something magical that would stay with me forever:

> *I'm on the bus headed to Roosevelt Field. I'm alone on this particular day. It's a sunny, dry, and beautiful warm summer day in 1977. The ride out of Long Beach and through Island Park are uneventful. As the bus approaches my usual stop in Oceanside, where I'm not planning to get off today, I look out the window from the back-row seat of the bus that's on the right side of the bus, or the same side of the doors, and I see my aunt Sylvia standing at the bus stop. She is wearing her light-brown raincoat, and she has a closed umbrella in her hand with the tip on the ground like a cane. Her beautiful blond hair is shimmering in the light as she just stands there gazing forward.*

The bus slowly drifts by her, headed toward a red light. I stand up, start frantically pulling the string to stop the bus, but it keeps moving. I don't take my eyes off of my aunt as I stand in disbelief, not just that she's wearing rain gear on a gorgeous day, but that she's there at all! It's been five years since she passed away when my parents took me on that cruise.

I keep pulling the string and start yelling, "Stop the bus! Stop the bus!" I'm panicked, excited, and anxious as I get up and run down the aisle to the front door of the bus, touching the seat backs so as to never take my eyes off her. Finally, we reach the red light, and the driver opens the front door, I take my eyes off her just long enough to look down and step off safely onto the sidewalk.

When I turn toward her and look up, I hear the door behind me close, the air release of the brakes sound, the bus starts to move, and my aunt is gone. She has completely disappeared.

My heart sinks, and my mind explodes with wonder and confusion. I suddenly start reliving memories of all the disappearing people I had seen as an infant and toddler.

My mind races to one particular memory:

I'm two years old, sitting in the basket of the shopping cart at our neighborhood Waldbaum's grocery store. My mom is pushing me around, filling the cart up with groceries. We come to the end of an aisle. The registers are behind me. I look to my left, and there is a man standing there. He's in a trench coat and hat, just standing still, doing nothing but looking at me.

I turn my head for one second to look at my mom, and when I turn back, he's gone.

I look back at my mother and ask, "Mom, why do some people disappear?"

Her response, "Melanie Beth, you're crazy! People don't disappear, and you should never talk like that, or people will think you really are crazy. No more talk of that!"

In that moment, although a bit dazed and confused, I somehow knew I could see things that other people couldn't, and I promised myself I would never talk about it with my mother again. It left me wondering why I was so different. I never brought it up again, and I never recall seeing another disappearing person until eleven years later, with my aunt standing at that bus stop.

That brought back another memory. I remember, when I was five years old, I'd wanted desperately to fly. Probably not an unusual thing for a child, but I knew that if I tried hard enough, I could do it. I spent a tremendous amount of time alone as a child, especially if my father wasn't home. I could spend hours in my room playing, imagining, wishing for a better world while being safely away from my mom.

One night, I had gone up to my room, which had a slanted cathedral ceiling. I'd gotten on my bed and started jumping. I'd jumped up, making my body parallel to the bed, and had fallen straight down onto it. Nothing. I'd repeated this behavior for almost three hours, jumping, falling, hitting the mattress. Nothing. It hadn't mattered how long it took—I had been committed to experiencing the sensation of flying and being weightless. I'd kept on.

And then something happened. On my next jump (I hadn't known it was going to be the last jump), for about three seconds, I'd suspended in the air, had felt completely weightless, and then again had fallen down in a belly flop onto my bed. I had known in that moment that anything was possible if I believed it strongly enough. I had not needed to do it again, and I'd realized that I wasn't victim to the body I was in. The world around me tried very hard and, to some degree, succeeded in affirming otherwise. I never told my parents about this, but I carried it inside of me like a proud secret.

Ever since I could remember, I had a recurring vision/memory where I saw myself as an infant being carried away from a woman by a man wearing a dark blue or black suit. Seeing the vision of my aunt prompted this memory again.

I'm wrapped tightly in a blanket with a little soft beige hat on my head. There's a woman standing down a cold and sterile beige hallway with a shiny floor. There are doors on both sides with little clips on them and papers hanging from the clips. She's staring into a long, rectangular indoor window. Her hands are on the windowsill, and she's crying very hard. Behind me is a small, thin woman in whose arms the man places me. I'm crying so hard I feel physical pain, and the pain in my chest is excruciating, as if it were being ripped apart. I cannot breathe, and I feel as if I'll explode.

I couldn't have been but a few days to possibly weeks old. (The first photo of me is at a month old, so I don't know exactly when I was sent home.) I was wailing in pain, feeling the most horrific sense of separation an infant could feel, but I didn't know that's what it was. I just thought it was an odd vision, maybe something I was making up. When I shared it with my mom as a very young child, she said it was just my very vivid imagination and that no infant could remember anything from that age. So I let it go, not knowing what was real and what was not.

I had two other memories of the first year of my life: one of my mother touching my genitalia in a way that was inappropriate for a child in diapers, and one standing in my crib clenching the railings until my hands were red and hurting hoping "the monster" wouldn't come in. If I heard my door open, I immediately became anxious, sick to my stomach, and fearful. I have no childhood memory at all of my mother ever cuddling me, stroking me with affection, or hugging me in a loving gentle way. She showed some affection when others were around but never at home. I have no recollection of sitting on her lap or her reading to me at bedtime, laughing or playing with me. Aside from the occasional craft she would help me with in school (which usually was pretty fun), the childhood memories I have of my mother are of a distant, cold, unloving, controlling, and demanding woman.

3

As my teen years progressed, I continued dealing with my mother lying to me and telling me inconsistent stories about my origins. If I asked a question about it, she clearly became uncomfortable, nervous, and oftentimes wound up with a headache or stomachache and had to go lie down. I continued to believe something was wrong with me simply based on the fact that I didn't seem to deserve to know my own truth. The ironic part of it is that I was raised never to lie, cheat, steal, or do anything illegal.

One way that I learned to cope was with food. My mother controlled everything in my life. She would snoop through my bedroom furniture drawers, read my diary, open my mail and so on. I had no sense of self, and I worked very hard at fighting back. One way I did that was to eat whatever I wanted when she wasn't around. My mother herself was a compulsive overeater, and she taught me well. She also stole from hotels and restaurants, things like salt-and-pepper shakers, sugar substitute packets and the holder they were in, towels that had our initial on it from specific hotels and so on. She was a dishonest person, so shortly after I learned of the adoption and had to swallow all the bitter lies, I found swallowing a lot of food a sweet way of counterbalancing things. I became an overeater myself. I was already chubby, and I remained one of the three fat kids in my grade. My mother made the rules very clear: I could not be fat, gay, or with a black-skinned person. She herself had thyroid issues, so she never became overweight, although she always said she felt fat. I would, without conscious effort, become a teacher for my mother merely by being who I am.

Throughout my childhood, both of my parents told me that I could talk to them about anything. My father wasn't present for the first five years of my life. He was driving a taxicab in Manhattan eighteen to twenty hours a day to support us, so he wasn't there to talk to. I learned early on that my mother wanted me to tell her everything, but she quickly reinforced that it's not smart or safe to do so, as when I did, the response usually was "What is wrong with you? Why can't you be like the other children?"

When I confided in her or asked her advice, these are the things she said. So I stopped going to her for any type of maternal support. I learned that what my mother wanted most was to control me. Feeling smothered and unsafe around my own mother made life very challenging. I learned by failure after failure that no matter what I did or said, I'd never make my mother happy. But like most children, I never stopped trying.

One situation that proved to me that my mother wasn't a safe haven was when I was seven years old:

I'm in second grade. My friend Beth and I are spending a lot of time together. She has Barbie dolls. Her mom bakes and does all the things most other moms do, but not mine. I never had a Barbie doll, only some cheap imitations. There are never milk and cookies in my house, no toys other than a few hand-me-downs, maybe a puzzle or two, and the only thing I'm allowed to watch on television are educational shows. To say the least, hanging out at Beth's is a treat.

Her mom taught me how to make homemade butter, which I just loved. My mother never invited me into the kitchen. One day, we're talking about my being an only child, and I tell Beth, in secret, that I have two half sisters from my father's first marriage. I'm so proud to have sisters, and sharing it with Beth makes me feel less alone and more normal, like her and the other kids in my class who have siblings. There are only a few of us only children in my class. Not long after, my mother finds out I told Beth about my sisters, and I get punished. I'm being punished for sharing a family secret.

I was in second grade, and I had no comprehension why my sisters could or should be a secret. They were my sisters, and I was proud to have them in my life, just as I was proud to be adopted. I was introduced to the family secrets and the skeletons in the closets at the tender age of seven, and I was expected to keep them in that closet forever. And so it went in my house.

There are very few people in my life that my parents approved of. Most of the time people were either "beneath me" (whatever that meant), not Jewish, not well off, not smart enough, and so on. Most of my friends over the years weren't good enough (for what, I'm not sure), and no one I dated was ever acceptable. I never saw myself as different from other people, and this got me in trouble more than once.

In second grade, I missed my bus stop because the driver didn't stop there for some reason. By the time I realized it, we were no longer on my block, so I got off at the last stop with my friend, Sara. I went into her house, called my mother right away, and immediately was told to "get out of that house" and wait outside for her to pick me up. Apparently being outside as a seven-year-old was a safer option for my mother than being inside with Sara and her family. I was told I was an idiot, and that I wasn't allowed into Sarah's house because they were Puerto Rican and it wasn't safe. I asked what that had to do with anything—it didn't make sense to me. And I was told that we didn't spend time with people like them. Period. I didn't get it. Sara was sweet and everyone liked her.

In fourth grade, my friend Karen developed a phobia of going into the classroom. My heart hurt for her, and I asked how I could help. I became her tutor. For three months, I went to her house after school every day and reviewed all the lessons. Then my parents picked me up, and we started over again the next day. I was so grateful they let me help her. Three times, we attempted to get Karen into that classroom. The first two attempts failed miserably, but on the third attempt, she walked over the threshold back into the classroom! And she never spoke to me again. I imagine she was embarrassed and humiliated, but I was crushed, and I lost my friend.

In sixth grade, I befriended Dawn. She was light skinned, so my parents didn't realize she was Puerto Rican, and I didn't say a word; for I was learning how to play the game. Dawn also had some learning challenges, so I helped her out as well, tutoring her during the times my parents thought we were playing. The day my mom found out about her background, she asked, "Why are you always drawn to the underdog?"

This question hurt on so many levels and totally confused me. I again felt like something was wrong with me because I didn't hang out with the rich, white Jewish kids. I was simply trying to help people in need. If there was something I could do, I wanted to do it. It felt good to help others. It gave me purpose and connection, yet I was being reprimanded with the idea that something was wrong with me because of the people I chose, as if they were less than other people. To me, everyone was the same in spite of skin color, race, religion, or finances. This clearly wasn't the case for my mother, although she professed repeatedly that she wasn't prejudiced.

My boyfriend James in seventh grade was, oddly enough, one of the great loves of my life, but dating him was wrong because he was Irish Catholic. My parents were so relieved when he was sent off to Catholic school. That same year, at one of my sleep-away camps, I became very close with the counselors. That wasn't unusual, as I was always mature beyond my years because of how I was raised. Counselors and other friends called to see if we could get together, but

I wasn't allowed to hang out with them outside of camping time because they did bad things, things that I wasn't told of, nor saw, and again I was left with a lack of understanding. Those bad things would come back to haunt my mother and ultimately change my life dramatically.

Another one of my mother's favorite stories was how the children in kindergarten always asked that I stay with them when they were sick. We didn't have a school nurse back then, and once everyone had been sent home, I stayed with the sick student until a parent came to pick them up, because they'd say I made them feel better just by being present with them. Why couldn't she see that helping my friends in other ways was the same thing?

As my teen years went on, I was filled with questions about my background. Did my birth mother know who she gave me to? Who did I look like, if anyone? What was my medical history? Why was my body the way it was? Was I product of rape? Was I left on a doorstep, in a dumpster, at a church? The questions were endless.

Each time, I approached my mother with these questions, I dealt with the nerves and lies. I stopped asking my father because he simply wouldn't discuss it. Somehow he thought lying by omission wasn't lying, which was laughable since not lying was one of the main rules of the house. I was left thinking something was wrong here; my parents were liars and hypocrites, my mother was clearly prejudiced, and I had developed a belief that they didn't really love me, because if they had, they'd have told me the truth. What parent lies to his or her child? What parent doesn't consider the child's experience?

Dad had three daughters. Two we kept hidden in the closet, and one, we didn't discuss her origins, a closet all in itself. What was wrong with us that we were to be hidden away, like shameful objects? These were the things that created the theme of my upbringing.

I was told by most of my older cousins that one day I just showed up, and that no one knew anything about me or where I'd come from, except for my aunt Mary. I slowed down with the questions as the years went by. I no longer felt safe in any way discussing my adoption with anyone. I didn't know what to believe, so eventually I believed nothing I was told. I had a very deep ache and yearning. I had a belief now that something was fundamentally wrong with me, and this was how I entered adulthood.

I turned sixteen in 1980. My parents threw me the obligatory sweet-sixteen birthday party. It was tremendous fun for me since I had so few birthday parties. We made gifts for everyone out of big lollipops with smiles on them and terra cotta planters, turning the lollipops into sweet, happy potted flowers. It was held at a very cool local restaurant, and I had all of my friends there. The friend who probably mattered most for me at this point in my life was my friend Miriam. Miriam and I had met the year before. She was also adopted, although she had been adopted within her family, but it was a bond we shared that made our friendship unique. We were like sisters from the start, and she was the first person who I felt understood my feelings and experience in any way.

Later in the spring of 1980, my parents "gifted" me with the news that we were moving to Florida because of my father's arthritis. I was heartbroken. This was no gift. The idea of not graduating with the friends and kids I've grown up with ate away at my heart. It was difficult to leave my friends behind. But when you're a minor, your life isn't your own.

4

It was early August, 1980, and we were living in Pembroke Pines, Florida. We moved into a fifty-five-plus community that allowed teens sixteen years and older. There were less than five teenagers living in the entire complex, but oddly enough, one of them was Lisa, a girl who I grew up with in Long Beach that had moved right after us into the same building in the fifty-five-plus community. We were in the same class, but never friends in Long Beach. She was part of the rich clique who were skinny, pretty, and feminine—nothing like me. We somehow found solace in each other, likely because of both of us being moved between tenth and eleventh grades. We developed a bit of a friendship and shared a familiarity that brought each of us comfort. And my mother, was she ever so happy that I was befriending a nice, white, pretty Jewish girl from New York.

My new school is the Cooper City Cowboys. A New York girl in a cowboy town? This was not a good match. Each time I spoke I was bullied. I didn't sound like anyone else at the school, so I went to work at practicing talking the way they did. Whenever I was alone, I talked out loud and said things the way the other kids at school did. I was determined to disappear as much as I could.

Over the last six weeks, I let go of my New York accent, as I stick out like a sore thumb every time I open my mouth, getting teased and the usual mean bullying that comes along with being different. I'm completely out of place. Making friends is nearly impossible, as I'm so different from everyone here. I've been spending some time with Lisa, but fundamentally we still are very different personalities.

I've found my way to one close friend, Pam. In just a few short months, I've been told that I cannot hang out with her anymore because of her mother and her aunt. It was the same thing I was told with the counselors at sleep-away camp in years prior in New York—that they do bad things. That's the entire explanation, which, like everything else, lacks any sense to me. The few times I've spent hanging out there were wonderful. I was comfortable with them. I could be myself. I was accepted for who I am. Yet I once again am feeling like something is wrong with me because anytime I find something that's a fit for me, I'm taken away from it, told that something is wrong with it, and me.

I chose to lose my virginity to Tony, a guy I'd met in New York before we'd moved to Florida. Tony was a perfect look-alike of John Lennon. He drove a Duster, which he was incredibly proud of. It was a pretty hot car, all souped-up, jacked-up rear end, and killer sound system. Tony had been dating a good friend of mine, and that's how we'd met. We weren't intimate until he visited me in Florida, and I don't regret choosing him as my first, as he was gentle, kind, patient, all the things that I do not get at home. But it came with a price, a huge price.

He called me almost every day. He was my last link to my life in Long Beach, which I missed desperately. Tony was doting and gentle, and he showed me love simply by his actions. But he looked like a thug to my parents, and he wasn't Jewish. To say the least, they didn't approve of him. Tony was one of a few people in my life that I truly felt saw me and loved me for who I was. Tony was my saving grace during this transition. He actually drove his Duster down to see me. To me, that was a big statement when you are sixteen. My parents knew he was visiting, but they didn't know that I was having sex with him, and when they found out, my world came crashing down.

I tell them I've lost my virginity to him, knowing this will send them both over the edge, which, I hate to admit, I like the idea of. I love the idea of hurting them the way they continue to hurt me day after day, lying to me, withholding information I know they know. It gives me sick pleasure to see them hurt, and hurt, they are!

My mother tells me I'm a slut, and my father promptly tells me in a very loud voice, "You are not my child. Get the fuck out of my house!" as he stands at the opened front door of the apartment. I don't believe he can say anything more hurtful than what he said in that moment. It fed my adoption wound tremendously.

So, like a typical teenager, I packed up my valuables—vinyl music records, Tony's vest that I was painting his Duster on and that my father ripped out of anger (which infuriated me), and the eight dollars that I had to my name—and walked out the door.

I went out the back door of the building and started walking through the golf course. I heard my mom yelling, "Mel! Mel! Come back." No way in hell was I going back to a house in which I'm told I'm not their child (even though it's true), where I don't want to be, and where I feel like something is wrong with me just because of who I am.

So I started running. I saw them driving in their car, trying to catch me, driving in and out of streets along the golf course. My mom got out at one point and started running after me, but I ran faster until I was out of their sight. I hitchhiked my way to the Greyhound station in Hollywood. I called Tony collect, and he was going to get a ticket for me in the morning. For the moment, I waited at the station, praying they wouldn't find me.

It's dark now. I'm hungry, but I don't care. I know I will be OK, but I'm not going back to that apartment. A man comes out of his taxi and asks me if I'm OK. He tells me the cops will pick me up if I loiter there all night and offers to take me home with him. My gut feels that he's a good man, so I agree. We get to his trailer and he feeds me, sets me up by his dining table to rest, asks if I want to have sex. I say no, and he respects that. He goes to sleep in his room. I sit in his trailer, knowing regretfully that I have to go home. I'm sixteen. If I want a future, I need to buck up and go home. I wake the taxi driver up and ask him to take me home. He graciously does.

As we pull out of the trailer park, I see a cop car drive by—my parents are in the back seat. They're looking for me. I can't help but take great pleasure in knowing they're worried sick. They brought it on themselves. When we pull up to the apartment building, my aunt Mary is there waiting for me, along with some of the neighbors. She puts her arms around me and quickly takes me up to the apartment.

When I was nine, Aunt Mary proved to me I couldn't trust her; she told my mother something I'd told her in confidence. Prior to that, she was always doting, loving, generous, and kind. I've always trusted people until I'm given a reason not to. But today, in this moment, she was the old aunt that I loved, and she took care of me. Until my parents came home.

They walk in the door, and instead of any sign of relief, my mother immediately starts yelling at me. Dad doesn't say much, but he is clearly very upset. She starts with "Do you know what you did to us? Do you know how you embarrassed us? What is wrong with you? That cab driver could have raped you or killed you. All the neighbors know now what kind of kid you are! Why can't you be more like Lisa!"

And, as usual, I sit here, not understanding why she was saying what she was, other than it's to be expected. My heart breaks even further. I feel completely alone and completely misunderstood. He told me to get out, and this is what I *did to* them?

This was life with my parents. And to this day, I wish I could find that taxi driver and thank him. He very well may have saved my life. I went to my room and cried myself to sleep, hoping tomorrow would bring a new beginning. But it did not.

My relationship with Tony was short lived due to our physical distance and we broke up amicably after a few months. Later that year, I was date-raped. It was another experience that I just thought I deserved. I wanted to be with him initially, but then it went on and on, and became very painful. I asked him to stop, but instead, he pinned me down on the couch with his arms, holding my arms over my head and his legs pushing mine open and continued for forty-five more minutes.

I could see the clock, watching, praying he would get it over with. I kept my head turned away from him, eyes closed except to peek at the clock. I was hurting terribly, crying in pain with each motion. Tears were running down my face, but he kept going. He never reached his destination, and I'm not sure why, but he finally did stop. I quickly dressed and ran out of there and ran home.

I never shared it with anyone until decades later in therapy when my therapist told me that qualified as date rape. I thought I had asked for it and that I deserved what I'd gotten. When I finally shared it with my mother, many years later, she said, "You're just making that up." There was to be no conversation about it. There was no support, just her telling me that I was a liar. And this was why I had stopped telling her anything many years ago.

My only real solace during my high school years in Florida was going horseback riding. I was an avid rider, and I became one with any horse I was with. When we'd lived in New York, my parents had taken me to a dude ranch in the Catskill Mountains. It had been the only time the three of us had ridden together, one of my few great childhood memories with them. I had been obsessed with horses since I was a small child. I drew them and fantasized about having one. I don't remember when I started riding, but it was always a natural thing for me to be with a horse. To become one with such a powerful beast, the animal I felt was the most beautiful on the planet, was an indescribable experience for me. I was grateful my parents supported me in this, especially during my late teen years in Florida. It was a very healing thing for me and got me away from my mother.

I had very few friends, and any time spent with my family was simply uncomfortable for me. I definitely was the black sheep of this family. And I was so different from the kids in this new high school. I felt as if I simply didn't belong anywhere.

I was a senior now in high school, seventeen years old. I didn't have many friends, but I got to know another Lisa. She was really easy to be around, and I quickly found out she was also an adopted, only child. We spent a lot of time after school together. I did sleepovers at her house, and I felt I finally had met someone who had some understanding of who I was, what I've felt and experienced, and who my parents actually liked and approved of. I thought it was because they knew she was an only, adopted child like myself. It was a miracle to me. I felt as if I had found someone who truly understood what I'd been going through, but I was mistaken.

Unlike my family dynamic, Lisa had a fantastic relationship with both of her parents. They attended church every Sunday, they participated in her life, they nurtured her, and she had no negativity or secrets around her adoption. In fact, she was completely peaceful about it. She had no desire to look for her family, and I, once again, felt isolated and alone in the world. In spite of that, Lisa and her parents gave me a huge gift.

It's Saturday night, and I'm spending the night at their house. They ask if I'd like to go to church with them in the morning—it's a Baptist church. I'd never been to a real church service, so I said yes, with the agreement that they wouldn't tell my parents because they wouldn't be happy about it, nor would they likely allow me to see Lisa anymore. They agree.

We enter the church. I'm handed a flyer, and we find our pew. I'm sitting on the aisle seat, and Lisa and her parents are to my right. We're about ten rows back from the pulpit. There is a huge glass window built into the wall above and behind the pulpit with water about halfway up the wall. I don't know what it's there for. I begin weeping before the service even begins, but I have no idea why. I'm moved so deeply, and I remain so during the entire service.

I learn what the water is for as I watch these beautiful baptisms being done in the pool set into the wall, and the entire hour I'm asking myself why I'm weeping so. All I can come up with is that Jesus is welcome in this place, but not in the Jewish synagogues I'd been raised in. I've never been moved in a temple like this. My heart has never felt like this. It feels warm, safe, expansive, and comforted inside. Strangely, I don't feel so alone for some reason.

I'm not moved or inspired by the sermon, but my internal experience is one that will change my future. I leave the church, never to go back, but I wonder now if I'm really Jewish at all.

In my senior year of high school, at the age of seventeen, I learned to drive and I got my first car. My dad bought me a brand-new, brown Chrysler LeBaron. It wasn't a hot car, but it was brand-new! At school, I was labeled the spoiled girl from New York. Couldn't really argue, as I was spoiled, materialistically—there was no denying that. The only way my parents could express their love to me was materialistically. I always appreciated what my parents gave me, but I would have traded it all, in an instant, for a hug, some compassion, feeling safe, unconditional love, and a happy, peaceful home (my parents fought often, and whomever was the loudest usually won). Something I believe every child should have.

Because of the advanced education system in New York, I was way ahead of my class and a straight A student for the first time. I was so ahead that I only had a few classes in my last semester of my senior year, so I started community college early while still living at home. That was a huge self-esteem booster for me. And it was at college that I met my friend John. That was January 1982. He made the entire semester worthwhile. We were wild and crazy, and our only goal was to have fun. We never got in trouble or hurt anyone, but we laughed all the time. We hated algebra and often cut class, ultimately dropping out of it, but we also managed to become very close friends, very quickly.

The freedom of having a car and going to college was immeasurable for me. I now had a way to escape being under my mother's rule. On an occasional Sunday morning, without my parent's knowledge, I started to explore this idea of Jesus possibly being what had moved me so much at that Baptist church. I went to Catholic mass, and although most of it didn't work for me, the Eucharist part of the service always moved me. Holy communion brought up the same feelings that I experienced that Sunday in the Baptist church. But I didn't continue because too much of what I heard and saw simply didn't make sense to me. I learned early and quickly that I will not and still do not support anything that judges or separates people in any way.

I made a few friends during this time of being in high school and college simultaneously, but none of them were really people I wanted to spend time with. My adopted friend Lisa and her parents moved to New England, and I spent most of my time with my high school sweetheart, Mike. Mike lived across the street from one of my girlfriends. He and I hit it off immediately. I thought he was the most handsome thing I'd ever seen. Oh, how I loved him. He was the cutest, sweetest, gentlest fifteen-year-old. Yes, fifteen. I was seventeen. I just knew he was it—this was forever.

As wise and mature as I was at this point in my life, I was still an adoptee and a teenager, desperate to be loved, accepted, and held onto. It wasn't too long before he wasn't allowed to spend time with me, so we snuck out in the early mornings before school, did what high school sweethearts do, and enjoyed every moment of it.

Graduating high school was very anticlimactic for me. I did not attend the prom since Mike was not allowed to go with me, and I never cared or felt any loss around that. At this point, I had few friends. Mike was my source of love and joy, and John was my source of friendship and fun. I had a desire to learn about the world, to become a responsible adult, and even though I was eighteen and a high school graduate now, my parents fully expected me to do what they wanted. Unbeknownst to me, I had a choice. I wasn't taught anything about choice, so when my parents said I was going to go away to a big-name college or university, I knew I'd have to go in spite of me saying I'd prefer to go to community college locally. So I applied to a few schools and was accepted at the University of Florida, Gainesville.

The first year of college proved to be more of a growing-up period than one of scholastic education, which is what I had wanted anyway. I was living in the dorms. Mike broke up with me after a very long and dramatic two-hour conversation of me begging him to tell me he loved me. In hindsight, it's sad how codependent, needy, and empty I was. I learned how to manage a checkbook, how to grocery shop, and how to party, drink, and try drugs. I spent my nineteenth birthday sleeping in the back of my car alone after doing acid for the first time. Not fun, no one to celebrate with and I felt horrid from the acid (not at all understanding why people did it). I remember lying in the car, wondering about my birth mother, yearning to have some connection to something that I could call mine. The car was the only thing at that moment that I felt was mine.

It was a year of learning about who I really was, without the constraints of living at home with my mother. I was very drawn to a few guys, who all wound up being gay. I started going to the bars with them, and ultimately, I came out of the closet and discovered my love for women, something that had been foreshadowed since I was twelve when my first sexual exploration was with a female friend. And it was during this year that I understood what it was my parents were keeping me from with the camp counselors and my friend Pam's mother and "aunt." My mother was terrified of three things where I was concerned: having a fat or gay child, or that I would wind up with a black person. She now had two out of three, which sadly gave me some sick pleasure. But I didn't tell them I was gay, nor would I for years to come, and that too would take a toll on me in every way.

I failed eight of the ten classes I took during my year in Gainesville. Understandably so, I was required to return to South Florida, which was a relief for me since I hadn't wanted to go to college in the first place. My mother said to me, "If you didn't want to go, you should have said something." That was laughable, as I had said something more than once. She confirmed that I wasn't heard, and that what I wanted didn't matter. I was going to do what they wanted me to either way. They truly believed that they knew what was best for me, but overall, they didn't.

In 1983 I moved into my first apartment, at nineteen years old, and I had a coworker as a roommate. He wound up being a thief. It wasn't a great year, but I grew up a lot. I was working for American Express, a job that I had gotten because of my friend John, who'd started working there while I was in Gainesville. but that wasn't where I was meant to be. After a year and a half, I was fired, which was a blessing. I made a choice to go into nursing school with a serious commitment this time.

I also met and started dating Vicky that year. Vicky was an unlikely match, although a mutual friend thought we were perfect for each other. Eventually I saw what our friend saw, and Vicky and I started dating after I gave her quite a bit of resistance. Vicky would teach me about intimacy, family, what it's like to have close siblings, what Christmas could be, and so many more things that I had not experienced before. But my mother loathed her, dad tolerated her, they felt she was beneath me. I still had no concept of what that meant, but I did understand it was nothing but judgment.

When I was twenty, I moved into a tiny one-bedroom apartment in Sunrise, Florida, that my parents were covering while I went to nursing school at the community college that I'd also attended while in high school. It was there that I would start doing some more searching for my birth family because of the privacy and solitude I now had. For the first time in my life, I had time for myself.

I find out about ISRR—International Soundex Reunion Registry. I send my information in, but feel absolutely hopeless. Would they even know my name? My mother said they did, but how could I believe it? Is my date or time of birth even right? I no longer am in New York. Do they know my parents' names? It feels futile, but I take the first step and pray. I join a couple of new New York adoption groups. I share my stories, but nothing and no guidance from anyone. There is little movement and nowhere really to go with things. I didn't have money to hire a private investigator, so I let it go.

Nursing school is a bittersweet journey for me. I love learning about the body, but the clinical setting, being with people, is really where I'm thriving. But it's a brutal schedule. Five days of the week, I'm in school, and five nights of the week, I'm at one bar or another, dancing, drinking, and partying with my friend John from community college. I spend much of my time studying for my psychology class, which is utterly horrid for me. I'm assigned to a state prison where the inmates are drug abusers, child molesters, and thieves. I spend my time there watching them urinate, defecate, masturbate, or fornicate in the open, and no one stops them. I cannot tolerate being around them at all. I feel sick to my stomach, anxious, and completely useless and hopeless for these people. If it weren't for Michelle (who goes by Micky), one of my fellow students, I don't know how I would survive. We become fast friends and create a study group, which literally saves me in that class and, ultimately, in nursing school.

Although I didn't know it at the time, I was extremely empathic. I wasn't capable of detaching and shaking off the disgusting things I experienced there. Nursing school was hell for me. Yet my parents told me more than once that they didn't understand how I wasn't an A student, because I was so intelligent. Mind you, neither of them had ever attended a college-level program. They really had no reference to how challenging it was, and they never considered that their daughter really wasn't cut out for traditional education. Despite begging, my instructor wouldn't let me drop out of the class. She said I was learning more than anyone else because how acutely aware I was, but it took a major toll on me.

When Micky and I met, we started studying together. I'm so blessed to say that to this day she is not only still in my life, but we really are sisters. After I left Florida years later, she, her mother, sister, and my parents all became very close, and they too became family. Not long after I moved, I returned for a visit. Micky and I took some time away just for us, and she and I agreed that we were much more than friends and declared our sibling-ship. We laughed, cried and hugged on it, and that was it. I had my first true sister. She is the sister that I wished to have with my adopted half sisters but did not, and as different as we are, we are best friends, and I love her dearly. Micky was and is a major gift to me in this lifetime. My adopted sisters are twelve and sixteen years older than me and never lived close by, or with us, so Micky filled a void that was precious to me.

John and I reunited after I came back from Gainesville. We spent five ridiculously fun years together doing what kids in their twenties do. I was becoming severely overweight, which is something I've been challenged by all of my life. Even as a child, I was chubby (and was reprimanded for being so, as if I had some control over it, leaving me again thinking something is wrong with me), and throughout all my formative years in school, I was remained one of the three fattest girls in class. But never was I more aware of how much my mother disliked it than on the day of my nursing graduation.

Everyone came to my nursing graduation, including Vicky's entire family, which was at least three times the size of mine. My parents, Aunt Mary and her husband Stanley, her eldest son and his wife (my cousins), and the rest of the crowd were friends and Vicky's family. I experienced the highest of highs when I was called up to get my diploma, and my friends and Vicky's family screamed louder than any other group in the crowd. I was gleaming inside and so proud of myself for making it through what was a hellish couple of years for me.

Nursing school wasn't easy for me. I had failed my OB/GYN class by one-tenth of a point, so I didn't get to graduate with Micky or my peers, but she was there cheering me on. Getting that diploma was a big deal. I was flying high, until right after the candle-lighting ceremony. Everyone came up to me, congratulating me, hugging me, sharing in my success as well as the relief of it finally being over. And then there was my mom.

The candlelight ceremony just finished, and everyone is coming up to congratulate me. Mom grabs my arm painfully and pulls me aside in the midst of it all and says in a strong whisper, with absolute disgust on her face, "I'm so embarrassed. You were the fattest one on that stage." No congratulations, no pride that her daughter is a nurse, only disgust for how fat I am. It's clear to me more than ever that I will never please my mother or be the person she wants me to be.

And being myself simply isn't enough. I'm twenty-four years old and a complete failure in my mother's eyes. I just spent two years in a grueling nursing program, losing too many friends to AIDS, being sick myself after failing a class by one-tenth of a point, and having severe irritable bowel syndrome and colitis because of the stress, yet there I am, being told I'm fat and a failure.

My heart sinks. I stand there, dumbfounded. I don't have any words, although I really want to say, "Fuck you. Go fuck yourself."

But I don't. I'm deflated, angry, and very hurt.

Nothing I ever did was good enough for my mother, I would never be good enough, and I never would feel love or appreciation from this person I called Mother. I know she spoke differently about me to other people. They thought she loved me to the moon and back, but they didn't know who she really was. She didn't deserve the title of Mother—there was nothing maternal about the woman, although I never doubted she loved me, only that she didn't know how.

A good aunt? Yes. A good friend? Sometimes. But a loving mother? Almost never. She certainly wasn't a loving mother in that moment. I ripped my arm out of her hand and walked away, fighting back the tears. I walked right back to my friend John, who lifted my spirits right up, and I ignored her for the rest of the day. I could see my father's pride for me, and disgust for her, as he knew she'd done her usual thing.

The irony of it all was that my mother's family always thought my father was crazy. It was she who could have used the emotional and psychiatric support more than anyone else.

But regardless of whether my mother was proud of me or not, *I* was! Graduating from that nursing program was an enormous accomplishment for me and has given me a solid career, for which I'm forever grateful to them. I wished my mother could have celebrated my success, but my mother never really was capable of celebrating anything. By this point in my life I was bitter. Very bitter.

Through the years, I had so much deep-seated hatred for my mother. I resented all the lies. I sat and wondered what my life would have been like had my birth mother not given me away. I imagine many adoptees have that thought at one time or another.

I also had so much anger toward my birth mother. I wondered if she knew who she'd left me with. Did she know the abuse I sustained? Did she know she left me with a father who lied by omission and a mother who just lied and couldn't love me for who I was? The anger and rage were so deep-seated that it was insane-making. As much as I'm ashamed to admit this, there was a very short period of time when I was nineteen that I was trying to figure out how to have my parents murdered because I just wanted them gone. A college friend and I discussed how we could raise at least $50,000 to hire someone to murder them. I figured it would cost at least that much (although I really had no idea at all about those things).

I became obsessed with the idea of life without the lies, the constant wounding, and the lack of love and acceptance.

The torture my mother brought into my life at times was just more than I could take. How could she do this to her child? Did she have any idea of the pain it inflicted and the damage it did to our relationship? The fact that my father would never speak drove me insane with feelings of betrayal because I knew he loved me and he taught me to never steal or lie. I was beyond frustrated and wanted the pain to stop, and the only way I could see that happening was to either know the truth, which I had zero control over, or to remove the cause of the pain for which I had at least that one option: remove them from my life.

I'm not proud of this piece of the story, and I dropped it immediately, but it was a testimony to the depth of pain that the situation caused me. Throughout my life, Mom voiced her disdain for my weight and body. I was never thin enough, polite enough, delicate enough. She restricted me and even reprimanded me as a small child from having anything sweet at all. My father eventually added snacks, candy, and coffee machines to his vending route, so I had a garage full of sugar to dive into daily, and I knew just how to leave no trace, that was, until right before we moved to Florida.

My mom found almost three hundred candy wrappers under my bottom chest of drawers when she started packing up my things. It wasn't the first or last time I would feel violated by her. That many wrappers would have been about a three-month accumulation, as I would periodically throw them away when I had a few minutes alone to do so. She was livid, and so was I!

Although my mother was a compulsive eater herself, she rarely ate that way outside of the house unless it was just the three of us. She indulged in large quantities of her favorite foods, for example; cream cheese and jelly sandwich with a quarter-inch slab of cream cheese on it. Or she made pasta with cottage cheese and margarine and ate the equivalent of two or three servings. This is how I learned to eat; by example. Yet I was never allowed anything that was a treat, so when I could, I stole, not just from her, but anywhere I could to have the forbidden foods.

Mom put lemon juice in almost all her cooking. Never was there a dessert or treat to be had in the house beyond graham crackers and the very occasional mandelbrot (an almond-like biscotti) she made. Even breakfast cereals were usually unsweetened and usually covered with wheat germ and skim milk (which to this day is the most disgusting-tasting drink to me). Food at home was horrid most of the time, although she did have one or two dishes that she mastered. But it was one of the many things she controlled me with, until I learned how to work around it.

I remember so clearly at the age of five thinking, "Now that I'm in school, this is the one thing she cannot control. I'll teach her!" Of course, there was no thought or awareness of the toll it would take on me. In general, no matter what I ate, I was sick after every meal, and the already-chubby child would remain chubby. (I didn't know at that time that I had some severe food sensitivities: wheat, corn, dairy, sugar, and as an adult, I learned of all of this, as well as the fact that alcohol is very toxic to me.)

I live in a body that is dense and bigger boned. I spent all of my life, thirty years of nursing, healing, and caregiving, and seeing hundreds if not thousands of different bodies, searching for someone with my body type. I didn't find anyone who had the similar quirky Flintstone toes, or my chunky hands, the indentations in my shoulder, or my puffy upper arms. I'm also quite busty. It never occurred to me that some if not all of my body issues were genetic.

To say the least, I'm not and have not ever been comfortable in this body, and my mother never helped me learn to accept or love myself in this way. She was always trying to change me to be thinner, prettier, different than who I am. She had me in Weight Watchers for the first time when I was ten. That was the first of at least six memberships. When I was twelve, she put me in Overeaters Anonymous. The meetings were in a church, and I was training for a bat mitzvah. I had a great sponsor, but over the six months, I didn't lose a pound and was completely confused about a higher power in a church—and I'm Jewish. I'm not sure twelve-year-olds can comprehend the twelve-step program very well. Everything was so uncomfortable.

It seemed the harder we tried to get me to lose weight, the more impossible it was. One summer in sleep-away camp, my parents paid the camp counselors extra money to literally starve me. I spent the summer watching everyone eat normal food, and I was given plain salads without dressing, yogurt and fruit and plain meat with naked vegetables and potatoes. I felt like a complete outcast being the only kid getting special diet foods. Sure, I lost weight, only to gain it all back with interest, like every other time she put me on a diet.

This yo-yo syndrome would go on throughout most of my life. As I have mentioned, and although she denied it repeatedly, my mother was prejudiced and very judgmental. Those are traits that I took on after being around it for too many years, even though knowing from a very small age that it didn't feel right to be like that. The race riots I experienced in high school in New York left me not understanding a world of judgment, separation, righteousness, and violence. It just isn't who I am. But I was taught to trust no one, that everyone is out to take advantage of you, that the world is not a safe place, and life is to be survived. In some ways, I can't argue, as we have a lot of evidence pointing toward that. Yet even as an infant, I knew when something was void of love just by looking at it. And as I've said, I trust people right off, until they give me a reason not to.

I'd be in my crib and watch or listen to my parents interact in the dining room through my doorway. They'd yell and fight, and they were just angry so much of the time. My father constantly tried to appease her, but there was no appeasing my mother. And once she got something she wanted, she didn't even take a moment to savor it or be grateful for it. It was right onto the next thing, never to be satisfied.

I could not be more than six months old. I'm standing inside my crib, holding the posts so tight in fear that my hands hurt. I'm praying the monster won't come in and will leave me alone. While watching them interact, I'm thinking to myself; "This isn't love."

In her later years, my mother shared with me that she had serious thyroid issues as a teenager, with a severe goiter and bulging eyes. She spent 13 weeks in the hospital at age

13 and again at age 15, having thyroid surgery in a teaching hospital because her parents did not have medical insurance. She shared feeling vulnerable, gawked at and about having a near death experience, which she said she never told anyone else. During that time she went for a walk in her neighborhood when two children were approaching her and when they saw her they ran away from her screaming, "Monster! Monster!" And in that moment, my mother believed it was true, and she became a monster. As an adult I could finally understand why she couldn't love or accept me as I was. I had great compassion for her because she couldn't love or accept herself. And as I believed all the untrue things she told me about myself, she believed she was a monster because of those kids.

Throughout my childhood there was a constant conflict between my parents about how to raise me. My father was the nurturer, and my mother was the strict disciplinarian who always wanted me to do the things she never got to. To be more accurate, she was the control freak. My mother did what she thought she was required to, was expected to, or thought she should, which were the basics of parenting: food, clothes, vaccines, education. I imagine it wasn't that easy for her to have a child such as myself. I did so many things that she felt were crazy. Different is not crazy. The fact was that she never really got to know me until the last few years of her life.

When I was four years old, I was given my Hebrew name by the rabbi at our conservative Jewish temple. The name was Mariasha. Hebrew names can be based on your birthday or the parents' birthdays, and often are chosen based on deceased family members, all depending on descent and tradition. I was supposedly named Melanie after my father's mother, Mini. I was born two days before the holiday of Purim, and there is no Mariasha in the story of Purim. Like the name Melanie, even as a child, I thought they both were beautiful names, but they never felt like *my* name. I didn't know why I felt that way, I just did, and I felt it strongly.

I was OK with people calling me Mel, but Melanie always caused an uncomfortable reaction in me. I asked my mother how she came up with the name, and she said I was named after Scarlett O'Hara's best friend in *Gone with the Wind* because of her nature, and it was my mom's favorite movie. That, too, just never sat well with me and made my gut nauseous when she talked about it. For some reason, it felt like another lie.

So, on the day I got my Hebrew name, while standing in the kitchen before dinner, I looked up at my mother and said, "Mom, my real name starts with an *E*!" And there was the face of horror and the usual response: "Why do you say these things? People are going to think you're crazy. Stop saying crazy things. People will never love you!" My mother proved over and over again that she and I were very different, and yet I must admit, it *was* an odd thing for a child to say. Yet, I knew something inside of me and would spend decades searching for my "E" name.

What brought my parents together is part mystery to me and part very obvious. My father told the story like it was magical for him, and for my mother, well, she had a very different perspective. Dad said they were at Grossinger's, a very popular Catskill resort in the late 1950s. Dad was a ladies' man—he just loved women, especially making them smile. He was sitting on a lobby bench with a woman on each knee having a grand time. He said my mother walked by him, and he was jolted. He basically threw the two gals off his lap, went over to her, touched her arm to get her attention, and when she turned around, he said, "I'm going to marry you."

I always loved his version of the story. Her version was quite different. She said that he did do that, and she thought he was crazy, but the family encouraged her to marry him because no one else had asked and she was in her late thirties. She said that on their first date she had to pay for the twenty-five-cent bridge toll, and all he could afford was two hot dogs and soda they had to share at Nathan's. I thought it to be terribly romantic. She thought he was poor and had no social skills. They were an interesting couple, constantly at odds about most everything.

Despite his frequent silence, I always felt safe in my father's arms, even as a small child, even though he didn't hold me often. Neither of them were affectionate that way, but Dad certainly was way more expressive than mom. When I was two years old, we moved from Brooklyn to Long Beach, New York. That was when Dad started driving a taxicab. One night when I was five years old, I happened to be wide awake at 10:00 p.m. for some reason, and it was a school night. I heard the car in the driveway and then the front door open and close. I rarely got to see my father because of his working eighteen to twenty hours a day—so I leapt out of bed and ran down the stairs into his arms.

Ah, safety, love, warmth. I hold on so tight. He says, "How's Melancholy?" (That is one of his nicknames for me, not necessarily an empowering one, considering its meaning, but he always said it with love. A lesser favorite is Big Mouth, and my very favorite: Kid.) Instantly mom is briskly walking out of the kitchen, wiping her hands on a towel and screaming, "What are you doing out of bed? Get back up there right now, young lady!" (I'm five, by far not a young lady yet.) My father does not put me down, and he says to her, "She is awake. I never get to see her. Let her be." And then the screaming begins. I'm in his arms, and I become the object of yet another shouting match. The last thing I hear before checking out mentally is my father saying, "She's my daughter too!"

My parents continued yelling for quite some time. My father eventually put me down. I went upstairs to my room tuning out the shouting. They switched from speaking English to speaking Yiddish, something they did often when they didn't want me to know what they were saying. They never taught me because of that. Many times throughout my childhood the phone would ring, my mother would start whispering and then would only speak Yiddish to my father about the phone call. I never knew who it was calling when she would do that. I felt this was a way for them to keep their lies and secrets safe, and, it was another thing that left me feeling undeserving and left out.

My mother always saw me as a possession, something to manage, manipulate, or mold into what she wanted me to be. Throughout my entire childhood, she touched me inappropriately. As a teen and even as an adult, she would poke my nipples and say, "Mel, put those away!" as if I had some control over them! Yet I felt shame about them. When she mended or measured my clothes to alter them, she'd put her hand in my crotch. It was well into my thirties before I became aware that this was sexual abuse. It was only 6 months prior to her passing that I finally had the courage to tell her to stop after poking my nipples while in an elevator and in front of my father. I was 41 years old. She made excuses that I had a button falling off, and stains on my clothes. Neither was true. Sometimes I don't know how I would have made it without my father. And I learned at a very early age how to tune things out and to become invisible, even in the biggest of crowds.

One day when I was twelve years old, Dad brought me outside to talk with me:

> *We're standing in the driveway, and he asks me, "Mel, if I were to live somewhere else, who would you want to live with?"*
>
> *I reply, "Don't you leave me with that bitch." I'm not afraid to say it to him that way because he knows who she is.*
>
> *He puts my face in his hands, looks at me with such love, says, "Ok." then grabs my hand, and we walk back into the house.*

Nothing else was said. Dad never left, and it was never brought up again. I don't know why, but I didn't ask. As long as he was there, I knew I would be OK.

My mother was one of those people who were so sad and unhappy inside of themselves that nothing ever was enough. She occurred to the outside world as the glue of the family, the matriarch, generous, funny and kind to others. But behind our front door she was a miserable person who had no self-esteem and took it out on the two people she should have loved and appreciated the most. My father, throughout their entire marriage, would give her compliments and she would say, "Oh Lary, stop the bullshit." But, he never did stop (one of the most amazing things about him in my opinion) and never once did I hear her say, "Thank you." My mother couldn't accept anything with kindness, as she was never kind to herself. When I was nine I saved up my allowance for three months and bought my mother gold hoop earrings with 14k gold posts. They cost three dollars, and she returned them. She never said why, but it stung to my core and broke my heart. It wasn't until I was eighteen that I ever gave her another gift, and it was to both of them, as I knew my father would graciously accept anything I gave him/them. As a child, I wasn't able to understand her as I do today. I was a child. I needed rearing, guidance, trust, love and support, which I didn't get very much of, to say the least. Thank God my father stayed with us.

8

I got out into the working world as a nurse at the age of twenty-four, only a couple of years behind most people with a two-year degree. I was a really good nurse, even I had to admit that to myself. Within six months at my first job, I was part-time charge nurse on the medical/surgical floor where I worked, and the rest of the time, I still took care of patients on the floor. I was asked to create and develop an oncology and chemotherapy wing with ten private rooms on the floor. I loved what I was doing and felt good about my career. It had its pitfalls like anything else, but at least out of the gate, nursing was a good fit for me.

The adoption was always running in the background. It obviously was my core wound and the context for which I operate everything in my life, even though I didn't know that back then. Seeing families gather, looking at people who look alike or act alike, it was always on my radar. I began looking at all the bodies I would take care of. Did anyone have my Flintstone feet? My hands? Or my eyes that people would say were so extraordinary? Maybe my hair, something, anything. But no, not one similar body type. It was another thing that fed into my experience of being alone in the world.

At this point in my life, for the last five years now, since I was nineteen, my mother has been asking me, on literally every phone call or visit we have, "Mel, are you gay?" and my consistent answer is "No, Mom." It was utterly exhausting to keep lying. It finally came time to tell the truth, which was what landed me in back therapy. More on that later.

I had gotten sick of living a lie, and was exhausted from pretending to be straight. My mother demanded that I make up a story about a boyfriend if I attended family functions. Vicky and I had now been together for almost five years. We were engaged and planning on having a holy union. Even at work, I pretended to be dating her brother. When we exchanged engagement rings, I told people he was my fiancée. I had become a liar like my mother because of her conditioning and instilling such fear into me that no one would accept me the way I was. I did it to survive in a not-so-friendly or accepting world.

I'm twenty-four years old now, it's 1988, and I still have not come to accept myself for who I am, living within the beliefs that my mother had taught me, still thinking who I am is not good enough. They've met Vicky. They think we're just friends and that she is "white trash." Today, though, for some reason, something is different within me; I've had enough. The lying is making me ill. This time, she poses the question, and my answer is "Yes, Mom, I'm gay."

Instantly, I'm once again dealing with this dramatic reaction of crying, wailing, and whining, "Don't say that! Don't say that! Oh God, why me? Why are you doing this to me?"

It's what I expected and was prepared for, just like the day I found out I was adopted. It angers me because I'm not "doing" anything to her. I just want to be me and free of the lies. It's a relief to tell the truth, and she obviously already knows. Getting honest was something my parents hadn't afforded themselves. I never understood why they wouldn't set themselves, and me, free.

When Dad heard the news, he simply said to me, "I just want you to be happy. No, I don't think Vicky is the best you can do, but if you're happy, I'm happy." Our home was so void of love and affection, intimacy and connection. I hadn't seen my parents ever touch each other until I was nineteen when they held hands for the first time in front of me. I almost fell over from shock when they did. And I was clear that it was all my mother who created it to be that way. Occasionally, a quick peck of a kiss would be exchanged between them after that point, but that was it their entire lives. Mostly, there was arguing, Dad trying to make peace, and Mom needing to be right, complaining, and asking for more.

When I was just shy of sixteen, my adopted half sister Sunny (my father's second birth daughter) was getting married. This may have only been the third time I would meet her that I could recall. I loved Sunny and admired how much she looked just like Dad, but with long hair. There was no question she was his daughter. It was the first time I was on a plane, and we were headed to Dallas. Dad offered to pay for the wedding, but she declined because her stepfather was covering it. Her stepfather just happened to be my father's former best friend, but that's all Gabby (my adopted father's first birth daughter) and Sunny knew.

The wedding was small and intimate in the rabbi's study. When the family was called up, everyone was called except my father and me. The stepfather and their other half sister were called up. My father was crushed. It was the first time I'd seen my father cry. He was extremely upset, he said more for the lack of acknowledgment of me than for him.

Sitting through the reception was horrid, as Dad never was very good about hiding his upsets. It took something to get him to that degree of upset, but when he was, it was ugly. He couldn't wait until it was over. We sat away from everyone and kept to ourselves the entire time. I didn't yet understand what was going on.

When we got in the car with my eldest sister, Gabby, and brother-in-law, Mike, our lives would all take a turn. Mike was driving, Dad was in the front seat, sobbing. I was in the middle of the back seat, Gabby to my right, and my mom to my left. Mike asked that we all just calm down, but my father wouldn't, or maybe couldn't.

Gabby is eight months' pregnant with my father's first grandchild, and she is shaking next to me in the back seat of the car. She says "Daddy, why are you so upset?"

He shares what happened in the rabbi's study, and that it's time they knew the truth, and so it comes out after decades of him keeping silent: he found their mother in bed with his best friend when he came home from work early one night.

Gabby is now crying, calling him a liar, asking why he would pick now to be telling her something horrible like that. He is crying, and I start to cry.

I try to intervene and calm them down. My mother elbows me, rather hard, and says, "Shut up, this is none of your business." The heat inside of me rises in an instant, and I look at her venomously and say, "That is my father and my sister. It is *my business!"*

She turns her head and looks out the window. As if what was happening wasn't already enough, she had to remind me that I wasn't really family! My head swirls with anger. I feel my face flushing, but I ignore her after that and just sit there crying helplessly, listening to my father and sister go at each other.

Gabby didn't believe him at first, understandably so. She was so close to giving birth, the stress was more than she could handle. She allowed us to stay the night, but then asked us to leave first thing in the morning. I was heartbroken. I loved having sisters, even if I couldn't tell anyone. They were a family secret that was to stay in the closet forever, so my mother said. My mother certainly had a very full closet; prejudices, judgments, righteousness, fears, insecurities. This spilled over into most every area of her life, and of course mine and my father's as well. Aside from my father and me, no one ever really knew or saw the degree to which my mother hid, nor the impact that had on Dad and me.

My sisters were so close, and they grew up with their other half sister from their mother and stepfather. I didn't have that, and all I ever wanted was to have them be close sisters to me. But that was the last I would see either of them for a very long time.

Many years later, after reuniting with my sisters, Sunny explained that she was young, wasn't thinking, and that there was no malicious intent. She called up her stepfather because he paid for the wedding and was the man who'd raised her. My father was really a stranger to her. It was understandable from my perspective and so easy to forgive.

Vicky came from a large Italian family. Her dad had passed away before we met, but her mom and six siblings were all very close. Half of her siblings were gay. To me, her mother was a new kind of parent. When someone walked into the house, they were expected to say hello to her, give her a kiss before anything else, including going to the restroom, no matter how much pain they were in! I learned that one the hard way! But her mom taught me about what a loving and accepting parent looked like.

I got to experience many holidays with a very large crowd. I was often very uncomfortable and overstimulated with all that noise and chaos, but it was fascinating to me. Christmas was over the top with presents, decorations, food, laughter, and fun. In all my formative years, my parents gave me only one Chanukah present: a Chinese checker set—that was it. So on my first Christmas with Vicky I was beyond excited. Like a child, I got caught peeking at my presents in the car. Boy, did I get in trouble, but she also understood what it meant for me. I was a kid who'd never had gifts because my parents said they bought me things throughout the year, which also fed into my feeling I was different and not normal like everyone else. I'd had only a few birthday parties: as an infant, my ninth, and then the required bat mitzvah and sweet sixteen. I didn't get a gift from them at any of these celebrations.

Vicky's family showed me what was possible, what I was never going to have with my mother. Her mom loved all her children equally. She knew who each of them were, and it mattered not if they were gay or straight, fat or skinny, only that they were kind, healthy, and happy. As I got to know her mother, I shared some of my story with her and told her I didn't think my parents really loved me because they never told me so.

She said I should start hugging them when I saw them and start telling them I loved them and that they eventually would start saying it back. I was terrified just of the thought of it, and I didn't believe it would work, but I trusted her parenting, as all of her seven children loved her to the moon and back. I hated my mother, so this was really over the top for me at this point in my life. Just a few years ago, I had been plotting her murder, so I knew I had made some progress!

It didn't take long, nor was it easy for me. But one day as we were ending a phone call, I told my mom that I loved her, and I heard the words "I love you too." on the other end of the phone. I was dumbfounded! Vicky's mom was right. That was the first turning point for our relationship, although it would not be quite enough for any real healing to occur. It had to come from me, and I kept on saying it, and so did she, and Dad eventually did too. For me, this was a miraculous victory. I moved forward in hopes that one day I would share real hugs with them, as Dad was very rigid physically because of his experiences and injuries in WWII. He was a good "patter," and Mom wasn't able to really connect even if she did hug. Her heart was never really open.

Setting myself free by speaking the truth didn't work completely. One would think that at age twenty-four I knew I didn't have to do what my mother wanted, but this was an unhealthy relationship at best, and I fundamentally believed something was wrong with me in many ways, so per Mom's request, I went into therapy, again. She put me in a few times prior to this to "fix" me. The first was when I was sixteen, as she read letters from my first real soul love—Ellen. We had kissed, and she was terrified of having a gay daughter. Now again, for the same reason. She thought this new connection we had would change me, and I could fix being gay.

After one or two sessions with me, the therapists asked my parents to come for a group session. Each one told my parents that nothing about who I was was abnormal, only that I was struggling with my identity and that I needed their help to come to terms with who I was. After that, we didn't go back. This time was no different. They told them that the issues I'd brought up weren't something I could heal without my parents taking responsibility for their part, and accepting me as I was, that there is nothing wrong with me, and that being gay was a natural and normal part of who I was.

As for myself, I never resonated with the words gay, lesbian, and so on. I'd always just felt like I was me, and whomever I was with, I loved them. It could have been a man; it could have been a woman. Labels had never been something I agreed with.

But in the therapist's office my mother started her wailing and drama right off. She refused to discuss anything that she had done, or her own past, said that it was all about me, that I was the problem and that she would not go to therapy, as he'd suggested, to deal with her issues.

We leave the therapist's office with nothing resolved, angry and not speaking. As we depart the office, the therapist looks at me with an expression of apology that he wasn't able to help. I nod in acknowledgment.

The ride home is silent, strained, and I feel sick and hopeless inside that my mother and I will ever find a common ground, that she will ever accept me just as I am. I don't care much about disappointing my mother at this point in my life, as it's inevitable that I will do so simply because of who I am, because I exist, but with my father, it's different, and I love him so for accepting me as I am.

But now a different set of issues were there. When I went to family functions, how was I to make up boyfriends and lie about who I was, who I dated, what I wanted in life? How could I continue that way? This would only compound the story that I wasn't good enough and that something was wrong with me, and I wanted to be done with that. I wanted to be free of my mother's issues. My father felt he couldn't fight her on these things, and I understood that. He chose to live with her, and unless you lived with my mother, you really didn't know who she was.

As I matured, I had more and more empathy for what he went through. He still was living with her and her insanity. I was getting more obese and had so many physical, emotional, and mental problems. I'd pass out and wake up projectile vomiting. I'd get sick after eating every meal, which had been happening since childhood. I had colitis on and off, and although the years of partying were slowing down, that never helped the situation. I wouldn't go places because of the fear of being seen and laughed at for how fat I was. I didn't have enough strength or awareness inside of myself to realize I had other choices, other options to deal with this, or life in general.

It's now 1989. I'm twenty-five years old. Vicky and I have finally moved in together after more than five years of dating. We have a two-bedroom, one-bath apartment in the building next to the one in which I was already living. At this point, I weigh about 280 pounds. I've been smoking cigarettes for eight years, and I'm always sick with digestive issues. Sometimes it's so severe I can't go out of the house. I'm miserable inside. I hate myself, I hate my mother and my birth mother. I hate the world. My mother and I fight often. I beg for information now and then, and she continues to lie, Dad remains silent. I feel it's finally time to get serious about searching without them knowing.

I had acquired both my hospital birth certificate and New York state birth certificate from my mother years ago.

The state certificate was handwritten (generally, they're only typed) and it said that my adopted parents were my birth parents, that my father was thirty-two or thirty-five when I was born (the numbers looks like both—he was forty-nine), that my mother was thirty years old at the time of my birth (she was forty-two), and that she was born in Virginia (she was born in Russia, although I didn't know that until much later on, she had told us she was born in New York). The Virginia piece baffled me because it was very random and something that I assumed was just another lie to keep me off track from finding my birth family.

I joined more registries. I eventually found some local adoption support groups, attended meetings, and heard many stories, none of which were even close to mine. No one knew how to guide me other than to keep showing up, keep registering, and keep sharing.

I went to special events where they had psychics. I didn't know how I felt about psychics, but I was open to any and every possible avenue that could help. (At this point, I had no clue I was a psychic medium, empath, or healer.) Something I was told more than once by multiple psychics at these events was that I'm in my father's family. One psychic insisted that my father (Lary) was my birth father and that my cousins (his brother's daughters) were my sisters. When I said it had to be one or the other, they insisted the girls were my sisters and that my father could be showing up that way because he really was my father in this lifetime. I brought some photos of my father and my cousins and me, wondering if my uncle Milton (my father's brother) was a connection here. (Over the years his daughters, my cousins, both told me he was a cheater, that he slept with his secretaries and other gals, so there was a chance that when my father said, "Mel, you really are a Shapiro through and through," that it was true.).

Both of my parents told me that my uncle Milton came to the house when I was an infant and, as my parents said, "kidnapped" me. I asked why he did that. They said it was so that he could show me off to the ladies. It didn't really make sense to me. Why would he have to steal me away instead of just asking to spend time with me? But I rarely got honest answers to any questions, so I remained in confusion and wonder about his role in my life.

I remember being held by my uncle and feeling so safe. I felt such joy when I'd see him. I can still feel it now. He always had a warm, safe, nurturing energy. I knew he loved me deeply. I always felt it. He died just before my second birthday, and all festivities were canceled because of that. As the years passed, I started wondering where he really had been taking me, as he was a married man with two daughters. What ladies would he be showing me off to? What was so special about me?

10

One rule I had with my searching was that I never gave up, and I left no stone unturned. Most of the time I spent at these meetings was bittersweet and painful. I was grateful to be among others who were searching and could relate to being adopted, but still, no one had my story. No one else had a handwritten birth certificate. No one had parents lying to them. I felt like no one could really understand my experience, and I continued to feel isolated and completely alone.

There were many times over the years that I talked to my birth mother either out loud or in my mind, hoping somehow she could hear me and wished for some reply from the ethers. I wondered if I looked like her? Did she love me? Did she ever think about me? Did I have siblings? I just cried, hopeless and frustrated, adding to my thoughts that something really must have been fundamentally wrong with me if I didn't even have the right to know who I was or where I came from. And so I made a commitment that I was going to search for the truth and not stop until I did, no matter what it took, and no matter the consequences.

I found a private investigator in Atlantic Beach, New York, with a good track record. I was twenty-four now, living as a responsible adult and ready to get serious about my search now that I was employed as a nurse and had my own income. The first thing he said when he looked at my birth certificate was "Why is it handwritten?"

I, of course, didn't know the answer, and he proceeded to tell me that no legally filed birth certificate in New York could be handwritten, that they all have to be typed. I was stunned, confused, and didn't understand, yet I was not at all surprised by another oddity in this story. But what I heard was interpreted in my mind as "Your birth certificate is fraudulent." And that was the fact. He said that there was no amended birth certificate, so ultimately there was no real proof of me. Boy, did that feed further into the something-is-wrong-with-me-and-I'm-alone story. In ways that most people have proof of their existence, I had none. In that moment, I felt more alone and isolated than ever. Nothing about my story was like anyone else's.

I chose not to tell my parents about any of my searching, but the more I learned, the angrier and more resentful I became. I felt that none of my four parents (birth or adopted) really cared about me as a person at all, which fed further into my feeling so alone and isolated in this world, connected to nothing.

After a few weeks, the investigator came back with nothing at all. The only thing he could find was the fraudulent birth certificate I already had. Once again, I was left feeling absolutely hopeless. I was finally able to afford a private investigator and—nothing. This only built up my anger and frustration toward my parents even further.

There were times I thought I would explode physically from the pain of the betrayal and the lies. I kept asking "Why?" I sobbed myself to sleep many a night. Sometimes I lay there in a fetal position, rocking myself and holding a stuffed animal for comfort. I wished to die. I cried out in frustration and anger to my birth mother. One night I was lying there, rocking myself, sobbing, and I suddenly saw a vision of a woman lying in the same position, rocking herself in the same way I was. A very dark-skinned man was yelling at her. I thought she looked pregnant, but mostly, she was crying in fear and in pain. I knew this was my birth mother. She looked like the woman I remember being carried away from. This would be a vision I'd continue to see for many years, though not necessarily understanding it, yet somehow I knew it was her.

At this point in life, I hated myself. Nothing in my life really worked. For the last six years after returning home from Gainesville, I spent most nights out drinking with John, going to gay bars, being a perfect example of a "fag hag." That actually was most of my year in Gainesville as well. I spent many a night in Gainesville passing out on the floor of the girls' bathroom after vomiting multiple times. Even then, I wondered why we all did this, yet we kept doing it.

John and I drove around drunk during the middle of the night, listening to music and having tremendous fun. Looking back, we both are grateful we never hurt anyone. I know I was hurting myself. Alcohol made me sick, but I kept with it. I went on a liquid, doctor-controlled diet, and in spite of that, on my birthday, I went out drinking and drank as I always did. I became violently ill from both ends of my body. I had alcohol poisoning. But I got in my car, pridefully not letting John know how ill I was, and sat there for forty-five minutes praying to be able to drive home safely. I had never prayed before going to church with Lisa and her parents, but I did periodically, usually to Jesus, but sometimes to a God I didn't understand, and only from desperation since then. This time I was praying to them both. I prayed the entire drive home, as I had to stop and vomit, and soiled my pants in the car. I promised them (God and Jesus) that if I made it home alive, without hurting anyone else, I would never drink to the point of being drunk again. I've kept that promise.

I tried quite a few drugs along the way too, but never the really hard stuff. I didn't really like most of them, and I was actually afraid of them because I had a such a strong desire to numb up and check out. But I sure did have a strong liking for poppers (liquid amyl nitrate). John and I did rounds of sniffing from these little bottles. We made up games with them. We even had a third bottle for us to share back and forth with our free nostrils. If I ever was addicted to anything (aside from food), it was poppers. They made you happy, laugh, and feel lighthearted. They were great for sex, and they were legal, cheap, and easy to get a hold of. I smoked pot when I could; it was much easier on me than anything else. But my early twenties really were about drinking, dancing, partying, and trying to numb out my life.

It's 1990. I'm twenty-six now. I've been on and off multiple diets, and I'm pushing three hundred pounds.

> *I'm constantly in physical pain. When I stand up in the morning, I have to wait a couple of minutes before moving so that my feet stop hurting. My back always hurts, from the weight and from multiple nursing injuries from lifting and moving patients who were overweight, bed-bound, and so on. I have skin problems in every skin fold, chronic yeast infections, urinary tract infections, back pain, and more. Life in this body is nothing but hell.*

My relationship with Vicky was codependent at best, and we fought often. She didn't make our relationship a priority; the priority was always her family, which apparently I wasn't considered part of, evidenced by her behavior (putting them before me or us) in spite of us being together for years and being engaged—another relationship that proved to me I wasn't really part of a family. I was absolutely miserable, and I saw no way out. I spent my days hiding at home, binging on food for hours, then being sick, gaining more weight. I was dying inside. But the deep pain I felt somehow became a motivator. I wasn't going to spend the rest of my life carrying it around. It created an anger in me that somehow fed a determination that I was never going to let go of. I was going to find out the truth no matter what it took, no matter what my parents had to say about it. Finding the truth would be my sweet revenge.

Vicky and I had our holy union in March; my parents didn't attend, actually none of my family attended. It was a lovely small affair. During the ceremony, as we stood up at the pulpit with the minister and in the process of saying our vows, I heard a voice in my mind say, "You will marry a man by the time you're forty." What an odd thing to be hearing in the midst of my wedding. I questioned if I should go on with the ceremony for a moment, and then looked at Vicky and completed my vows. But that message would never leave me. We had a short honeymoon in Disney World and went right back to our life of arguing and being miserable together. We truly did love each other, but neither of us had any relationship skills.

In my twenty-seventh year, now 1991, a lot of things started to change. I started the year off by joining the Alma Society: Adoptees Liberty Movement Association in New York. I put myself on their search list as well as their mailing list and started attending local meetings. No matter with whom I connected, although there was great compassion, no one understood how my situation could happen, nor were there many suggestions other than to keep myself "out there."

My time at the hospital had come to a close after three years. I could no longer handle what I experienced there, especially with the cancer patients. I saw doctors encourage one more round of chemotherapy, knowing all too well by their lab work that it likely would kill the patients. But they wouldn't tell the patient or families that and I couldn't handle the lack of integrity and dishonesty around it.

And who got to give that last dose of medication? Right—me. I was a legal murderer. I couldn't do it. The deceit was more than I could handle. I transferred to telemetry and did some time in the ICU and CCU. But the final end to my hospital years was when I was reprimanded for consoling a terrified patient who was ninety-two years old and going in for heart surgery. She was just one of too many, but I pulled up a chair next to her bedside, held her hand, and listened to her while she cried and shared her fears. When we were through and I walked out of the room, I found the nurse manager standing there, arms crossed, clearly angry by the look on her face. She said, "If I ever see you sitting on the job again, you'll be written up and disciplined." She had my resignation within a few days.

I quickly found a job with hospice, but this was a specialty position; all of my patients were HIV/AIDS. This was during the early years of the disease. I had already lost friends, and in the nine short months I worked there, I lost many more as well as friends of friends, infants, toddlers, and young men barely starting their lives. It was the most difficult work I'd done in my life and remains so to this day. I risked my license repeatedly, telling them to use marijuana for the symptoms. They would thank me profusely because it was the only thing that made a difference for them. And I did that often, happily so, aware that I could have lost my career. Their comfort came first.

All of my friends thought what I was doing was wonderful, and they had great respect for it. On the other hand, all my mother could say about the job was "You're too young to be around so much death." It was futile, but I attempted to explain to my mother that death was only one moment of the time I spent with these amazing people, and that most of our time was spent focusing on their quality of life and celebrating their lives. She simply could not grasp these concepts, likely because of her own beliefs and lack of experience .

As with any job in medicine, if you have a truly caring heart, you cross paths with patients, families and caregivers who touch your heart. Some become friends, family, or even more. This is the nature of the beast. Fernando was one of those patients. His mother was precious, and his partner David and I became very good friends. When Fernando died, David had no one and nowhere to go. He had no resources left, and his career as a chef left him with limited financial resources with Fernando having been sick for so long. Vicky had met him, and we agreed to let him move in with us. This crossed a line that thankfully was never caught by the hospice, and it would be a lesson I would learn about picking who you welcome into your home and your life.

David got a part-time job and agreed in return for staying with us to play private detective for me. His job was to call every single one of my family members, pose as a PI, record the calls on cassette tape, and follow a list of questions. He played the part brilliantly. Most of my adopted family talked with him. I had asked that he request they not share the conversation with my parents because of how it would upset them. Most of them were awesome about it, agreeing that I had a right to know, but none of them knew anything except for my aunt Mary, who at the time would not share anything. Neither side of the family knew more than the other. The common story was that they knew my parents had wanted a child, had tried adoption agencies, and then one day I'd just shown up.

He spent hours on the phone, day after day, for weeks until he'd spoken with everyone. We then went over the recordings, sentence by sentence, listening for inflections, fear, anything that would sound like someone was lying, hiding, or misleading. But they all sounded genuine and honest, truly wanting me to find the truth and have peace around it, as they all knew, especially my close cousins, how much pain this issue brought me.

But I didn't just hit another wall. I hit many in a very short period of time. I wrote vital statistics in New York, requesting a copy of my original birth certificate. After weeks of waiting, I received a letter informing me that there was no other birth certificate than the one already was in my possession confirming what the P.I. had told me. I forged a letter in my mother's handwriting requesting a copy of their marriage certificate to see if that would give me any information, only to receive the response that their records weren't on file with the state. The more stones I turned over, the less hope there was. I was obsessed at this point, ravenous for the truth, and angrier more than I'd ever been because I had gotten nowhere.

My resentment toward my parents continued to grow. Mom found out about the interrogations, and she was furious with me. She wouldn't tell me who told her, but I was fairly sure it was one particular cousin. We fought every time we interacted. I hated my mother more and more with each day. She had the keys to my freedom and would likely never give them to me. The issue was taking over my mind and my life.

I became obsessed with adopting a child. I looked at many options: in-vitro, in- and out-of-country adoption, and other avenues that were all far beyond my means. But if I had a baby, it would be mine. My blood, or legally my child. I would buy baby dolls and pretend they were my babies.

I was treating myself horribly with food, horrid thoughts, and poor behaviors. I wanted to die many times over the years, but this time I couldn't stop thinking about death, begging God to kill me, but I would never kill myself. For some reason I had a belief that I'd only have to come back to this horrid planet and do this again, and I knew it wasn't a solution, but I thought about it often and still prayed God would just take me. My life often felt like I was living in a soap opera and the drama was simply too much. I needed help. I was tormented. It was time to find a counselor, this time on my own.

11

In March of 1991, I found this fantastic therapist through work: Sandy. Now, mind you, I was twenty-seven years old and taking an action on my own, for myself, for the very first time to take care of me. It took a few sessions to really get the therapist caught up on what life has been like for me, the dynamics between my parents and me, and the struggles I face on a daily basis. I was now three hundred and thirty-three pounds and experienced little joy. I didn't go outside unless I needed to now. I wouldn't go to a beach or anywhere that I might have gotten gawked at or teased. I wasn't alive. I was living in darkness, anger, shame, resentment, and anguish and had no hope for anything different. Well, Sandy would be the one to help me with my first major breakthrough.

After just a few sessions, she encouraged me to write a letter to my parents since I had not tried communicating in that way. This was right around Vicky's and my first wedding anniversary. The letter was written very carefully with Sandy's guidance. The premise of the letter was sharing with my parents what it had been like for me to not have their unconditional love and acceptance about being gay, being overweight, and to consider that my weight was a sign and measurement of that pain. I shared how hard it was for me to deal with the lies around the adoption, and that I couldn't understand why they have handled it the way they have. I told them what I wished for in our relationship: emotional intimacy, support, respect, and exchange of love and acceptance. I told them that if they could not accept me for who I was, then I could no longer have them in my life, and that choice was up to them, and at that point, they would no longer hear from me unless we could find a common ground. I sent the letter, and I let go as much as I was capable of at this point in my life.

I was very anxious and terrified, but I was also enjoying the absence of those difficult conversations with my mother, all the time, about who I was. I started to wonder if that was the end of our relationship, until a few weeks later a letter came in the mail. I immediately had a reaction of anxiety and nervousness as I walked up to my apartment looking at my mom's beautiful handwriting. Dare I hope that this would be something good? That things could actually be different now? Well, they would be, one way or the other.

I closed the door, sat on the couch, opened it with shaking hands, and read the most disappointing letter I could have hoped to receive. I was, in fact, baffled, reading with disbelief about all they had done for me, and what I was doing to them and the pain I'd caused them and that I was the worst child that ever lived. I actually chuckled out loud at that last one, as it was absurd to me.

She said that I wasn't worth the $10,000 that they paid for me, but most painfully, she included a full-page list, both sides of the paper, of all the ways they had spent money on me, with the dates, the amounts, and the details of each item. She pointed out all that they had done for me, that I was ungrateful, and that she just didn't know what to do with me anymore.

For me, I felt that nothing they had ever given was without some type of string attached, some expectation. And little did they know, I had been grateful for them from the moment I knew I was adopted, but my mother couldn't and wouldn't allow it, see it, or accept it. After reviewing the letter with Sandy, it was clear there was nothing left to do but let go. I grieved, but at the same time, not having my mother poke at me brought solace, relief, and freedom from a pain I thought I would never be without. Another pain was present with the loss of them, but grief was a much more manageable pain. Finally, my heart would have a chance to heal.

Ten months passed. During that time, Vicky and I went to Colorado on a summer vacation. We went to visit my closest friend at the time, Rick (and his partner Skip). Rick and I worked together at my first nursing job in the hospital. We were instant friends, and the four of us spent a lot of time together, and in a way, we were like family. Rick and Skip had moved to Colorado six months prior, and I had always wanted to see Colorado, dreaming of it as a child, so this was our chance.

We had a layover in Dallas, and as we ran to the gate, I stopped at a payphone, flew through the phonebook, found my sister Gabby's name and number, ripped it out, and barely got on the flight. I would call her when I returned home. It had been twelve years, and I missed my sisters and wanted them in my life. I wanted any family that would have me. If I waited for my father, it was likely I would never have contact with them again. The one thing about my father that I feel was detrimental to him is that if he felt he was right, he remained in that righteousness to the death. He never communicated with me after my letter, likely because he was very hurt, and he had to keep peace, living with my mother. Now that my parents were out of my life, I felt the freedom to do what I wanted.

I fell completely in love with Denver. The moment I got off the plane and felt the dry air on my skin, with its sweet scent, I just knew I was home. I only felt more strongly about it each day we were there. As soon as we got back to Florida, I asked Vicky about moving, and she hesitantly agreed. She was hesitant because she'd be leaving her family who continued to be more important than me.

Nevertheless, I put the plans in motion, and our last day in Florida would be February 28, 1992. What better a present for my birthday than to leave a place I had never wanted to be in the first place? I felt hope. For the first time in my life, I felt I would be truly happy, one day. My life was in my hands now, finally.

I called Gabby right after our return. She was thrilled to hear from me. It was so good to hear her voice and to hear that I not only had one nephew, but four! She had two boys, and Sunny had two boys, and they were doing very well. We caught up. I told them I would be moving to Colorado, and we agreed to meet in Dallas when I drove through on the way to Denver. Dad had repeatedly said he wanted nothing to do with them. I doubted that he would ever forgive them for what had happened at Sunny's wedding or ever realize that he was the reason that there was so much distance between them now. But for me, I was overjoyed to have my sisters in my life again.

The holidays had passed, it was January 1992, and we were six weeks away from our departure day. I had given my notice at the hospice and apartment complex, and we were full swing into packing. I was home, packing, and the phone rang. It was my cousin Beth in New York. Beth and I had grown up together. Her mom, my aunt Bea, was my mother's youngest sister and they were very much alike (my mother and aunt). Beth and I had always remained close, even in challenging times. We had the same family values and were very like-minded. She had always been the only one in my mother's family that truly had gotten all of who I was and loved me anyway.

We got caught up on what had been happening in our lives. I was expecting to end the call, and then she told me, completely out of the blue, that my mother wanted to talk to me. I replied the same reply I'd been giving for the last ten months: "If she wants to talk, she knows she has to call me, and she has to be prepared to accept me as I am and stop trying to change me."

Beth said, "OK, I'll tell her." I figured that was the end of that. It wasn't likely my mother could ever refrain from those behaviors.

It took courage, but I didn't stand down. I did what was best for me, no matter the consequences. I had thought about my parents daily for quite a few months, then it started letting up, and one day, then two, then three, and then months went by without thinking of them. I had a sense of space and freedom in my life that I'd never had. It was a relief. Certainly, I thought about what it would be like if I got a call that one of them had died, but I would deal with that when and if that time had come. I made a choice and I stood by that.

Twenty minutes later, the phone rang again.

I answer and say, "Hello?"

"Mel, this is Mom."

My heart sinks. My head swirls, my adrenalin rushes through my whole body, and immediately I'm in a fight-or-flight mode. With great control, I say "Hi."

And she replies, "Beth said you wanted to talk to me."

And in this moment I know I've been duped. Beth has set us both up. I'm furious with her, but here I am, on the phone with my mother for the first time in ten months.

We quickly went over Beth's shenanigan and start to catch up.

She said my father wouldn't come to the phone, which was typical of him when he felt hurt. Two years after the incident with my sisters, Sunny called him, and he pretended he didn't known who she was, said he couldn't talk, took her number saying he'd call back, and never did. When he'd gotten the announcement of his first grandson's birth, he ignored it. He was great at cutting his nose to spite his face. This was my dad. This is why I felt their separation was now in his hands.

I was very tentative, but Mom wanted to meet. She didn't want me to move to Colorado without saying goodbye. I told her they had to come to my place, they had to be OK with Vicky if she were home, and she quite surprisingly agreed.

It's a couple of days since our call. Mom is knocking on my door. She is alone, Dad refuses to get out of the car. She comes in. We visit for a while. It's awkward, yet surprisingly good to see her. Through it all, she is still my mother, a fact that cannot be changed.

After a bit we walk down to the car. Mom wants Dad to come up, but he won't even look at me.

I say, "Hi, Dad."

Looking forward out the front windshield, he says, "Hello," in a deep solid tone. The energy is thick; it can be cut with a knife. It's terribly uncomfortable, but he did drive her here, and I know inside he is writhing in pain.

I ask him to please come up. Nothing. Mom asks again, and he finally concedes. The ride up the elevator is awkwardly silent. I'm anxious inside and afraid to say much of anything. He won't look at me, and he will not say a word. But he is here. That is a miracle, and I choose to look at this whole thing as very positive.

We sat and talked for quite a while. I got them caught up on what was happening. We agreed Beth had done the right thing, and it was a gift for which we never would really be able to repay her. I knew they were still disappointed. I was heavier than I'd ever been, married to and living with someone they thought wasn't a deserving match for me, but they did it. They were able to be good with it just enough that it didn't get in the way.

There was no attempt at trying to get me not to move, or to leave Vicky, or anything at all of that nature. It was a moment I had only hoped would happen because of my actions ten months prior. I was grateful and felt as if, even though we'd be eleven hundred miles apart, the lines of communication were open again, and something different may be possible now for us. I got my parents back, and I had hope for the future. I could not have anticipated just how much things were about to change.

12

For the next six weeks, we visited on the phone at length and talked often. Dad warmed up gradually, and by the time I departed for Colorado, we agreed that a visit would not be too far in the future, as they'd never been to Colorado and knew how beautiful it was there. For me, if I never returned to Florida, it would be OK with me!

One thing I didn't share with my parents at the time of our reunion was all the searching I had done up to that point. I was feverishly searching for the physician who'd delivered me at birth: Sidney Malet, MD. His was the only signature on both the hospital and state birth certificates that could possibly lead me to where I wanted to go. I contacted the Division of Professional Licensing; they had no record of his current location or anything past. I had gone to the library and gone through microfiche of phonebooks from the 1960s. I searched until I found an old address. After much work, I got a phone number for that address, and after some deep breathing, I mustered up the courage to dial the number. I reached a family who said that the address had been a residence for the last twenty-nine years. Dead end.

I called Kings County archives and inquired about any records from Interboro General Hospital, only to be told that the hospital had been turned into a nursing home and then closed decades ago and records would not have been kept that long. Dead end.

I contacted the New York City Hall of Records, Brooklyn Family Court, the Brooklyn Adoption Clerk, and Kings County Surrogate Court. Dead ends. So as the time approached for leaving Florida, I packed the adoption binder I had been filling up for years in a box, and hit the pause button on my search.

David, Vicky, and I departed for Colorado. He agreed to come with us, find work, and help with rent and expenses. We made our way to Dallas and met with my sisters and nephews. It was a joyful reunion. As an adult, I could see them differently now. Gabby was always a sister I looked up to. She had created a wonderful life with a new husband, Ron, whom I adored right off the bat. Sunny was still married to Marty, and she looked more like my father now than ever before. I joked that she was "Dad in drag." I couldn't stop staring at her. She was always beautiful, but after not having my father (whom I loved so much) in my life for the ten months, here "he" was in front of me with long, wavy, brown hair, radiant, and clearly alive. We had a wonderful but short visit and agreed to stay in touch.

On March 2, 1992, after four and a half long days, I drove the U-Haul up to our apartment in Aurora, Colorado. We had a wonderful view of the front range, Mt. Evans, and the Rocky Mountains. I solidified a job I had interviewed for while still in Florida at a wonderful hospice house in Denver, David found a job as a cook around the corner, and Vicky started job searching.

Eight weeks went by, and my best friend, Rick, called me while I was at work. It was my third week into this job, and he told me that he couldn't sit on this information any longer. He just didn't feel it was fair. He told me Vicky hadn't been looking for work at all, that she had been lying to me the entire time since we'd arrived and that she was going to give me two weeks warning before moving back to Florida. He said that David knew because they had been goofing off instead of her looking for work. He said that on his days off she had been taking him to adult book stores, and he'd been fooling around with strangers, in spite of having HIV, and he wasn't disclosing it to these other people, and that she was planning on going back to Florida to be with her family. That infuriated me more than her pathetic "two weeks' notice"! It was a sucker punch out of nowhere!

I sit in the basement stairwell at work with the six-foot coil phone cord stretched as far as it could go so as not to be heard. Getting through the shift feels as if time has slowed to a sloth's pace. I'm livid and angry beyond measure, partly at Rick for choosing to tell me this while I am at work, but more so at David and my wife, for lying and more importantly, putting her family before me/us yet again.

I hang up with Rick and immediately call her, asking her if this was true. She says yes, that she is planning on giving me two weeks, and confirms what Rick said she and David were doing with their time.

I reply in a clearly enraged voice, "I'm not a job that you give two weeks' notice. I'm your wife. And how can you with any consciousness help David spread a deadly disease around? Are you fucking kidding me? I want you out of the apartment before I get home, both of you, and I do not want to see either of you ever again!" and I hang up.

As I drive home, I'm banging the steering wheel, asking God why this happening. In the next moment, I'm thanking God for this happening, as I know, being honest with myself, that this is the best thing for me. I'm listening to Madonna's "Express Yourself" over and over again. The song has always been a favorite, but in this moment, it has personal meaning.

I drive up to the apartment, I see her car. They're home. My blood rushes to my head. I can feel myself getting more and more angry. I walk into the apartment, screaming, "What the fuck are you still doing here!" David is sitting in my recliner, not saying a word, looking down at the floor. Vicky comes out of the hallway and starts giving me her excuses: wanting to say goodbye, wanting to know if I'm OK.

I can't help myself, and at the top of my lungs, I start screaming, "Get the fuck out of my apartment!"

She continues to try and talk me down. I escalate more and more, telling her I would have been fine if she had left as I asked. She continues to placate me, and I start throwing things: our wedding rings, our wedding pictures, anything breakable I can find.

I lock myself in the bedroom, and Vicky calls Rick and his partner, and they agree to come over and be with me. She comes to the door to tell me they're on their way. I open the door and tell her she needs to leave, which she finally does. The guys arrive and just let me cry myself dry. They had been in our wedding, so they know the journey we've been on. They're godsends. Her leaving is the last good deed she does for me.

The guys do a great job at calming me down. I get them set up in the guest room, and I go in my room and call my parents. It's four in the morning in Florida. When Mom answers, I tell her it's me, and she says very anxiously, "Mel, are you OK?"

I reply with, "Mom, if I ever needed you, I need you now. Please don't lecture me. I just need you to listen." And by the grace of God, she just listens for the very first time! We talk for two hours, and by the end of the call, they agree to come for an extended visit. I lay some ground rules about this time needing to be a healing time for me, and they agree.

A new day began. I slept only for a couple of hours, merely because of exhaustion. Unfortunately, it didn't begin well. Vicky called and said she and David were leaving to go back to Florida, to "be with my family," another gut-wrenching dig. She asked if she could come get a few forgotten items and say goodbye. I figured, "Why not?" as this is the last time we would see each other and getting it as complete as possible would be good.

After she grabbed her belongings I walked her out to her car, I gave her a hug, without tears, without emotion, and as I turned to walk away, she said, "I know we will be back together, this is only temporary." She was clearly not in reality, wasn't remorseful, was not responsible for the fact that she may have assisted in transmitting HIV to innocent people, nor responsible for lying to me.

I turned around and replied, "No, Vicky, we will never be together again, nor is it likely you will ever see me again," and I walked into the apartment and closed the door. I never looked back. (I did meet Vicky once in Florida four years later, it was a good visit, and although she never did pay her debt to me, I was grateful to be free and complete.)

A couple of weeks later, my parents arrived. They had driven cross-country to be with their daughter, who was devastated, feeling abandoned, lost, and alone. The visit wound up being eight weeks long. Prior to this moment, I would have suffocated at the thought of being in a small two-bedroom apartment with my mother, but somehow, she had risen above (maybe she was just happy Vicky and I were over, but either way, she was amazing) and was supportive and comforting in ways I'd never thought she was capable of. She even gave me a very surprising gift: my father's war medals. I had always wanted them, but she had this odd belief that certain things only should be gifted after someone is dead or it's an omen they will die sooner. Well, there they were, put in a shadowbox frame, lined up perfectly with a small war photo of my father below them. I burst into tears of gratitude and hugged her. She was becoming a better mom. It was miraculous!

On the days I went to work, they would go sight seeing around Denver, and once I had built up enough vacation time, we took a vacation around one of the most beautiful states I'd had the pleasure to live. One thing we always did well was road trips. That eight weeks was exactly what I needed, and I think it was what they needed as well. Only a few months before that, I'd thought I'd be leaving Florida and would never see them again. I may have lost a marriage, but I got my parents back, and in a way I'd only dreamed of. My wish was fulfilled: the visit was nothing but healing.

A few months after their return home, my parents agreed to help me purchase my first home. They managed the deposit for an FHA loan, and the monthly mortgage was mine to take care of.

13

In August 1992, I moved into the most adorable 1925 brick bungalow in south Denver. I had already started letting some weight go. I was 333 pounds at my highest. My goal with this house was to be able to get up the basement steps without being short of breath. This house would be my sacred space, my cocoon, and the place I would do a tremendous amount of healing.

For the first few months in this house, I was working, nesting, decorating, and enjoying having a home with no limitations on what I could do with it. I started shedding some weight naturally, but I started thinking about reaching out for help, as my grief over the end of my eight-and-half-year marriage, especially ending the way it did, wasn't going well. Vicky and I had no contact except to discuss her share of our debt, which she clearly wasn't going to pay, so I stopped communicating with her altogether.

It's the end of February 1993, and I just turned twenty-nine years old. I'm loving my job. I'm starting to have unusual experiences with the patients, and those experiences somehow seem quite comforting to me. In the last few months, I've noticed while in a patient's room (this hospice house has a hallway of eight private rooms, and the rest of the house parallel to the rooms is a kitchen/dining room, living room, and sunroom and office in the front) three figures moving through the hallway together. They're always lined up, and they float across the hallway floor. I never see walking motions. I never feel afraid of them, only curious. They're gray-shaded figures in the shape of humans, but flatly dimensioned versus three-dimensional.

It happens a few times, and I realize that on the nights that I see them, a patient dies. So I start to pay attention to when I see them, which is more and more frequently as time goes by. Every time, when I return to work the next day, a patient has passed. I eventually realize that I'm seeing angels. Maybe death angels, but angels. This opens me up to a part of myself that I had forgotten, and I recall the situations of disappearing people when I was younger.

Seeing these beautiful beings float the hallways also sparked a hunger for me that I'd not had in a long time as well; the hunger for God. My human experiences as of late had taken me away from all that. I realized it was time to really find myself, so I found a great therapist, whose name was Ted. I start working with Ted in April 1993. On our very first session, he suggested to me that I go to an Overeaters Anonymous meeting. My past rushed in full force: twelve years old, training for my bat mitzvah, and going to these twelve-step meetings in a church, and most of the participants say Jesus is their higher power. I shared my confusion with Ted, and he requested that I go to a meeting that was not at a church and to go with an open mind as an adult of my own accord now.

Ted also asked me how I felt about things. I was like a deer in the headlights; I truly had no idea what he was asking me. How was I feeling? No one ever asked me how I was feeling. I told him I was pissed at my mother, that most of this was her doing, I was pissed at Rick for telling me about Vicky the way he had, and I was most pissed right now at Vicky for what she did with David and lying to me.

He again asked me, "So how do you feel about that?" Deer in the headlights. He had a huge dry-erase board in his office and wrote the following on it: *happy, angry, sad, fear, joy, disgust, grateful,* and so on.

I just looked blankly at these words. In that session, for the very first time, like a moment of enlightenment, I realized I never was allowed to have feelings at home. I had not been in touch at all with the anger I was carrying around with me since I was a child, and at first glance, I realized it was a huge amount of anger. I had a lot of work to do to heal, so I agreed to go to an OA meeting, read *The Dance of Anger* by Harriet Lerner, and then *You Can Heal Your Life* by Louise Hay. Both, most especially the latter, would wind up being books I would use for the rest of my life as needed. Both changed me dramatically, brought tremendous healing, and in hindsight, were also training grounds for the work I would do in the future. Ted also helped me learn how much

I had taken on my mother's patterns and behaviors. I had a lot of work to do on myself to unravel the "mini me" Sylvia successfully created.

It's May 23, 1993, and I walk into my first OA meeting as an adult. I'm instantly home. I hear people speaking my story of their relationship to food: It doesn't hurt. It doesn't talk back. It doesn't argue. It never abandons me. It comforts me. I'm floored and ever so grateful to have found a place where I belong.

Little did I know that I had just planted, watered, and sprouted the roots of my spiritual foundation. I started working with a nutritionist, and was immediately on a steady downward motion with my weight. I was steadily losing a pound a week. I spent my time off walking and hiking, and every three months, I went to Grand Lake, Colorado, to enjoy a little slice of heaven. The time there was spent hiking, reading, journaling and doing my inner work. My parents continued to visit, always spending an extended amount of time with me, and the time always included a road trip.

It's their third trip to Colorado now. It's mid-1994, I'm thirty, and I absolutely love life in Colorado. I'm still working at the hospice house. I'm the charge nurse for the evening shift. On this one morning, my mom is helping me paint the basement floor of my new home. I have a work meeting today, so I have to be done early and get to work by 2:00 p.m. We prep the floor, and I start painting as Mom keeps me company.

Dad is upstairs in his usual position: on the couch, watching television.

Out of nowhere, my mother asks, "Do you ever think about your birth family?"

Instantaneously, much like the night when Vicky left, I have a surge of energy go through me, and I'm immediately reacting, and I ask, "Why are you bringing that up!?"

She says, "Have you thought about what it could have been? Like maybe you were a child of rape? Or maybe there are racial issues in the family? Or maybe there was some kind of abuse going on? Do you ever think about that?"

I'm already fuming on the inside, aware now of my anger and rage. I cannot believe we're having this conversation, once again. She just cannot leave it alone.

I look at her. I stop painting the floor, and I say, "Mom, there is no scenario that I've not gone over in my head, that I've not thought about, not dreamed about. But most of all, nothing is more painful than not knowing and being lied to. Why are you bringing it up again?"

She tells me that she was just wondering, and goes into her stories about my birth father being Jewish, and that they made her promise never to tell anything, and that it pains her to know I'm hurting.

I remind her that I'm hurting because she won't tell me the truth! I remind her that nothing is more painful than not knowing, that no truth could be worse than that, and that her stories and lies are what hurt the most. The conversation escalates to the point of screaming. The painting ceases, and we're having a full knockdown, drag-out fight.

I begin crying, asking her why she can't just leave it alone. "Why do you have to keep bringing this up?"

She has no good answer. I'm aware it's her guilt, but her guilt is not my problem, and I had enough healing and growth to know how to handle this now. But I'm too upset. and after about ten minutes back on the old merry-go-round, I go upstairs an absolute wreck, crying (really more like wailing) and unable to calm down.

Dad asks me what's wrong, and I tell him, "She brought it up again. She just can't leave it the fuck alone!" At this point I don't care if they don't like me cursing. I'm a grown woman, they're in my home, and she has violated me once again with her lies, upsetting the peace and impacting all the good work we've done up until this point.

She comes up from the basement behind me. I sit on the couch, trying to calm down. The couch is a candy-cane-shaped couch. Dad is sitting on the curved end, facing the television. I sit at the opposite end and try to gather myself so I can get to work. She comes and sits next to him. There are at least two spaces between us, and he just looks at me, then her, and says nothing.

And then she starts in again saying "Mel, I know how you feel. Remember I told you when I was a kid I thought I was adopted. My sisters and brother all told me that, and I really thought I was. I understand how you're feeling."

My blood boils. My mother had said this so many times throughout my life time, and this time I just couldn't hold back. "You have no fucking idea how I feel, and I'm sick and tired of you saying something so stupid. No one has a clue how I'm feeling. You aren't me. You aren't adopted. You haven't been lied to by your parents and God knows who else. What the fuck is it going to take for you to shut up about this and stop bringing it up!"

She continues to spew out the lies about the whole story, repeating all the inconsistent information she's given before, and I'm now having a complete and total breakdown. There is nowhere safe to go, so I sit there falling apart emotionally. I can hardly breathe. I cannot see out of my eyes because they're so red, painful and swollen.

She finally stops talking. Neither of them say a word. Neither of them reach out to comfort me. Neither of them do anything to correct a situation that they have created and allowed since agreeing to adopt me. They sit there staring into space while I fall apart completely.

As if the issues itself weren't enough, I now have two parents who do absolutely nothing to console their child. What kind of parents do this? They weren't suited for the job, and no matter how much I loved my father, I'm equally as angry at him right now as I am with her.

I miss my meeting at work. I'm almost late for my shift after getting up from the couch, looking at them and pleading ever so venomously: "This is the last time you will ever bring this up until you're ready to tell me the truth. We will never, ever discuss this again. If you ever do bring it up, I promise you, you will lose me again, and this time forever."

They never move. They don't look at each other. They keep looking down at the floor when I leave.

I have a lot of painful memories with my parents, many more with my mother, but this was by far the most painful moment I shared with my parents together. As I have said, life often felt like a very highly dramatic soap opera with her, often times as if my life wasn't even real. I simply could not and still cannot understand how parents can watch their child in that much pain, inflicted by their own actions, repeat offenses and not even reach out to comfort them. Never in my life have I felt so alone, and I had felt alone *a lot.* In that moment, I knew that there was nothing to do but let this issue go and stand by my promise that if they ever brought it up again, I would end all communication with them. I finally was able to stand for myself, but boy, did it come along with an insurmountable amount of pain.

When I got home from work that night, there was little conversation. Dad was already in bed, and Mom had waited up for me, but there was no further discussion about the forbidden topic. The rest of their visit was tainted at best. I forgave the conversation, but it was a bittersweet relief when they left this time.

14

The next time I saw my parents was in Florida, 1995. I was thirty-one now. We had been doing better. My life of recovery was going well, although certainly not without pain. Abandonment was my core issue, I was still desperate for love, but I was starting to develop some of that for myself now. On my visit that year, I asked my parents if we could have a very short conversation about the "forbidden subject." They agreed.

We're in their apartment. I'm standing in the dining room, facing the living room (it's really one large room), Dad is sitting on a chair in the living room, Mom standing next to him, and I say, "This really will be the last time we speak of this topic, but I'd like to ask that whatever you know, whatever information you have, please, for your daughter's sake and sanity, please leave the information with your wills."

They look at each other. A little nod up and down occurs for both of them. They look back at me and, at the same time, say, "OK."

I thank them, and that is the end of the conversation.

I knew by the nods at each other, and the way they said OK that they knew more than they were ever going to tell me. Although my heart sunk once again with such a deep sadness that my parents were still not going to end this misery for all of us, all I could do now, for my own peace of mind, my own sanity, was to leave it alone.

I had done all the searching I knew to do. I joined registries as they came up. Now that the World Wide Web was becoming a more commonly used thing, I got online and spent hours searching for anything I could find about adoptees in New York. It was always futile, but as long as I stayed in action, I believed the universe knew that I was serious about finding my birth family and the truth. The depth of the pain and emptiness that came with it never lessened. I learned to just accept it and let it be, although some days were easier than others, as the wound was still there.

It was June of 1996. I was thirty-two years old, and for the last nine months, I'd been dealing with the most severe physical pain in many years where being a woman is concerned. Since my teen years, my menstruation has been an irregular, painful source of anguish and frustration. My first two days of my periods, when I have them, are spent in bed or in the bathroom. After biopsies, ultrasounds, CAT scans, blood tests, and nine months of two extra-strength Vicodin every four hours (rendering me nonfunctional except for the first few hours of the day in which I'd rush and see my patients and come home to chart for the rest of the day) and it being the day before my hearing with the insurance company to fight them on allowing the surgery, they call and agree to let me have the surgery. What a crazy system we have! Nine months of suffering, finally comes to an end.

I was never one of those women who felt menstruation was a beautiful cleansing process that arrived every twenty-eight days on the dot and left me cleansed and empowered afterward. For me, my period was disgusting, painful, very irregular, dirty, and foul. This was a day of celebration. Tomorrow, I would be free of this unhappy organ living inside of me. But there was one thing I'm suddenly confronted with: I for certain will never carry a child of my own.

I was standing by my bedroom door, and all the years behind me come flooding in. During my years with Vicky, we had talked about having children. The year prior to moving to Colorado, while I wasn't in touch with my parents, I investigated more choices in adoption, artificial insemination, surrogacy, and so on. I became obsessed. I went to toy stores and held baby dolls, imagining what it would mean to hold a baby that shared my DNA, whose skin came from my skin, who may have my blue eyes, my funny toes, heavy build, curly or wavy blond locks. I would imagine what I may have been like at that age to the adults my life. I became completely entrenched in it until the move which broke the obsessive cycle I was in. Financially, I didn't have the means for any of those avenues. I talked with Rick, and he and his partner agreed to donate their sperm, but with the irregularity of my cycle, it seemed futile to try.

So here I am, frozen in time, with all of these memories flashing though my head. The grief of what is never to be floods through my heart right to my eyes, and I begin to sob. I'm standing behind the couch where I was sitting just a couple of years ago when I'd had a complete breakdown. But this time my mother gets up, walks over to me, and for the first time in my life, at thirty-two years old, she wraps her arms around me, pulls me tight, and lets me cry myself empty. She is being the mother I yearned so desperately for, even if only for a moment.

I understand why of course, as she had a hysterectomy when I was five, so she understood exactly what was going on inside of me (aside from the desperate need to have someone who shares my DNA). She is compassionate, patient, understanding, and loving. I'm surprised, confused, but deeply grateful.

The surgery and recovery went well. And no sooner was I back at work when the doctors called to inform my mother that the reason she has been having so many digestive issues (which she has had for decades, but they had only recently become critically chronic) was that she had forty-two pre-cancerous growths in her stomach, and they needed to do a complete gastrectomy with pouch construction from her small intestine. This was going to be a major operation. She would not be able to stay on her thyroid medicine, which she had been on for decades, and she would be in the hospital for at least a week. I flew to Florida in August to support my parents.

It's the summer of 1996. Mom is seventy-five now, Dad is eighty-one, and I'm thirty-two. Mom's surgery goes very well, and thankfully, Micky (my "sister/friend" and amazing nurse) is working at the same hospital and keeps a close eye on Mom. Micky has become a full-fledged family member. My parents tell the doctors she is their granddaughter, and she becomes my rock during these times.

As the days progress, Mom becomes more and more irrational, agitated, and much like the monster of my childhood. We have cots brought in the room today (day two) to stay with her because she became belligerent and paranoid last night, calling us at home after we were in bed and past midnight, saying the staff was trying to kill her. We get little rest.

On the morning of day three, she wakes me up and says, "Mel! Get up! The doctors and interns are coming, and my bed needs to be made. The room needs to be cleaned and straightened up. They can't see it this way."

I sit up with a start and floods of memories from my childhood come back to me of her saying similar things because it was more important how things looked than if we were happy, cared for, rested or nurtured. This is my mother.

I think, "How am I going to get through this?" and clear as day, I hear myself say, "You're going to eat your way through it."

Over the next eight days, I gain back eleven of the one hundred pounds I lost. But something very interesting happens in this moment.

I realized that the monster was out because she wasn't on her thyroid medication. My heart sunk with compassion. For the first time, I put together the children running away from her screaming, "Monster! Monster!" when she was a teenager, with my perception of her as a monster, and realized that all these years she was this way because her medication was never managed properly.

While on a break I went outside and sat in meditation, eyes closed. I got a vision in my mind of the inside of her stomach, and I saw these forty-two growths—each one has a lie attached to it, and they festered from her swallowing them. My spiritual and metaphysical mind is connecting the dots now, and again, a wave of compassion comes through me, and I can feel my mother's suffering for the first time as any another human. I feel her suffering as if it were my own.

A week passed, and Mom was home again, back on her medication, much less the monster and more her balanced self, and I headed home to Colorado with some insight, understanding and a lot of forgiveness in my heart.

Mid-October, my father had some routine tests that the cardiologist requested, and as a result, they scheduled a cardiac bypass for him. He happened to be in the hospital of my first job, on the same telemetry floor that I worked. Talk about going back in time! I flew back to Florida again to support my parents, this time in reverse. This time I was more stressed because I was spending 24/7 with my mother, and once again, I asked myself, "Mel, how are you going to get through this?" Same answer, "You are going to eat your way through it." Eleven more days, another eleven pounds gained. I was a master eater, and my mother was my food guru.

Mom was losing weight rapidly. She was as worrisome and nervous as ever. She never relaxed, always unsettled, constantly doing something, and what she couldn't do herself, she then ordered me to do. Thankfully, she had given up badgering me about my sexuality, and my weight was coming off, so most of the negative attention toward me was now based on what needed to be done instead of her trying to change me.

She had been given a very specific diet to follow with her new tiny pouch of a stomach, and not one day since the surgery had she followed it. She was looking pale and was weak, not getting the nutrition her body needed. Nor could it digest or assimilate what she was putting in it, so those of us around her had to suffer the results of these actions. I spent a lot of time cleaning carpets and gagging on disinfectant spray and cleaners, as her bowels never were to work right again as long as she didn't change her diet. Wearing diapers didn't even do the job. There were times of indescribable humiliation for her, and great frustration for me.

Dad made it through surgery just fine. The few days post-op that we spent at the hospital were similar to Mom's hospital stay, with me being ordered around to tidy up the room, get Dad snacks, but he reigned her in enough to give me some relief. We got him home, and again I was relieved to go back home to Colorado. This wasn't the year for our amazing extended vacations together. It was a rough few months that I was grateful were over.

15

September 14, 1997. It had been quite a while since I had done much on the adoption. It had gotten very painful to look at, and with nothing but dead ends, my frustration level had gotten too high. But on this day I felt it was time to rekindle the search. I had enough of a break from it to recover and build up some strength, so I got on the internet and found seven support groups in the Colorado area and joined them all.

After that, I decided that this was the day I was going to confront my aunt Mary, Mom's sister: the one who picked me up at the hospital and brought me home to my parents. I called her. We were catching up. Up until that day, we never talked about it openly. She honored my mother's secrecy all these years, but this day felt like the day to ask her. I no longer cared about what other people's needs were in this situation.

"Aunt Mary, you know how hard this adoption has been on me."

She says "Yes honey, I do."

"Would you be willing to tell me anything you know?" I replied.

She said, "Melanie, I've wished your mother would tell you the truth since the beginning. I hate that you don't know. She is going to hate me, but yes, I will tell you what I can remember."

I was full of anticipation and hope in that moment. It was as if for the first time a bank vault door was unlocked. I felt excited, and for the first time in a long time (if not forever), I felt someone actually cared more about me than themselves.

Aunt Mary then shared that Dad had brought her to my birth mother's house in Brooklyn once to give her money for a phone bill. Aunt Mary couldn't recall if it was a brick warehouse-type building or validate that she went up one flight of stairs to the second floor to get to the apartment. (These were things that I had seen in visions for many years) She couldn't recall if the phone payment was cash or a check, but she did recall that when my birth mother opened the door, she was quite pregnant with me.

My birth mother was about five foot, two inches in height, and she looked a lot like me, with my coloring. There was a three-year-old boy with her (he is my half brother), and she believed there possibly was an older brother as well, and my grandmother. Aunt Mary couldn't recall where it was in Brooklyn, or names, but she was certain that I had a brother three years older than me, and in that moment all I could think of is "I have a brother. I—have—a—brother. *I have a brother!"*

I'm as still as an oak tree, planted firmly in my seat, ears open, pen in hand, with my adoption-search binder, and she shares with me that she was in fact the person who came and picked me up at the hospital and brought me home.

I share with her my memory of being carried away from my birth mother, and she says, "How on earth do you remember that? That is exactly how it happened!"

I tell her it's likely that a child never forgets the moment he or she is ripped away from his or her birth mother, even if they bury it and are not able to pull it up at will.

Aunt Mary tells me that it's also true that my birth mother did assume my adopted mother's name during her hospital stay. I wonder how on earth that was even possible.

As she shares, I'm revisiting memories I have of the building: red brick, black wrought iron railings, exterior stairwells and fire escapes. I see inside the apartment for some reason: kitchen as you walk in on the left, dining area and living room past it, a little hallway with two bedrooms on the right, and a bath in the middle. I've no idea if what I'm seeing is real, right, or just my imagination, but as she speaks these visions come in so strongly.

At the same time, my chest is welling up with emotions. Tears are in my eyes. My heart is pounding, racing, knowing some truth about where I come from for the first time in this life. For some reason, I notice I'm not as excited about my mother (I felt that she made her choice in giving me away), but my brother and I didn't have that choice. I never really had a thought at all about my birth father (this was likely because of the fact that he was never part of the story related to the lies, only mentioned as being the reason as to why I was Jewish).

I always felt a pull toward my grandmother for some reason, but I'm fixated on the thought of having a big brother. I immediately start wondering if my brother knows of me, or am I a secret to him as well? Thoughts and emotions are flooding through every part of me, I'm tingling, excited, and at the same time angry as ever that, for thirty-four years, I've not known anything at all.

Until now.

Although this was all that my aunt Mary remembered, it had a major impact on me and got me revved up for more searching again. It also seemed to have opened me up because I started having more of the same visions of my birth mother. It was something that helped me start to realize was a connection to my birth mother of some sort, but like most of my story, I may never know if it's true.

Aunt Mary told my mother what she shared with me. On the next call with my mother, I confronted her in spite of the agreement (there was no choice—I couldn't let this go now that I actually had something tangible), and she was furious at my aunt. But she was backed into a corner now and admitted that they did pay the phone bill and what my aunt shared was correct: I had a brother!

In spite of barely being able to breathe, I didn't hesitate a second, and the inquisition began: "Did you pay the phone bill, Mom?"

"Yes."

"Did you pay by check or cash?"

"I don't remember."

"Did Dad drive her?"

"Yes."

"Where did he drive her to?"

"I don't remember."

Every question from that point forward that led to a final answer ended with "I don't remember."

When I asked my father, he gave me the same response. I knew he was lying because my father drove a cab in Manhattan and he worked the five boroughs of New York on a major soda company vending route after that. Dad could pretty much tell you what street he drove at any time with a client in the car or where his soda machines were. He was from Brooklyn and was a door-to-door salesman at one time as well, but this, this was the one place he couldn't remember driving to? I think not.

My life had just changed forever. Shortly after these conversations and learning I was, in fact, not an only child, I was at home in Denver, working on a painting, and the song "Somewhere Out There" from the movie *An American Tail* came on the radio. I was listening to the lyrics, and I found myself in tears. I was singing along, singing to my big brother, praying, and hoping, one day my dream will come true. (The movie is animated, about a family of mice who immigrate, to New York of all places, to find freedom.

The main character gets lost and goes on a search to find his family.) This became my song for my big brother. Every time I heard it, I cried like a baby, yearning, wondering, hoping, and praying that one day I would be able to share it with him. At night when I saw the first star, I wished upon it to find him, coinciding perfectly, without intention on my part, with the song.

Never a night has gone by without wishing on the first star for him when I see it, and then singing the song, even if only in my head to a brother I wished for more deeply than anything else ever in my life.

I attended a couple of meetings of the support groups that I had found, and nothing had changed. Any suggestions were things I'd already done; any leads led nowhere. Then one day there was a psychic at one of the meetings, and I figured, "What do I have to lose?"

My reading only repeated what the previous psychics had told me: my father was either my adopted dad or his brother Milton, that within six months my mother would tell me some answers, and that when I come to a dead end and it seems as if there is no other place to go, somehow all will finally come out.

I laughed at the reading, disappointed once again.

16

Another year passed, and as 1997 came to a close, I got a very strong feeling in my gut that it was time to leave Colorado. In January 1998, as I was putting my home on the market and packing, I spent much of my free time on more searching. I continued to search for Dr. Malet (the doctor who'd attended my birth). I wrote the Albany Registry requesting any non-identifying information they had at all. They had nothing. I wrote the *New York Times*, the *Herald Tribune*, the *Daily News* for any archives in 1964. The little I received had nothing that would turn into a lead.

I sold my home in February of 1998 and did some traveling, and only a year later found myself back in Colorado. During that time away, while I was living in Fort Wayne, Indiana, from June until December of that year, I resumed my efforts. In July, I called another private investigation company: Priority One Investigations. I spoke with a gentleman named Rick, who heard what I had to say and felt that there was enough to go on, but of course, there were no guarantees. The flat rate of the search was only $300, which was an inexpensive and worthwhile investment to me. I hired him and prayed that this is the direction that will finally reveal something: anything.

While I waited to hear back from Rick (the PI), I reregistered with the ISSR: International Search Soundex Registry, since I'd moved a few times. I wrote the American Adoption Congress, People Searching News, Independent Search Consultants, the Department of Social Services, and the Adoption Reunion Registry. Anything I could find that had anything to do with family, adoption, or searching, I went for it. But nothing.

Rick got back to me within a few weeks, and he said that the only thing he could confirm for me was that the adoption was either black market or illegal, as there was no amended birth certificate or anything anywhere that would indicate I was adopted. I don't know why I felt as I did, as I thought I'd be used to the disappointment by now, but this felt like the greatest of dead ends to date.

I went into counseling again and started on some herbal supplements for depression that was partially caused by the gray weather of Indiana and partially from the adoption situation. After six months in Indiana, I was thrilled to go back to Colorado—I missed the sun! I took a travel nursing job that got me housing in Aurora, Colorado, and within a few months, I found a great home in Arvada, Colorado. In late 1999, I started a job at another inpatient hospice.

I was in my thirty-fifth year of life now. There have been no further occurrences with the adoption story. I avoided thinking of it as much as possible, as the pain was excruciating at times. I still had a very hard time dealing with my parents lying to me, and although I'd forgiven them, it was a constant source of contention. It was the elephant in the room that would never be removed. It was to be there forever, and I finally had come to some sort of acceptance of it.

I'd done all I could do. I'd talked with everyone in the family by this point; I confessed about David being the private investigator. Most of the family were so understanding. A few couldn't understand why I couldn't just be happy with such great parents. These relatives didn't know of how my mother would treat me, touch me, talk to me, lie to me. They just saw this amazing woman who was generous and kind. And she was: to them.

It was in my new Colorado home that I really start exploring my spirituality more deeply. I'd already read so much on the Native American culture, which was what pulled me the most at this point in my life. I met a shaman at a metaphysical fair who introduced me to my first spirit guides, two Native American parents of a past life, and three angels: Lily, Lanie, and Anna. I worked with them for months in meditation, getting a deeper understanding of past lives, the beauty of the Native American culture, and what it was like to have angels with me all the time. This spirituality felt like a perfect fit.

I had a channeling done with a fellow nurse who'd lost her left eye when her third eye opened. She told me about my healing stone (in her readings, she told you what your personal healing stone and healing animal was, not like a birthstone or pet, but tools to help you in your spiritual journey), and what I was here to do in this life. I learned about chakras, numerology, Reiki, and smudging. I enrolled in a reflexology program. It was time to really walk my spiritual path.

I went back to OA meetings after a few years out of program. I had hit a plateau after the year of all of our surgeries, and I knew I needed to focus on it again, so in January of 2000, I walked into a meeting and met my sponsor and forever friend Ann. She was the last person in the room my ego wanted as a sponsor. I wanted someone who looked a certain way—young, fit, and obviously successful, but knowing how my ego sabotages, I chose her. What a gift I gave myself that day! Ann was an elder woman, with long, straight, gray hair, thin, and attached to her knitting bag, always busy creating something. But when it was time for her to share, she stopped and was fully present with everyone. I felt good about choosing her, and she said, "Yes!" So, I was now on a clear path to more healing for myself. I chose to take a break from relationships again and really focus on myself.

Although I was still on a weight plateau, I was doing a lot of inner and physical work. I had been having severe nerve and neck pain since 1988 when I had been in a hit-and-run accident with my friend John. We had been rear-ended by a vehicle that came out of nowhere while we were trying to save two drunk people who were staggering in the middle of the road. I became a living example of "no good deed goes unpunished."

I had undiagnosed whiplash and spent year after year with neuropathic pain going down my arms that ultimately led to a diagnosis in 1996 of fibromyalgia. I lived with chronic, horrific pain, but the headaches were getting worse, and my shoulders were locked tight in spite of physical therapy, massage, and any other treatment I tried. I went to the doctor, who suggested I consider a breast reduction to relieve the extra weight, stress, pressure, and tension they were putting on my neck and shoulders.

This, of course, wasn't something insurance would cover, so after the doctor's recommendation I asked my parents how they would feel about covering the expense. They said they would, and I was so grateful!

It was the end of October 2000; I would have these large, pendulous breasts taken down as small as the surgeon could get them. The idea of having perky breasts and having less pain is unfathomable to me. My breasts had been pendulous since I was twelve years old, and I hadn't seen my feet since then!

I was excited, but I had no idea what was really in store for me. The surgeon told me how it would go and that, because of the type of surgery, I would not be able to get a private room for recovery. My parents weren't going to be with me for this surgery, so I set an intention silently to have that private room and told him so! (I was very committed to my spiritual path at that time.)

During my study of numerology, I realized that my life path number was eleven, which a master number, and also a two (11: 1+1=2). Ever since I could recall I've had this odd, some would call it compulsive, behavior of doing things two or three times. I'm very drawn to the trinity, whether Celtic, Christian, or any other path. It simply resonates as a power number for me. And the more the number was multiplied, the stronger it got (i.e., 333 or 9). This ties into the following experience:

It's early afternoon, and I'm being prepped for surgery. I'm in a holding room, lying on a gurney. I suddenly experience a tremendous amount of anxiety. I go into meditation, affirming the transformation I'm going to go through, knowing I will be changed forever. I'm freezing to the bone, an experience I have not ever had before. I'm shaking from the inside out. I do some deep breathing. The nurse comes in and starts my IV. The doctor and anesthesiologist come in soon after, we go over the final paperwork, and off to the operating room, I go.

The nurse helps position on me on the very cold operating room table. It's freezing and sterile in here. It's a large room. The table is in the center of the room with all the usual equipment surrounding it. The nurse straps my limbs to the table, and the anxiety suddenly subsides; I stop shaking.

The anesthesiologist asks if I'm ready.

I say, "Yes!" and close my eyes counting backward: one hundred, ninety-nine, ninety-eight, ninety-seven...

I suddenly find myself sitting at the head of the operating table with a head in front of me. I see a blue surgical cap on the head, the drape coming up over the rest of the body. The heart lung machine is to my left, the IVs and anesthesiologist are to the right of my head. I have no awareness that this is me on the table, nor that it's me sitting here observing this. In this moment, there is no me.

After a moment of assessing the surroundings, I start to gently float to the ceiling, as if someone pushed a button on an elevator, still in a sitting position, although there is nothing underneath me. I rise to the ceiling, float to the right of the room, and am gently released into a reclining position as if resting in a recliner. I turn my head to the left, look down, and see a lot of chaos and shouting going on in the room. I can hear alarms going off, but they sound muffled in the distance. I watch the surgeon start doing chest compressions. The nurse runs out of the room. The anesthesiologist is putting something into the IV. I still have no awareness that this is me coding on that table. I'm void of feelings or emotions.

I suddenly feel the sense of rising and falling, very gently, no more than a few inches up and down. I get a sense of three sets of wings behind me that are causing this rise and fall. A huge wave of energy, much like Reiki (a healing technique based on the principle that the healer can channel energy into the body, activating the natural healing processes and restore physical and emotional well-being), comes through me from my feet all the way to my head. I feel a sense of relief as if I can breathe for the very first time.

Then, in an instant, everything goes pink. I'm standing in an immersion of deep pink. It's as if one is immersed totally underwater, but without the feeling of being wet while being able to breathe. I become aware of this pure sense of peace and freedom I've never felt before. I see sparks of light in the pink, floating down, hundreds of them, glistening, sparkling, shining as if they're on strings of fishing line coming from and going nowhere. I feel as if I spend a long time in this pink. I just take it in, feeling a growing and immense sense of love that completely overtakes me.

I hear someone calling my name in the distance. I choose to ignore it, but it gets louder. The pink starts to slowly shrink into a circle. Behind it is nothing but darkness, a black background. The yelling of my name is getting louder. I'm yelling, "No, I want to stay in the pink, please let me stay in the pink!"

And then slam! *I feel a horrific pain in my chest that causes me to scream out loud. I can't breathe. I'm gasping for air. The pain is excruciating. I open my eyes, and the first thing I see is a clock—it reads 4:06 p.m. I feel two people pull me up into a sitting position while on the gurney. I let out another scream, again gasping to catch my breath as they push me back. They put a cold, hard X-ray panel behind me that's causing more pain. There's chaos all around me. I realize I'm in the recovery room and have no idea what's happening.*

A cardiologist introduces herself, tells me that they lost me on the table for ninety seconds, that it took one shot of epinephrine and some compressions to get me back, but they're very concerned and needing to do some tests. I am told the horrific pain in my chest is from the surgeon cracking my sternum while doing compressions. She says he heard it crack when it happened.

The pink has completely faded away from my mind, and the pain has taken over completely. In an instant, my experience changes from complete love and peace to total pain and chaos, one I liken to heaven versus hell. I realize that I'm never going to be the same, and not in the way that I had anticipated.

I was medicated for the pain once all the testing was done, and the next time I opened my eyes, I was in a private room on the medical surgical floor. I had gotten my wish; I just had no idea it would happen this way! I looked down at my chest, and for the first time I saw, even through the bandages, that my breasts were looking forward for the first time since I was about eleven years old. I had a sense of femininity flow through me that I had never experienced before. I felt like a woman, and aside from that, the feeling in my chest was full in a way no breasts ever could have been.

Once I was home, my pain was from my cracked sternum; the surgical site was healing quite well. I reviewed the experience with a dear friend who came with me to my post-op visit. When I shared what I'd experienced with the surgeon, he confirmed everything as 100 percent accurate, and was even a bit stunned by it. Plastic surgeons generally do not lose patients on the table. I was the talk of the office for quite a while. He answered some questions I had and allowed me to look at my records.

The surgery started right around 1:30 p.m. They lost my heartbeat at 3:33 p.m. That means if I woke up at 4:06 p.m., I was out of my body for thirty-three minutes. I was clinically dead for ninety seconds. All of these were divisible by three. No coincidences, although I don't necessarily get what it means, if anything.

During my recovery, the doctors had me do an echocardiogram and a stress test. As I had told them, they would find nothing, and that was the case: all tests were normal. This was a pure spiritual experience: a shaman's death. A shaman's death is one that is not meant to be a final physical death, but one that merges spiritual and physical, usually bringing growth, change, and advancement spiritually to those who experience one of its many forms. I liken it to walking both worlds at the same time (the spiritual world and earth).

There was no scientific explanation for what had happened. I also now knew my theory of death was correct. We do not die. In fact, all we do is let go of these bodies to go back to our true essence: love.

The near-death experience had left me so open, yet exhausted. I was almost two weeks post-op, and I couldn't bounce back. I went see my regular doctor. I had just started working with Monique earlier in the year because of my fibromyalgia diagnosis. We had alleviated the fibromyalgia completely by cleaning up my diet, identifying food allergies, doing heavy detoxing, noting what foods caused my inflammations, and treating what I've learned is chronic candida (systemic yeast overgrowth) and that it was the culprit of my horrible periods, inflamed and boggy uterus, and certainly all the other digestive and painful symptoms I had.

The doctor told me I had two heartbeats. Literally, she heard two heartbeats, like an echo. She said she didn't know what that meant, and told me to call a man named James, and he would help. (My doctor was a D.O., a doctor of osteopathy, an integrative doctor, open to alternative methods and treatments.)

I called James immediately when I got home, he happened to be free, so I told him about the near death experience, the doctor hearing two heartbeats, and that I didn't understand why I wasn't healing. While on the phone, he proceeded to tell me that breasts represent maternal nurturing, which I seemed to lack tremendously (how the heck did he know?), and I'd literally cut that off, so we needed to retrieve the energy of the breasts and reunite it with myself. It sounded a little crazy, but in a way I totally knew what he was saying. He told me he traveled in his mind to the hospital, located, and pulled the breast energy back to me and sealed it in.

Part of me was thinking, "Seriously?" and another part of me somehow knew exactly what he was doing, but I didn't know how. He said I had deep, deep wounding around mother issues that needed to be addressed. I was astounded. Within thirty minutes, I was feeling like I could run a marathon.

He was doing all this funny-sounding breath work, making odd noises, and yet I could feel things shifting inside of me while he was doing this. I felt forgiveness come through me like never before, and I had a clear thought, as if someone else was saying it for me: "If he can do this, I can do this."

And so began my shamanic path, my journey as a healer. And I learned very quickly that healers are often people who have been through a lot of pain in their lives, be it spiritual, mental, emotional and/or physical, and are survivors with experiences that strengthen them and prepare them to help others. It would be this fact that made all I went through more acceptable as time would go by. I would even learn to embrace my difficult experiences because I knew they had a higher purpose other than my own personal growth.

17

I had been hearing, and ignoring, a faint whisper in my right ear for three years that said, "Shaman, shaman, shaman." I'd always disregarded it, with the attitude that I was a blond-haired, blue-eyed chick from New York. I laugh at it now, but that was my belief then: no way could I be a shaman. Then I remembered the shaman who had done a few readings for me a few years ago, telling me about my Native American parents: Sandra Marie. She was African American, from New York, and was a shaman. I realized it was time to pay attention.

I set up a private session with Sandra Marie at her home. During that first session, she took me through a regression process to the moment I agreed to come into this life. Now, mind you, although I was very open spiritually at this point, there were things I didn't imagine I was personally capable of, nor would ever experience. I wasn't even really clear what being a shaman meant, only that a shaman was like a medicine man/woman, of an indigenous culture, and that they were healers. But I was committed to keeping an open mind, because in my gut, I knew it was time to face whatever this meant.

I close my eyes and allow her to direct me through the regression. After only a few moments, she asks me to go to the moment when I agreed to come into this life.

Immediately I'm floating among cloud like formations, and I have no sense of a body.

She asks if anyone is with me, so I look around and see a male figure, dressed in a brown robe with sandals and a twisted rope like a gold belt. He has Mediterranean-colored skin, long, dark hair, long beard, and deep but gentle chocolate eyes. He has a loving energy about him, with a warmth that pulls me to him. He reminds me of Jesus Christ.

We start to talk. He tells me his name is David, that he is my spirit guide for this lifetime, and that he was the one who has been with me from the moment I agreed to come in to this life and that he will be with me until the moment I leave. He asks me if I remember all the times I felt someone behind me, especially when I turned off the bedroom light.

Oh, yes I do! As far back as I can recall, every time I turned off the bedroom light, I felt someone behind me. It terrified me, and I ran into bed so that something else would be at my back, and it would go away. It never hurt me. I never saw anything. I only felt the energy of it behind me.

David says this has always been him. I immediately know it is so. He asks if I'm ready to review my agreement coming into this life.

I say yes. A scene immediately flashes in front of me, as if I'm hovering above what's happening. He and I are in the same cloud like formations as we are now. He says there is an opportunity for me to go back to earth one more time to complete all my lifetimes, and it's my choice; I would not be required to come back if I choose it. (Meaning, this could be my last lifetime if I'm willing to do the work to be complete with human experiences.)

I ask what it is I would have to do. He tells me that I will be born of one family, but given to and raised by another family. He says the lifetime will be very hard, unjust, painful, and that I will feel very alone for much of it.

I ask him what the point of doing this would be. He says that I will be ready at that point for advancing to archangel training. (As the observer, I am quite taken back by this, as from my human awareness, this is the highest level of angelic being. I am surprised and impressed.)

I look at him and say, "Who wouldn't do that?"

He requests clarification that this is a yes, and I say that it is. Instantly I turn into a small ball of golden, flowing, and sparkling light that starts to descend down and away from us toward earth, and I see myself as the ball of light immediately in my birth mother's womb.

And that is how this journey began.

This experience had a profound effect on me. I didn't realize how easily I was able to detach and leave my body. It also validated so much of my life up until that point.

During the second session she wanted us to explore the moment I was born;

I am in a hospital surgical room. I am hovering over a birthing table. There is a woman on the table with legs in stirrups and a drape over her to her knees. There is a male doctor and a female nurse present. She starts screaming and pushing, and as the baby comes out I am gasping for air. I can feel and see the experience at the same time.

I am hanging upside down and everything is cold. My head and ankles hurt and I am being shaken a bit and then my butt is slapped. I am wailing now, my eyes hurt, it is so bright. The woman on the table looks like me, and she is crying heavily, she is keeping her eyes closed, her head turned to her right. She is clenching her hands to the side of the birthing table. They look just like my hands!!! She keeps saying, "Take it away, please just take it away. I can't do this, I just can't." I feel her heart breaking as the doctor hands me to the nurse. I float to the other side of the table and can see her now as the nurse carries me away. She is clearly broken hearted and in a lot of emotional pain, gripping the table so tightly as the doctor receives the placenta and finishes taking care of her. Everything fades away.

In that moment, for the very first time, I had compassion and forgiveness for my birth mother. I had been crying, and when I came back into my body I realized it. In that moment I also knew that she did not want to give me away, and doing so was killing her inside. This was a huge shift for me, as I had hated her and was angry with her for so many years. Just this little window of time brought such healing. I learned a lot about the value of regression in these experiences.

Also, during the first regression, David showed me (with Sandra Marie's guidance) the most important lifetime related to this one, and I was in fact a very powerful shaman who was shunned, thrown out of my tribe, and murdered for my gifts at the age of 48. (That lifetime was in the Coconino forest of Arizona, where I would eventually move to in my 48th year of life!) Over time, I learned of many of my lifetimes as a Native American, yet I struggled deeply with the idea of being self-proclaimed, as traditionally, it was always an elder shaman who initiated the next one in line. David assured me that the things weren't the same as they once had been: living on reservations, in tribal situations, and that the new generation of shamans had to come in to bring the healing work into the ever-growing world.

We had one more session together. Three sessions with Sandra Marie was all I needed to get me up and running. The rest of my training came over the ensuing years, mostly through my spirit guide, David. I did work very briefly with two other shamans, also Caucasian people from New York, who helped me get comfortable with the idea of being a "white" shaman, and release the struggle of calling myself one.

It took three years more for me to get comfortable with calling myself a shaman. I was proud of it, and grateful now for what it brought to my life, and others. It's a major ingredient of all that makes me who I am today.

David worked with me both in and out of body. He taught me how to leave my body at will and how to walk both worlds. He reminded me of what my purpose is here: to love as Christ loves, to walk a similar path of both worlds, and to carry the responsibility of grieving for the planet. He shares that this is why he is dressed in biblical-style clothing, and that there are many spirit guides like him who are teachers of love, compassion, healing, and forgiveness just as Christ taught. There is no accident that I wound up in hospice at a young age, or that I have a love and passion for death. That is my personal shamanism.

So the world occurs as a very different place for me now. Since my near-death experience, my heart is open in a way it had never been. I realized that the color pink was one of the colors of the heart chakra. It made sense that my heart would be as wide open as it is now. I felt gratitude for being alive, and for the first time in my life, I didn't have a strong desire to die and go back home.

As far back as I can recall, I've hated being here. I found life confusing, painful, even torture at times, lacking love, and I felt completely misplaced. The idea of dying was always a welcome one, one that I often wished for. Unfortunately, after only six months, the effects of the earthly life took its toll again, and that feeling of pure unconditional love dissipated to a degree. But I was left with an awareness that changed me forever. I now know what is waiting for all of us, and it is indescribably beautiful.

18

The year 2001 was a year of learning, growing, and continuing my training. I earned a certification in reflexology. It made more sense to me as a nurse and shaman than massage therapy, as reflexology impacts the entire body, so I chose to start there. I also took courses at a community college for my certificate as a holistic nurse. I learned about any modality I could. I read books on mediumship and being psychic, and I found myself at home in every one of them. I continued to work with my doctor on the candida, and the weight started to drop off again with ease.

I started online dating, with men. The message I'd had when I married Vicky about marrying a man by the time I was forty never left me, and the time was now. I was the healthiest and most confident I had been in my life. I had lost 175 pounds and I knew myself in a way I never had before. My parents and I continued our long visits and taking vacations together. Although they couldn't make the drive anymore, they flew into Denver, and I went to Florida as well. I had finally come to a place of peace with the adoption conversation, and on very rare occasions, I asked a question, but the "I-don't-remember" response was a constant now. It was futile, but I wouldn't give up, even though I had, at least to the furthest degree possible for me, let it go and turned it over to God.

In May, I lost an adopted cousin who I'd once thought might have been my birth mother: my uncle Milton's daughter, Zelda. Multiple times, both Zelda and her sister Faith had admitted to Uncle Milton cheating with his secretaries and likely others. I had asked them if DNA testing were ever available, would they do it. They both said, without hesitation, "Yes." They were so much more like sisters than cousins, and I looked very much like them: blue eyes, dirty-blond hair, and Zel and I were built alike. I had often wondered if she was my birth mom, but she adamantly denied it.

Her death was the first really painful personal loss in my life. Zel advocated for me and my parents over the many difficult years we had. She was a solid force in my life. Unfortunately, she was plagued by cancer for twenty years. She fought a hard battle and was one of the most powerful women I'd ever known. She once told me I was the most courageous person she knew. That not only stuck with me, but it motivated me to always keep going.

Shortly after the near-death experience, only six months after her passing, I came across a local medium in Denver. I made an appointment with Deb for November 17, 2001. I wanted to see a medium in action, live and in person. This was for personal reasons, but would also be part of my training.

I walk into Deb's home, and it immediately feels safe and comforting. We go up the stairs to her reading room. There is a video recorder set up and a candle lit, with two chairs facing each other. She shuts the door, we sit down, she says a prayer, and then she gives me a short explanation on how things may go; sometimes the recorder goes on and nothing records, same with the cassette player, as apparently Spirit has its own agenda. I leave it up to them (Spirit and Deb), but I take notes, just in case, as best I can through what is a very amazing experience. (Both recordings showed up fine!)

Deb knows nothing about me, yet it doesn't take long for her to start sharing about my being adopted. She does some general reading on how difficult this path has been for me, but that my spiritual aspirations and goals are tremendous and affirms I'm well on my way. She mentions in the reading that she sees me being a psychic medium as well. I just smile.

She says that I'm only at the beginning of knowing who I truly am. She had asked me to prep by calling in whomever I wanted contact with, so of course, I talked to Zel as if she were right next to me between the time of setting up the appointment and this present moment.

Deb says someone is here, and I know it because I feel this whoosh of energy come past my left side and stand at her right side. She describes Zel to a T, and then shares the following information:

"Your birth mother has passed. You have three brothers. Two are older, one is younger, and one of them was also given up, and I feel you all have different fathers. There was abuse and possible racial issues within the family. There are activities that go on within the family unit that are very destructive to the children."

This is the first time I have some confirmation that what my aunt Mary said about possibly having an older brother was probably true. But this is the first I'm hearing of a younger brother. Three brothers. Three?

I can hear everything Zel is saying before it comes out of Deb's mouth. I'm awestruck by this ability, yet not completely surprised for some reason. I begin to understand all of the times that I'd seen the "disappearing people" throughout my lifetime. It all starts sinking in while becoming illuminated in my mind that I truly do walk both worlds.

And I now have been told that I have two other brothers! I recall the visions of my birth mother and the dark-skinned man. Was he the racial issue or the abuse she was referencing?

So much is going through my head now I'm spinning, but with joy, elation, curiosity and wonder.

Deb ended the session by encouraging me to consider that I was blessed to not have been raised with my birth mother. Although she didn't get a lot of detail, it was a strong intuition she had, and in my gut, as much as I may not have wanted to give up the fantasy, I knew she was right somehow.

By this point, I've had so many wonderful spiritual experiences, and the training with David has left me very clear that spirit never lies. I knew Zelda was telling the truth. I knew instinctively that I had these two other brothers, but when asking my mother, she gave me the expected, "I don't know. I don't remember that."

I knew I was breaking my own agreement when I'd come to her with these things, but I had to ask no matter what the consequence. I had to follow every possible lead. I also had become strong enough inside of myself that I could deal with her ongoing lies, and the impact was much less.

Thank God, my mother, at this point, had stopped bringing it up. She was finally allowing the scab to heal a little more. Although she said she didn't know or remember, I somehow knew the likelihood of having three brothers (again, three!) was correct. I had little faith I would ever know for certain, meaning, would I ever have physical proof? I had no trust in my parents keeping their word and leaving the information in their wills.

But I kept my search going. In 2001, I also joined FindMe.org, Heartland Registry, New York Adoption list, and four more adoption email lists. Although I was putting out a lot of energy, my return, aside from my reading with Deb, was nil.

Later in the year, I came across a show called Crossing Over, starring John Edward, the psychic medium. I watched the show and learned and listened, not realizing I was actually getting training during those shows. Eventually, I started hearing what he was hearing and realized I could do what he was doing, just as I had in Deb's office during my reading. When I became aware that John Edward did tours, I found the closest location and purchased my ticket to see him in Wichita, Kansas. That was in February 2002. As I finalized the purchase of the tickets I had a feeling come over me that took my breath away. Something major was going to happen to me, and I knew it wasn't going to be that he would be reading me. I had no idea what it could be, what it meant, but I knew it, and I knew it without a doubt.

The three months leading up to his show were full of continued growth and learning. My friend Lill decided to tag along, and while no tickets were available, I knew she would get one at the door. The more I trusted my intuition, the more it proved me correct. We drove east through Colorado, stopping close to the Kansas border for the night. It was an easy drive to that point, but when we got on the road the next morning it was typical Kansas driving: the wind was horrid!

I spent most of the next five hours holding onto the steering wheel so tightly my arms, shoulders, and neck ached. But we made it to our destination in plenty of time to get in line outside with umbrellas and sit in the rain, waiting for them to open the doors. We were shaking and shivering. But Lill got her ticket with ease, and we finally made it inside.

We find our seats. There are three sections on the floor and a full round of balconies over us. We're in the right section, of rows, row six to be exact, all the way to the left side of the row so that I'm sitting in the aisle seat. Lill is to my right. John comes onto the stage promptly at 7:00 p.m. He has an aura of light around him like I'd never seen before (considering I only see energy and not light or colors in a person's aura, this was literal and impressive). He has a glow about eight feet in diameter all around him that moves with him as he moves.

He explains various phenomenon to the audience right away because many people see things in his presence that they hadn't experienced before. And then he goes right into giving messages to those from the other side. He is fascinating to watch. It's a gift to see the healing, although deeply emotional, that comes from people connecting to loved ones they have lost. I'd experienced it myself with Zel, so I feel grateful, honored and privileged to be experiencing this live. At this point, I've completely forgotten my intuition that something huge was going to happen for me here, and I'm completely absorbed in the moment.

It's about twenty minutes into the evening. I suddenly start feeling pain in my chest. I notice it changes into pressure and moves into my left shoulder, arm and jaw. I choose to ignore it, somehow knowing it's not something really happening to my body. Over the next twenty minutes, the symptoms get stronger. I now have pain all the way into my left hand, I'm sweating, nauseated and feel like I may pass out.

Lill looks at me and says, "Mel, are you OK?"

I say, "Yes," continuing to ignore the symptoms as best I can, still knowing I'm not really having something physical happening to me. I feel frustration, anger, and struggle to stay present. I start taking deep breaths, attempting to ease the worsening symptoms.

Lill says I'm turning gray now, and after another twenty minutes of this, I'm furious that I've come all this way to see this man in action, and whatever this is, is taking me out of the experience. I'm completely distracted by it now.

I do the only thing I know to do: I close my eyes, take three deep breaths, and I ask spirit to please help me get over whatever this is so that I can enjoy being in the room. The symptoms don't let up. I gently and slowly open my eyes, look up at the stage, and to my surprise, there is my birth mother standing on the stage to John's left.

She looks exactly as she did when I was being carried away from her: wearing a hospital gown with long, wavy, dirty-blond hair. She is illuminated much like John is, except that the light comes from behind her instead of surrounding her.

I look at Lill and tell her I will be right back and make a mad dash for the restroom. (Historically, if I pass out I often wake up projectile vomiting, and I certainly didn't want to have that occur while in the audience.)

I quickly find a stall. I'm the only one in the restroom. I lock the stall door, sit on the commode, still feeling as if I may pass out. I'm very short of breath. The sweat is dripping from my face. I feel like my heart is being crushed by an elephant, and I just try to breathe through this.

Suddenly, I look up, and hovering over the stall is my birth mother. She still looks exactly as she did when I was carried away from her all those years ago. She looks down at me and smiles warmly. The first thing she says is that she passed from a heart attack. Instantly, every one of my symptoms disappears. I'm stunned, relieved, gasping for breath, and physically exhausted. I'm also now aware that this is the first conscious contact I've had with her since February or March of 1964 when I was carried away from her!

She starts to talk. I tingle all over, feeling deep love and gratitude in my heart, much like my near-death experience. She tells me many things, the first being, "He is coming in June."

I ask in my mind, "My brother?" and she simply repeats the same thing. She then tells me that I need to go home, take out a pendulum, put it over an alphabet to get her and my brother's name, and to also put it over a map to find out his location.

I do not speak at all. I sit, listen, and forget the entire world that is outside of that bathroom stall. I'm with my birth mother! She has a glow about her that I'm in awe of. As she finishes sharing a few personal things about herself, and that she is sorry for all the pain that I've had to endure, she retreats from the stall and fades away. I take some time to gather myself, get up, go wash off my hands and face, and leave the bathroom.

As soon as I enter the hallway, she floats over to me. No one else is in sight, and she is hovering in the air in a prone position. In her hands is a small infant-sized, white-lace Baptism gown.

I ask her in my mind if that was meant to be mine, already knowing it was, and she says, "Yes." I begin sobbing. Now I know my intuition about not being Jewish was correct. I don't know the path they followed for certain, but I do know my gut has always been right. And here is my birth mother, knowing exactly what I needed to validate who I am. I slide down against the wall into a squatting position, and I just sob, ever so grateful for her visit and messages.

Once I empty myself of all the emotions, I pull myself together, stand up, and she fades away again. I walk back to my seat and look at Lill in utter exhaustion.

She says, "I guess that was the 'something huge' that you were feeling would happen?" That was an understatement!

Never would I have guessed something like this would have occurred. My birth mother accompanied us the whole way back to Colorado the next day. Lill, who is also a psychic medium, felt and saw her in the back seat of the car as I did.

I dropped Lill off at home, and I was in the car alone again. My birth mother told me, from the back seat, that I wouldn't see her again, but to know that she would always be with me, watching over me. In an instant, she faded away like a cloud dissolving, and I can no longer see her or hear her. I will forever be grateful to John Edward for being the conduit to allow for this to happen and I wrote I'm a letter of thanks.

As soon as I return home I take out my pendulum, write the alphabet on a piece of paper, and start hovering it over the letters. The names I get are Irene and Tony Torres. I somehow know that these aren't correct, but I go with it anyway. I figure what else do I have?

I get out a map of the United States, and again start hovering the pendulum over it. I start over the state of Washington, slowly going right to the east coast, then back to the west coast, and again back to the east coast, and once again back toward the west.

The pendulum isn't moving at all, and then, as it approaches northern Arizona, it starts to swing in a clockwise motion, which is the pattern for 'yes' for me. I stop there, and the circular swing gets bigger and faster. I've hit something, but don't know what.

I got on the computer and looked for every Torres and Torrez I could find in the state of Arizona. I started calling everyone on the list. Those I reached were dead ends, and the rest I left messages for but didn't hear back from them. In my heart and gut, I knew the names weren't correct, but as always, I could not leave any stone unturned. I was disappointed, but not without hope. I knew someone was coming in June, I knew that I'm not completely Jewish, and I knew my birth mother was with me now and always. That was so much more than I had had up until this moment.

In May, I found myself at wit's end with the dating thing, and I decided to go on two last dates and then I would be done! I had been dating men for a while now, feeling that it was the right direction for me at this point in my life. I had still not forgotten the voice I'd heard when I'd married Vicky, and I was approaching forty, but I made the change because internally I felt this was the right thing for me at this juncture. Yet every date seemed like a repeat of the last; every guy said he had a great time and would like to see me again, would call, but they never did. It had gotten old, and I was ready for a break from it. Little did I know the last date really would be the last date. I met Paul, my future husband, on June 2, and as my birth mom had said; he arrived in June. And with that, her messages had come to a conclusion, or at least I thought they had.

After so many dates going the same way, it took me by surprise that Paul actually followed through. He kept his word, and that little sign of integrity caught my attention. My mother was over the moon happy that her daughter was now "normal." My father remained steady with just wanting me to be happy. Paul wasn't Jewish, but he was white, and he was a "he," and that made my mother content. Well, as content as she knew how to be.

Paul and I married on September 6, 2003. I was thirty-nine and married to a man before I was forty. Another intuition fulfilled. At this point, I had three of my four skin reduction surgeries. I was at my thinnest, and felt great, but it took working out nine times a week and eating very consistently and with restrictions that often made life a challenge. Sometimes I felt like I simply replaced one addiction with another, but it was a grand accomplishment for me to say the least.

I wasn't sure the doctor would be willing to do any more surgeries, but he agreed that what I experienced after my breast reduction wasn't physical in nature, I had no concerns moving forward, and so we continued on with the transformation process. I had one more surgery during the early part of the marriage to complete my transformation. I lost over 150 pounds on my own, and the surgeon took off twenty-two pounds of skin. I was completely transformed physically.

It's a bit difficult to describe what being in my body is like now versus before these surgeries, but my choices were to keep the extra skin and stay a larger size or to remove the skin and have scars. I made the right choice. And although I have put back on about one fifth of what I lost, I remain healthier and happier in my body. With each surgery, I felt more feminine, more whole, and more at peace with my physical existence. I had friends who supported me through each surgery, and my parents also came to help me after most of the surgeries. It's hard to describe how far we had come by this point, but I felt that aside from the adoption topic, we had nurtured our relationship beautifully, and I loved that we were able to have some kindness with each other. They were so generous in paying for all of the surgeries, which I'm eternally grateful for. It was truly the start of a rebirthing; I was at the crux of truly discovering who I truly I was. It was the first layer of the onion, peeled away, and now the mental, emotional, and spiritual healing and transformation would follow.

In early 2004, because of a friend pushing me very hard to do so, I started doing psychic readings at a bookstore in Denver. For the last few years, I had spent much of my time learning not only about my spirituality but also how to use energy for healing, studying to be a holistic nurse, becoming a reflexologist, and learning many more modalities. I completed all of my skin reduction surgeries, and it was because of my own healing that I was able to learn so much as others healed me. I attended the Church of Religious Science in Lakewood, Colorado, and learned so much about mind over matter. I basically was a spiritual student in every situation I was in. I would go to metaphysical fairs annually, and with each bit I'd learned, I opened more and more to my gifts of being a medium, eventually coming to realize I was extremely empathic, intuitive and a really good psychic. I spent a long time learning through spiritual guidance and meditation how to do my own unique healing methods, and I had many amazing experiences myself and doing trades with others.

This same friend insisted that I start doing psychic readings because she said that during my healing work, I was doing it anyway. I felt I was reading the body, but she said it was much more than that. My thoughts were that the world didn't need another psychic. I was a bit of a pessimist about psychic readers at the time, as there were so many out there already, and so many I'd met weren't the real deal.

And she replied, "But there is no psychic like you!" I conceded, and although I had never just sat down with someone and read them, I felt I didn't have much to lose, so I applied for a reader job and was hired immediately, much to my surprise! The store manager and I quickly connected, and she was one of the three shaman teachers I worked with. (I had one other session with a friend who was also a caucasian shaman from New York.) My readings were going so well that I had repeat clients right out of the gate. She frequently talked about a guru from India she had been following and eventually asked if I would like to meet this guru. Absolutely! Anything I could learn from any path was a welcome addition into my mind and heart. I had read so much on so many paths, all in the face of finding myself, each one adding to the recipe of who I was. I would take what worked for me and leave the rest.

So, in June of 2004, I was introduced to Amma (meaning "Mother"), also known as Ammachi or Mata Amritanandamayi. I was very curious to know what a hug from the Divine Mother would be like.

It was a long, six-hour drive down here to Santa Fe. My friend gathered a group of us together, and we all carpooled down here for the day. I'm very curious to see how today will go. Amma is known as "The

Hugging Saint," so her darshan (gift to her devotees) is in the form of a hug, followed by a flower petal and a piece of candy (in this case, a Hershey's Kiss). She has been coming to the United States since 1987.

I'm standing outside a fairly large tent on her ashram grounds. There are a few hundred people swirling all around me. People are mostly wearing white cotton clothing. I smell aromas of curry and chai spices from a table in the tent that draws one in closer. There is music playing, but it sounds nothing like anything I've heard before, yet clearly is Indian-style music. I walk into the tent with the crowd, my friend directs us to a person who gives us a little laminated "token" with a letter and number on it so we know when to get in line for our hug.

I step back for a moment, looking down at the line I see people sitting on the floor surrounding the stage in front of me. There, on a small bench decorated with silk and flowers, is a small, dark-skinned woman dressed in a pure white sari. She is laughing, talking, and hugging people one after the other. Many are in tears. Some are laughing, some in quiet meditation. There is, to say the least, a lot going on around her.

After some time goes by, my token number comes up, and I get in the darshan line. Suddenly, I feel tingling all over, and a bit of nervousness comes over me. It takes quite some time to get up to Amma, and I use the time to observe the miracle of her being able to sit for hours on end, no food, no breaks, and few sips of any liquid while she hugs hundreds of people, one after the other. I have heard so many stories about her, but in this moment, I'm focusing on being present, open, empty, and receptive. I want to understand what it is that thousands and thousands of people all across the world experienced with this woman they call "Mother."

I move along the line until finally I'm there. A woman on my left directs me to kneel down, which I do, and immediately I'm overwhelmed with the scent of rose, the sweetest scent I've ever smelled of a rose in my life. (I would discover later that Amma wears a rose oil/sandalwood oil blend of her own making.) As the person in front of me backs out and stands up, I'm guided into Amma's arms. I'm already so moved by the love and compassion she has been showering on everyone who comes to her, I can't imagine it getting any better.

She pulls me in, places my head on the right side of her chest, my left ear toward her and right one facing out. I'm intoxicated with her scent, and as she wraps her arms around me, I close my eyes, and I fall into her bosom. I feel her left hand softly rub my back. Amma is talking to the swami next to her and others—it seems as if she is discussing business, but I do not understand her native language of Malayalam: the language of her home state Kerala in southern India.

She holds me for a while and then suddenly she holds me closer, leans into my right ear, holds my face with her left hand while still holding me with the right and starts saying, "Daughter, daughter, daughter," repeatedly, then "Ma, Ma, Ma" (which I'm assuming means "Mother" or the "Divine Mother").

I'm vibrating, my heart chakra is opening, and I'm overwhelmed with love: unconditional love. I'm melting while being rocked in the soft arms of a mother like I never had before, feeling a sense of love that was completely unfamiliar to me. Amma holds me for quite a while, and I focus on staying open and receptive while still observing everything around me best I can. I feel full and almost unable to breathe. Emotions are welling up at a rapid pace.

She lets go with a gentle release, gazes into my eyes, smiles like a very pleased child, places a flower petal and Hershey's Kiss in my hand, and I'm being guided to back up. I do so.

My friend comes to me immediately, aware that I'm in quite a state, and guides me up and around the back of the stage. She has me sit about three feet behind and to the right of Amma's right shoulder. I sit here for over ninety minutes sobbing my eyes out, releasing so much of the past. I feel as if all the love she instilled upon me in those short few minutes is pushing everything painful out of my being. It takes the ninety minutes for me to feel complete. I'm not sure what exactly just happened, but I'm aware that this is only the beginning for Amma and me.

I saw Amma two more times in 2004. On the first visit I recalled a vision while meditating that I'd had before I'd met her in person. It was of a small dark skinned woman dressed in a white sari, sitting in a chair under a tent with me. She was giving hugs, and I was doing healing work and giving donations to these people after she hugged them. I had completely forgotten about this. It felt to me as if she had been calling me to her long before I met her. It would be on the second visit, which was a full weekend retreat, that I received a personal mantra from her (a short phrase used in repetition to focus on God), which symbolized the commitment of me taking her on as my guru, and I as her devotee, or child, as she says. Amma sees us all as her children, even those who have never heard of her. She would become and remains the greatest example to me of what God is fully in the body. She is egoless, tireless, and she shares an endless stream of love, compassion, and healing to all. She is and will always be my example of who I want to be.

Paul and I had a couple of good years. We built a custom-home construction business—he was the contractor; I did the interior design—and I also had a private healing practice. But, like many marriages, things begin to quickly fail. He met Amma and said it was "no big deal." He proclaimed to be beyond her, which was very laughable since Paul didn't practice any type of spirituality. It eventually became an abusive marriage. Paul ultimately wound up being verbally and physically abusive. He embezzled many thousands of dollars from our custom-home construction business and my personal accounts. He had addictions he wouldn't admit to and had zero interest in integrity or being responsible for himself, his life, or his actions. But more on all that later.

In January of 2005, just before my forty-first birthday, I met Sierra. I was working at a metaphysical book store part-time in the mountains. She had been struggling with intense dreams and was looking for a shaman to support her with them. When she came to the doorway of my treatment room, I was stunned. There stood a six-foot-three-inch-tall Amazon goddess. She was breathtaking. We started a professional relationship that quickly turned into friendship, but we kept training together. She told me about a program called Landmark Education. We had an instant trust and pull toward each other. Because of that trust, I went to a Landmark Education introduction as soon as I could. Paul went with me. Landmark Education promised that I would be free of my past within a three-day weekend. Impossible. But they gave me a money-back guarantee. What did I have to lose? I immediately registered for the April program, and with hesitancy, Paul did as well. I had high hopes it would help with our marriage .

In March, I found out about a new company that was doing DNA testing. They could tell what your DNA is through the maternal lineage, as well as the percentage of your ancestry origins. It wasn't going to necessarily help me find my birth family, but it would give me more information about myself genetically. I immediately ordered the test and, when it arrived, immediately sent it back with my DNA.

On Friday, April 8, 2005, I started the Landmark Education program that would change me, my life, and my relationships forever: The Landmark Forum. By Saturday at noon, after sharing a gut-wrenching seventy-five minutes at the microphone, sharing all that I had experienced with my mother (the abuse, judgement, lies, deceit, etc.) I became aware that *all* of my suffering was based on the story I had made up about what happened in my life, right from the very moment that I was carried away from my birth mother.

For me, I had lived with the story that I was not enough, never would be enough, and that something was wrong with me because I was given away, treated poorly, and touched inappropriately. I had two mothers, and I didn't feel loved by either of them. In three short days, I had the power to recreate my life from a clean slate.

I continued training with Landmark for quite a few years, but it was this initial weekend that gave me the ability to have my parents in my life in a way I'd never dreamed possible. I was able to forgive them and open my heart in a way I never thought I could. The key was me being willing to consider that my interpretation of what happened wasn't the truth, and inside of that, I took my power back from them. I never realized how disempowering not being responsible for yourself and your life was. Everything changed for me.

The course was a full three days, Friday, Saturday, and Sunday, and then resumes to complete on Tuesday evening. This gives people a couple of days to put their breakthroughs to work. So, Monday morning I called my parents to share the changes that Landmark had orchestrated. I thanked them authentically from my heart for the first time for all they had done for me. I authentically expressed my love and gratitude for them. This somehow opened up a conversation I didn't expect. My parents proceeded to tell me that in their forty-plus years of marriage that they never once had been intimate. This news wasn't a tremendous a surprise because of their lack of intimacy, and it answered some things about their loveless marriage. Even as a small child, I somehow knew things that I was never told or overheard. I believe it was intuition.

After they told me about the lack of intimacy, I had a sudden flashback to when I'd found out I was adopted. I would tell people that there was no proof that my parents had ever made love, not even once.

My parents shared so much in that conversation that enlightened me, but the most important was understanding now why my mother would touch me inappropriately; she had never had that connection that lovers share. She had never allowed herself to open up to love. My heart broke for her. During the conversation, my father said she was a cold fish, a prude. She blamed him for being sterile after the war, but the truth was, she could not bring herself to be vulnerable enough to open up to someone and be loved. She was unable to express her love and affection and was so shut down. She was still a virgin, at eighty-three years old, and would likely die that way. I was heartbroken for her, and grateful for a deeper understanding of their humanity. I was also heartbroken for how empty a marriage my father chose to stay in.

I asked them if they could come to my Tuesday evening session, just the next day, and they said, "No," to me for the very first time since we reconnected. They said they weren't physically able to make the trip anymore. A flag immediately went up for me, and I knew this was it. It was time for hospice. I was going to lose my parents, and it would be soon.

In May, I received my DNA test information: 85 percent European, 12 percent Native American, 3 percent East

Asian, and zero percent African. I was thrilled to see I was one-eighth Native American, and the rest was really no surprise. What I did find most interesting was that I had a marker that was an exact match for a sequence reported in northern Portugal. This could explain my olive complexion, but I didn't feel any connection to Portugal. I searched inside of myself for anything that felt like an affirmation, but nothing.

When I had traveled to Europe, it was the United Kingdom, Ireland, France, and Holland that called me. Greece was also a place I dreamed of seeing and was very drawn to, but Portugal had no pull whatsoever. It was a physical fact that seemed to have no value. I had no desire to learn about Portugal or the Portuguese people and customs. I figured maybe one day I would visit there, but there was a complete disconnect as far as identifying with it in any way. But I was glad I had done the test, and I wished for the day that they had more information available such as what tribe of Native American I was, where in Europe I was from, or possibly matching to other people's tests, but that did not exist, at least not yet.

I started flying to Florida monthly. Dad agreed to hospice right away; he was very much a realist, I think that was likely because of his experience and injuries with WWII. Mom, on the other hand, was the problematic one, as always. We admitted her to hospice, and she would call 911 to get herself discharged. She was terrified of death and felt hospice was a death sentence, in spite of all I had shared and educated her about my professional experience, witnessing Zelda's hospice experience (which was the first time my mother saw a dead body) and in spite of it being a beautiful transition. I finally gave up and focused on my father, who was declining rapidly.

One day, he called me and said, "Hey, Kid, do you realize that this will be my ninetieth birthday?"

I replied "Yes Dad, of course, I do. Would you like to stick around for it?"

He said, "Well, yes, I would."

And so the party planning began. We had a wonderful family reunion. I called his birth daughters (my half sisters Gabby and Sunny) who came in from Texas. Five years prior, after twenty-one years apart, and nine years of me encouraging Dad to talk with his daughters, he had finally agreed to talk with Gabby, and eventually Sunny as well. It was one of those moments you don't think you will ever witness. It was a true miracle. They had visited a few times in those five years, and Dad had met his four grandsons, which just lit him up, which in turn lit me up. It had been a gift he'd really given himself, with a lot of prompting over many years, but it had been a joy to witness. His niece Faith (Uncle Milton's daughter) from New York also came in. My in-laws from Montreal, and all the local family, including Micky, her mom, and sister all joined us at his restaurant of choice to celebrate ninety years of life. It was a very special time.

I knew his time would be very short after this last hoorah, maybe three months, and I knew my mother would likely be within three months after him. I had seen this pattern enough in my hospice career, and I was as prepared as I could be.

In mid-August, my visit with him was bittersweet. I say "with him" because my mother happened to be in the hospital again for respiratory issues and had gotten herself off hospice again. He remained at home for the rest of his journey. I took advantage of this alone time with my father, and it was very sacred. He was on oxygen at this point, and really was failing because of age—not a specific condition. His mind was clear, and he gave me the privilege of doing his life review with me one evening. (Life review is a process where one reflects on their life, attempts to resolve incomplete conflicts, reflects on things and often shares to facilitate healing. It is different than what people experience as seeing their life flash before their eyes during traumas or near death experiences.) He talked until one in the morning which was highly unusual, as my father never saw the midnight hour, let alone anything after that, so I knew this was a sacred moment in time, and that his departure was only a few weeks away at best. It was a privilege to be his witness.

During the conversation, he said a few things that would never leave me. He asked, "Mel, was your mom sicker (in the mind) than I ever allowed myself to believe?"

I replied simply with, "Yes, Dad." We both knew. He knew that she had touched me inappropriately, he knew she abused me, and I knew how painful it was for him. There was no need to say anything further.

During his review, he said "Kid, no one will ever know what you and I have been through." I replied, in agreement, "No Dad, they won't." He then explained to me that he never talked about the adoption because he didn't want to do it and was afraid that I would think he didn't want 'me'. I told him I never would have thought that. After losing Gabby and Sunny with his first marriage ending in divorce, he was terrified of possibly ever losing another child. My heart melted. It was then that I realized he had stayed with my mother because of this, because of me. I couldn't have loved him more in that moment.

I mustered up the courage to ask him if it ever were an option, would he do a DNA test for me, and he said, "Yes." And somehow I knew in that moment, he wasn't my birth father, but he was my real father, the man who would do anything for his daughter. I never did follow through on the test, nor did I ask anything further about the adoption. His willingness to do one satisfied something inside of me.

He also said, "I want you to know, you were the only one." I just started to cry. I held him, and he held me in a way that I never thought he would. The rigid, cold embrace was gone, just a melting away of all of his past, his heart wide open and at peace. It was something to witness and was so inspiring.

I knew he loved his birth daughters deeply, the years they were separated were horrid for him. But he was validating me in a way that my inner child needed, and he knew it. And who was there with him? Me. I'd called my sisters and told them to come if they wanted to see him again, but they declined. One said she didn't want to see him "like that." What was interesting to me was that he was no different than he'd ever been. My father was clear and alert through the entire journey until two days before his passing when the hospice staff started giving him some morphine to support his difficult breathing. He never declined physically, other than getting weak until those last two days when he gently fell asleep for the last time.

He gave me that hug I had waited all of my life for. There was an understanding between us that was unstated in that moment. My father and I had fallen in love with each other, and we were complete. I left Florida knowing I would never see my father alive again.

A week later Hurricane Katrina arrived. My mother had just come home just in time. I wasn't able to get down to Florida again even if I'd wanted to. Although Hurricane Katrina left the scene on August 31, the airports were closed, and Dad passed away on Labor Day, Monday, September 5, 2005, only three weeks after my visit.

I'm sitting in the passenger seat of our car. Paul is driving. We're heading home from vacation in Yellowstone and Grand Tetons National Park. Dad insisted we go and live, repeating his "Do-it-while-you-can" mantra. We're on a small, two-lane highway. My phone rings. I see it's my mother, and I ask Paul to pull over, as I know what's coming.

I answer and say, "Hi, Mom!"

And she says, "Dad just died."

I gasp, put my free hand on my chest, and instantly begin to sob. It was over. The greatest man of my life left us to be with God.

My mother said she and the hospice nurse's aide had been with him. He had just fallen asleep, which was what I'd hoped for. As much as I'd wished he wouldn't leave first,

I knew it had to be that way. I had work to complete with my mother, and this was the only way it could happen. She became my responsibility now, and unbeknownst to me at the time, I was to be faced with the most stressful and difficult time of my life.

21

The airports opened in time for me to get down for the funeral. The process of packing up my father's things was extremely difficult in itself, but my mother and her dramatic personality and attachment to every material thing she owned only made it worse. She wailed and cried, holding on to things, not willing to let them go. At other moments she was stoic and strong and very deliberate about what simply had to be done. One never knew which personality would show up with her.

Paul and I made over one hundred trips to the trash chute with things she'd collected over the twenty-five years they had been in that apartment. She had stacks of plastic food containers hidden away that were 25 years old and shattered into pieces simply by trying to hold them. She was a Great Depression survivor, so she held onto anything and everything. (Dad didn't care for material things, all his concern lied with the people he loved and their well being. Very opposite from my mother.) Little of it was worth even donating, and things that were got driven over to the thrift store. The apartment was quiet in a way that was uncomfortable and eerie. The laughter and love in my primary family unit were gone. Aside from a few times on vacation or at family events, life at home had always been grim. My father had done all he could to boost my mother's morale, but she had just called him a "bullshit artist." If it hadn't been for my father, I would never have felt any love at all from a parent. Mentally I knew my mother loved me, I just rarely felt it. Although she could be quick witted and funny, overall she was a depressed, angry, and difficult person. He had been the jokester who had brought levity to everything, and he'd cared not that people hadn't understood him or thought he was "Crazy Lary." He had been a wonderful father in spite of dying with the adoption lie unrevealed. Now it was time to manage things for my mother.

I got home health aides set up around the clock to help my mother and keep her safe, although she firmly believed she didn't need any help. Her dementia had gotten bad enough that even before my father's passing she was leaving the stove and coffee pot on and doing other things that compromised her safety, but she wasn't going to make it easy. She called me, saying that they'd sent another *schvartza* (Yiddish for a "black person") and she didn't want them in the house.

But the hardest piece was my mother scared them with her behavior. They got glimpses of "the monster" and quit. The longest I could keep a gal in service was three weeks. I spent four to eight hours Monday through Friday on the phone during the week, trying to manage everything. My mother had become my full-time work. I wanted to get back there as often as possible, but another mother, Mother Nature, wasn't going to make this easy either. Just a couple of weeks later, and a week before my mother's eighty-fourth birthday in September, Hurricane Rita came through south Florida, once again shutting down the airports. The devastation was again horrific. So I played the waiting game.

As soon as the airports opened again, I flew down there. I had to get her out of that apartment. I felt horrible about doing this while she was alive, but I had no choice. She simply wasn't safe to be on her own. Letting her belongings go was excruciating for her. Paul surprisingly had suggested we get a new home that would accommodate her living with us, so when I was back in Colorado, I searched feverishly for a house. The first contract fell through, and then I found a place with a basement that easily could be an apartment on its own. It would be perfect for her. I was packing and dealing with a move at home and in Florida. Micky was helping me wherever she could, continuing to be the solid "sister" and support that I needed. She checked on Mom in between my visits, helped with her medical needs, and so on. Mom's nephew Frank (my aunt Mary's eldest son of two) visited her at times, and her cousin Walter (he was her first and my second cousin) also checked in on her, and he reported to me what was going on. I appreciated Walter a lot during this time, as I was not really close with any of my cousins now except for Beth.

As I made plans for my October visit, Florida was hit once again, this time by Hurricane Wilma. The airports closed again, and although I was beyond frustrated, it was very clear that in some way, this was God's way of taking care of me by not allowing me to be around my mother much at this time. Mom finally allowed hospice to provide her care. I still was working full time on the phone while moving, managing our construction business, seeing clients, and trying to have a life. I was utterly exhausted and emotionally drained, and felt terribly guilty that I wasn't there with my mother.

In November, once the airports were open again, I planned to fly down before Thanksgiving, as we had standing annual plans to be in Montreal with my in-laws for the holiday itself. My mother wanted us to still go, so I was going to see her before. We closed on the new house and started moving in. On day two of the move, I was carrying a banana box full of glasses and dishes into the house. I couldn't see my Rottweiler on the floor and tripped over him, planting my face right into the glass. I received a major cut on my left eyelid that was gushing blood. Twelve stitches later in the ER, the doctor told me I should count my blessings, as I was a hair's width away from losing my eye. He also told me that I wasn't allowed to fly anywhere, once again being thwarted from going down to take care of my mother.

The hospice at this point could not keep her any longer, as she wasn't having a crisis that met general inpatient status, nor was she actively dying. I didn't know what to do. She had used up every resource we had, every agency had sent out every possible aide to be with her, and they all refused to come back in spite of my begging. So I made a decision I hoped never to have to make for either of my parents: I put her in a nursing home. As a hospice nurse, I'd been in too many nursing homes to know that the care my mother would get would be subpar to what I wanted her to have.

It was only for two weeks, she was totally good with it, but my heart broke with guilt for doing this. I had no choice.

During this time, from August until December, I was participating in the last of a series of three programs with Landmark. I would not have gotten where I had if I hadn't had that support. Paul wasn't participating in this last program, but I was to make lifelong friendships there, and these people carried me through this extremely difficult time.

Finally, the house was done, and I was given the clearance to travel for Thanksgiving. I had some family members giving me a very hard time about not being with my mother, others were upset with me because they didn't like the situation around my father's death, yet none of them were there, none of them were contributing, only generously offering me their judgment and complaints about what was already the most difficult time in my life, as if it wasn't already hard on me. I knew after my parents were gone that most of these relationships would fall away, and I would be relieved.

It's Friday, December 2. I fly out to Florida. I get the rental car. I spend my last night at their apartment, making sure it's clean and ready to put on the market. I finalize things with the realtor and close out my parents bank accounts. When I take my parents safe deposit box into the private cubicle to pack it all up, I go through things one by one. As I'm sifting through everything a small, white index card with rough edges falls onto the table face down.

I curiously pick it up, turn it over and find it has old-fashioned, typed letters on it. On the top right-hand corner, there is a date: 1/21/64. I gasp. As I start looking over what is on that card I realize it's all the information that is on my birth certificate, with incorrect ages of my parents, just as they are on the certificate, and most surprisingly, a due date of 3/15/1964, approximately three weeks later than I was born.

I'm in shock. I suddenly recall my parents promising to leave me something with their wills. This was it. Nothing more. Nothing helpful or useful in my search. But one thing it did confirm: my adoption was well planned and thought out long before I took my first breath.

The next morning, I picked up my mother from the nursing home. I chose not to say anything to her about the card, as it was futile at this point. She asked if I would take her to the cemetery to say goodbye to my father, as she didn't remember anything of the funeral because of being in shock that day. We got her discharged and packed everything she had into the car.

As we were driving, she started to cry. She placed her left hand on my right arm and said, "Mel, I don't know what I'd do without you."

My eyes welled up, and I looked over at her and said, "Mom, you have taken care of me for the last forty-one years. It's my turn to take care of you now." And I meant it. I could see a vulnerability in her I'd never seen before. My mother was, in my opinion, like an army tank. I'd never seen her weak or vulnerable before. She was becoming more confused and forgetful, and more dependent, which was extremely difficult for her, and in that moment, all that was present was love, compassion, and gratitude. The visit to the cemetery was emotional:

I assist my mother from the car over to where my father's crypt is. My mother's future resting place just next to his. I point to show her where he is.

She slowly looks up and instantly begins to cry. She falls into my arms and weeps, saying, "I don't remember the funeral. How am I going to live without him?"

My eyes fill with tears. I begin to share with her what the funeral was like. She clearly has blocked it out. I feel such compassion for her pain.

My mother states she has no purpose now. My heart feels broken for her. She gets very quiet, and we just weep for a few minutes. After some time, she says she is ready to go. She thanks me, and off we go to the Fort Lauderdale airport.

I requested a wheelchair at the airport. I got us through security, and we were sitting at the gate, waiting. We were close to the door; I was in one of the regular chairs, and I pulled her wheelchair up close to me. We were knee to knee. She looked so frail. She weighed eighty-eight pounds, was pale and almost fragile looking. It was hard to recognize her.

She looks at me and says, "Walter talked to me. He said that if I remember anything at all about your adoption, that this was the time I should tell you, and that you have a right to know. He's right, and there are some things I want you to know."

I'm rendered still and speechless. I presence and brace myself.

She continues; "I don't remember a lot, but I do know that you have more than the one brother. You have three. Two are older than you, and one is younger. You all have different fathers. She (my birth mother) never wanted you to know or to be found, and they made us promise to never tell you anything. That was part of the deal. Otherwise, they weren't going to give you to us."

I had little faith this would ever happen. But I could see the honesty in her for the first time. She was unburdening herself of this forty-two-year nightmare, which left me wondering if she was going to join my father sooner rather than later. I then remembered the forty-two tumors in her stomach. It was as if she had one tumor for each year of my life (as I was in my 42nd year), each being a lie. I was filled with compassion for what she had put herself through, not just me or my father, but her as well.

I asked her a few questions, but it truly was all she could remember at that point. I was so in shock, and equally as grateful. I knew Walter had been talking to her. He had told me he had been encouraging her to tell me what she remembered. What Deb (the medium in Denver) and Zel had told me in that reading had been true, and I suspected so was the rest of it. And the elephant that had been in the room for my entire life finally started fading away. I felt a love and closeness with my mother that I'd never felt before.

She had always told me "they" didn't want to be found, but she never told me that they wouldn't have given me to them unless they'd agreed to hide it. That piece may have made things easier on all of us if they had. But one thing that didn't enter my mind at this time was how she knew about a brother who was younger than me.

On the flight to Denver we held hands a lot. I felt a closeness to my mother that was new and different. I knew something had changed between us when the stewardess bent over and said how touched she was by how close my mother and I were, and that she could see and feel we had a beautiful connection. She did not know how new it was, but I was grateful she said something. I was a different daughter from then on, and it was a simple outcome of my mother speaking the truth and unburdening her heart. It was one of the most special moments I'd ever had with my mother, and now something different would be possible between us.

22

We got home to Colorado and got her settled in. I was very excited to start a garden with my mother. She had a green thumb, and we had great fun creating together. I had warned Paul that I had a vision of coming home and finding her on the floor with a broken hip, and that that would be the end. I told him that once I started giving her any morphine or Ativan (very standard routine end of life medications for pain, anxiety and difficulty breathing), she would let go because she would be out of pain for the first time in her life. I had seen it many times as a hospice nurse, and those who thrived on pain could not let go until the pain was alleviated. It was just a matter of time. We just didn't know how much time.

We did everything we could to set up some safety parameters. I had hospice come out the next day and admit her and go over everything with me for safety and logistics. I got a nurse's aide twelve hours a day. And that evening, Monday, December 5, three months to the day after my father passed, as I completed this last program in the curriculum with

Landmark, I told everyone, "Although I don't know what this means or looks like, in this moment, I'm declaring myself complete with my mother." And so it was. I went home that evening, and something really had shifted dramatically.

When we started the day the next morning, as every morning, my mother cried for at least three hours. She ached for my father, she ached for her apartment, and she ached for her quilt, her flashlight, all the little things that kept life familiar. I'd brought what I could with us, but her physical things gave her more comfort than anyone else could. She felt she had no purpose. I just held her as she cried, being so grateful I was able to leave the past where it was and just care for her as I would have any patient, with pure, unconditional love.

As things often do when parents age, the roles had reversed, and I had now become the parent and caregiver. This is not always an easy transition, but thankfully my hospice career prepared me. She wasn't able to use the coffee maker, even though I purchased the same exact one she had at her apartment to make it easier for her. She couldn't figure out how to use the toaster oven, or the microwave, which had a simple turn dial on it. It was heartbreaking.

But there was no more angst inside of me. I could love her as I would anyone: without conditions. I held her when she cried. I cooked for her and made sure all her needs were met. We reinforced her not coming up the stairs without help, but she would not remember. We found her on the floor upstairs the first time we went grocery shopping. We had been gone only forty-five minutes. Thank God, she hadn't hurt herself. She couldn't remember so many things, or connect so many dots, but she certainly knew exactly when we left so she could come up and play. My mother always had a sneaky personality in that sense. That meant looking through cabinets and drawers (she had no boundaries) or eating food out of the fridge, drinking milk right from the cartons, or eating with her fingers from unwashed hands. She had a full fridge of food in her downstairs apartment, but the grass always seems greener.

That next Saturday, I had my annual holiday party. Most of my friends had met my mother multiple times during their visits to Colorado. She was napping, but my friends requested that when she awoke, they wanted to see her. Something unimaginable happened. All of the ladies came down to the basement. We were in her kitchenette, and a circle naturally formed in the room. One by one, each of my friends acknowledged her for being who she was, for raising me as she did. They thanked her for her contribution to me and to the world. I was rendered speechless. My eyes filled up along with my heart. This was the one and only time my mother was in a circle of powerful, awakened women who were holding her up to the light. It was incredible.

After they all went upstairs she looked at me, threw her arms around me, and said, "I'm so grateful you have so many wonderful friends and people around you. It comforts me knowing that they're there for you." Because of my mother caring more for me than herself in that moment, I knew the time was close.

Sunday evening, Paul and I again run out to shop and do some errands. He had gotten home after the aide left so Mom would have to be alone again for an hour at most.

We needed food and supplies for her. When we returned, the interior basement door was open, and my mother was nowhere to be found. We were walking around the entire house, yelling her name, but there was no response. All the exterior doors were locked and closed. After almost ten minutes of looking, I finally saw her on the living room floor hidden between the couch and coffee table. She was awake, but not responding other than looking up at me.

I said, "Mom! Are you OK?"

She said, "Yes," but clearly she was not. I called Paul over who helped me get her up. She was in pain. He carried her downstairs to her room and laid her on her bed. She cried out as he put her down. I got her personal needs taken care of, and asked her if she wanted some pain medication. She nodded yes. My mother wasn't one to ever take pain medication (this was a woman who did root canals with nothing at all), therefore lived her life in almost constant pain to some degree. Tylenol would be a breakdown for her, so I knew for certain this was the beginning of the end.

I go to the box of as-needed medications that hospice left in the home as they routinely do. I give my mother a single dose of liquid morphine and Ativan, and I sit with her until she falls asleep. I somehow manage to get a decent night's sleep.

It's morning now, and I go downstairs, and she is barely awake. I gently whisper, "Mom."

She opens her eyes and says she needs to use the bathroom. For ten minutes, I watch her trying to sit up on her own, but the pain doesn't allow it. I offer to help, and she pushes me away repeatedly. She finally concedes after another five minutes or so.

When I transfer her to the bedside commode, she lets out a cry that breaks my heart. When she is finished, I take care of her hygienic needs, and as I pick her up to transfer her back to bed, her body fully surrenders to me.

She starts to cry and says, "Mel, I can't do this anymore." More words I never thought I'd hear my mother say, and they would be her last. The look on her face is one I've never seen before. She looks completely defeated, surrendered and lost.

In that moment, I know it is time.

I called the hospice nurse to come assess my mother, and we discussed the situation. We agreed that she'd either broken a hip or her pelvis. I gave her another dose of pain medication, enough to make up for the hours that she missed while she slept to give her a good loading dose and get her out of pain which the hospice nurse and I agreed on. I waited until the nurse's aide arrived, and then I had to leave the room, as it was all more than I could take in at that moment. With her not being a surgical candidate, weighing eighty-eight pounds, the hospice nurse and I agreed that a trip to the emergency room would only be a futile, stressful, and painful experience for her. It would be a matter of time now—one of keeping her comfortable.

I was a nervous wreck throughout the day. The aide would report to me every few hours and I would go down there to give her more medication to keep her comfortable as needed. I'd never seen my mother free of pain before, so it was a bit surreal for me. I found myself doing whatever I could to keep busy. The hours ticked away, but my anxiety did not. I could feel my inner child, whom I call Emmy ("she" wanted that *E* name!), full of anticipation of a life without the woman who'd perpetrated her in so many ways, most offensively by lying and continuing to rip a scab off a wound that never got to heal.

My mother was her stubborn self to the end. Almost twenty-four hours had passed since her fall. She was taking breaths every seven minutes at the end. Just when the aide thought she was gone, she would take another few breaths. In all my fifteen years of hospice, I had never seen seven-minute pauses, it was supposedly humanly impossible, yet here she was. She finally took her last breath just before eight in the evening on Monday, December 12, 2005, three months and one week after my father died.

I ask the nurse's aide for a few minutes alone with my mom. I close the door, and crawl into bed with her. I put my head on her chest, and for the first time in almost forty-two years, I cuddle with my mom. She is cold, empty, no heartbeat. I couldn't feel her in the room as I had with so many people. When she finally let go of that body, she left quickly.

I'm feeling things I don't believe I have before. I'm afraid this isn't real, that it's some kind of a joke, that it can't possibly be over. How can it be that my mother, the strongest person I've ever know, is dead? I lie with my arms around her for quite a while, and tears continue to involuntarily leak out of my eyes. I feel as if I'm in an alternate reality.

After some time, I gather myself up, have the aide come in and clean her up. I call the hospice to send a nurse here, and then I go outside. I'm standing on the grass of the front yard. I take off my shoes in spite of it being quite cold outside, and with bare feet, I find myself dancing, spinning, whirling, and twirling in celebration of her freedom and mine. I do so until I almost fall over from dizziness. We're both finally free, and peace will now come. Both of my mothers are in heaven now. I'm beyond grateful to know that the wound will finally heal.

A few days passed, my mother's body was flown to Florida, and another funeral began. This entire part of my life was so surreal. Paul traveled with me, and only a few family members attended. Of course, Micky was by my side as always.

I find myself in Florida again, standing in front of another coffin in the same spot where my father was just thirteen weeks prior. This time it's my mother's face I'm looking at. This is a private viewing for only me before the service, as in a typical Jewish funeral the casket remains closed.

She looks better than she did when she was alive. The embalming has made her soft and beautiful. (Soft is not a word I would have ever used with my mother before today.) This time, though, I feel terror.

Emmy (my inner child) is looking at her mother, the monster, and just knows in any moment she is going sit straight up like a vampire, look directly at her. and say "Ha-ha, it's all joke!"

My rational mind, my nurse-mind knows better, but the little girl inside of me cannot believe the nightmare is over. I'm shaking with fear. The little girl is finally free of the monster; the adult daughter is now without any parents at all.

The service is brief. We head out to the mausoleum. I stand there and watch them push her coffin into the opening, fully expecting to see her hand come out like a zombie. I still can't believe on some level that it's over. The final screws are placed into the marble plaque outside of her mausoleum drawer, right next to my father's.

A slamming completion comes through my body, especially my chest. I take a deep breath, exhale in a way I never have before, and walk away.

It was over. Neither of them would lie to me again. I'd never told them about the insurmountable effort I'd put into my search, but now they will both know. I've missed my father terribly over the last few months, now I was curious how I would feel about the void of my mother's presence as well. I felt like an orphan with no real family to speak of. Micky was the closest thing I had, and my cousin Beth, who had set us up all those years ago. From this point forward, my adopted family, except for Beth, would no longer be much of a presence in my life. A chapter of chapters was complete.

The year 2006 was a big time of spiritual growth for me. With my parents apartment sold and all their affairs being complete I was free to focus on myself again. I found Kabbalah very serendipitously through a reunion with Ellen, my dear childhood and soul mate friend from New York. She studied a bit and showed me a few things that immediately caught my attention. I very quickly found a study group in Denver and started attending. Paul joined me as well. He seemed to enjoy it, but when it came down to the truth, like most things I had interest in, he was only going because I was going. He was quite controlling and manipulative, and I was clearly not happy in the marriage. I'd hoped the study group might have a positive impact.

But that didn't interfere with my studies. I couldn't get enough of it. Kabbalah was a blend of all the traditions of Judaism that I loved, but without most of the religious pieces that turned me off. I took on working with a teacher right away. I was doing service work and having functions at my home, and I even traveled to the center in Los Angeles to see where it all began. So much of the Kabbalistic traditions—the focus on astrology, numerology, the energy of the day, how they respect women and honor the natural spiritual attainment of women, and that they follow a lunar and solar calendar—all aligned with my personal belief system. I felt at home.

One of the many things I love about Kabbalah is the belief in the power of names and the energy behind them. It's said that when someone calls your name, there is an energy in the vibration that is imparted upon you, which I had come to believe after many years of searching for my *E* name, and knowing how I felt when someone called me "Melanie."

When someone speaks your name, the idea is to have it align with the vibration of your soul, and for it to be empowering. I had been given spiritual names through multiple paths that I studied. In the Lakota tradition, I was given the name Star Dancer. In a Navajo past life, I had discovered during my shamanic regressions that I was named Morning Star. I had been asking Amma for my spiritual name for years, but it apparently wasn't my time yet. Either she chose not to give names at the retreats I attended, or I didn't make it in the line (she usually only gave so many names each time). But the names I did get weren't names that I felt comfortable being called, although I loved them and the meanings behind them. But it didn't go unnoticed that both names had the word *star* in them. I have such a strong connection with the night sky, always seeing it as "home" for some reason. I loved stars so much that I'd had them on my bedroom ceilings since I was sixteen years old. It left me curious.

As I continued with Kabbalah, I learned that each Hebrew letter had a specific power and meaning behind it. There was a list of names called the seventy-two names of God that were made up of Hebrew letters in a very specific way. The applied science behind the seventy-two names was encoded inside the biblical story of the Red Sea. There were three verses, and each of those verses contain seventy-two letters. The Hebrew letters of these verses were combined (the first letter of each of the three verses, the second three letters, the third three letters and so on) from each verse to create a three-letter combination, or name, although it was really a symbol, as you cannot pronounce the name as they're spelled. The names are similar to Native American names in such a way as they are more descriptors, such as Fearless, Healing, Soul Mate, and so on. My name "just happens" to be *Lost and Found!*

My immediate reaction was thinking that you can't make this stuff up! How could that be! When I read the meaning of the name, it hit home powerfully and profoundly. The Hebrew letters from right to left are *resh, aleph, hey.* The name means "Wisdom to find and not lose sight of direction."

I've often thought that this name was my saving grace on this adoption journey, as if it was the power to help me navigate, that I would always come back to myself somehow. It affirmed for me that this was my soul's journey in this lifetime, to find myself, my truth, my spiritual way home through life. I never lost sight of the "Found" part. It gave me hope. My entire life up until now had been a series of my losing myself and finding myself, whether it be to my mother, through a difficult time, relationship issues, health issues. I would lose sight of who I truly am, and then come to a higher place in my self, with a sense of feeling like I found myself again. This cycle truly would be the theme of my life. Little did I know at the time how profound the name really was and how it would continue to play out in my life.

But Kabbalah also strongly encouraged everyone to have a biblical name, or Hebrew name. I immediately stopped using Melanie and started using Mariasha, the name I had been given as a child by the rabbi from my childhood temple. I used it even though I knew it wasn't the right name, which my teacher agreed with. But it wasn't Melanie, and that was a step away from a past I was long ready to take. Not one of the teachers or leaders, either from the United States or Israel, had ever heard the name Mariasha, but they also felt it was better to use than Melanie. I had looked up what Melanie meant many times, and it meant "black, dark." This affirmed my dislike for the name personally because I had been told for most of my life that I had a strong light and that there was brightness about me when I walked into the room. I resonated with that, but not with the dark. The dark was my teacher, but certainly not who I was.

So, after much conversation with my Kabbalah teacher and two friends who had changed their names, along with a very long and loud fight inside my own head with my ego, I filled out the form to get my name. It was highly encouraged that the name be used, but still we have the freedom to choose. From the moment I handed over the form, with much trust and great anxiety, I started praying, "Please, not Ruth or Esther, not Ruth or Esther." These were names of old ladies when I was growing up in New York and many people saw it as that type of name, including myself. So, although I was trusting, I clearly had not really surrendered completely.

The highest healing of Sabbath's, Shabbat Pinchas, was coming up on 7/7/7, just a few weeks away. I decided that was when I would get my name. The teachers said I should not get my hopes up, as they did not give names out on holidays, and I told them that I wasn't going to fly all the way to Los Angeles without getting my name! My intention was set, strong, and I had certainty.

That morning, in the midst of the service, the study group teacher turned around to look at me and gave me a thumbs-up. Immediately I was anxious, jittery, and my legs started jumping up and down. Again I began repeating in my mind, "Please, not Ruth, not Esther!" I was begging God for a gift, with conditions. Being human is so laughable.

The Shabbat service just concluded. The study group teacher is walking over to me. I'm jittery and nervous.

He says, "Are you ready?"

I stand there looking at him breaking out in a sweat, knowing that everything is about to change for me, again. Another defining moment in my journey on earth. I plant my feet solidly on the ground, look at him, take a deep breath, and say, "Yes."

He says, "Hello, Esther," and smiles at me.

I feel an energy go through my body that makes me shudder. My knees give out, and I get full-body chills. My eyes well up involuntarily, and I know. I just know. In that moment, I came home to myself, to my soul, in a way I never knew or could have expected. I knew it was my name, my correct, true soul name.

I sat down after thanking the teacher. Still shaking, I closed my eyes, and all I saw was the letter *E*. I had gotten my *E* name ever so perfectly. I took out my smart phone. I looked up the story of Esther, and was reminded that Esther was the main character in the story of Purim. I was born two days before Purim! I talked with the teacher and rabbi more about this, and I had in fact been named incorrectly as a child. Esther wasn't only a queen, but she most importantly saved her people from a dishonest and manipulative man who'd wanted to kill all the Jews. It was an honor to have this name and it felt right.

On a personal note, what really got me was that Esther means "star." It aligned with my Native American names. My name meant that I was a source of light (not darkness), something I strive for all the time to be for myself and everyone. My ego immediately dissolved around the attachment to not having Esther or Ruth as a name.

It took about two weeks for me to completely fall in love with the name. I loved and still love when people called me Esther. It felt different and so very right. I felt free. I put my application in immediately to change it legally, and two months later my name journey was complete.

The years I was married to Paul would become the years of overseas and international travel for me. Running our own business afforded us the freedom to set our own schedules, so we enjoyed a few big trips during this time. Of course, I had done some traveling up until this point. As a small child, my parents had taken me to New Orleans, to Florida a couple of times to see family, and to experience Disney World. They had taken me to New England and to many places in New York. We'd visited Wisconsin, Texas and everything east of there at some point. We usually had a wonderful time when we traveled, as Mom wasn't stressed like she was at home with getting everything done and doing it perfectly. But for some reason the one place they had never allowed me to go is Coney Island in New York. It had angered me because my friends reported how much fun the rides were and how cool a place it was, but they had never given me an explanation—I simply hadn't been allowed to go, and that had been the end of it.

When I had been a teenager, they'd taken me on a road trip throughout the Midwest and southern states. The best breakfast I'd ever had was at a train depot in Savannah, Georgia. Our main destination was Nashville. I had been a closet country music fan as a teenager, as country music was totally uncool, so I'd never told any of my friends. But I had been excited to go to Nashville, mostly because I wanted to go to the Grand Ole Opry. I had seen it on TV a few times, and there had been something about it that had a hold on me. I'd felt pulled to it, curious and excited to sit in the theater, but for no particular reason.

The day we'd arrived, there had been no artists playing, so we'd taken the tour, and then I'd asked my parents for some time to sit alone in the theater, not even sure why—I'd just felt like I needed to be there alone for a while. My parents had gone off on their own as I'd chosen a seat about six rows from the stage toward the right side of the theater. I'd just sat, looking at this empty stage, blankly, wondering why I was there. Nothing had come to me, and after about twenty minutes, I'd gotten up and hesitantly left the theater. Whatever it had been that had me visit was strong, but it was to remain a mystery.

We'd also taken a trip to Dallas for my sister Sunny's wedding that I'd shared earlier, and the cruise when I had been eight, just before finding out about the adoption, as well as an Alaskan cruise and quite a few road trips around the Colorado area. Once I left home, my parents had started to do some traveling, which I had been thrilled about. My father had worked very hard to give us a good life, which he had. They'd spoiled me materialistically with clothes and necessities (and on rare occasion things like a radio or a turntable with some records) as a kid, and helped me with vehicles and the down payment on my first home as an adult. As I'd gotten older and learned to appreciate the value of a dollar more, I'd wanted them to enjoy life and the fruits of his labor.

When I'd been sixteen, after moving to Florida, they'd gone to Israel. Many years later, they would visit China and Japan, but that had been it. My mother always dreamed of an African safari, but once she'd lost the ability to really walk on her own for any good distance, which had been in her late seventies, she hadn't gone anywhere. To her, it had been worse to think of being seen in a wheelchair than to not see the places she'd wanted to see. As I mentioned earlier, my parents had both said to me, "Mel, do it while you can." They'd said it repeatedly, and after witnessing their unfulfilled dreams, I took them seriously.

In 1995, I took my first trip overseas to the UK. I did a tour because I was still too insecure and fear driven, and it was a great first taste of international travel. I loved England in spite of the gray, wet weather and eating dinner at 9:00 p.m. I felt at home there, especially in the countryside and at high tea. I loved high tea like it was in my blood. Everywhere we went this was what I would want to experience most. My favorite spot was a small cafe across the street from Harrods in London. It was the best high tea I'd ever had, and remains so to this day. I was very drawn to Wales but we only had one stop there. Scotland too was lovely, but I wasn't quite as drawn there.

After Paul and I married, we honeymooned on a cruise to the western Caribbean. That would be the first of many cruises we'd take in the five years of our marriage. We cruised the inner passage of Alaska, the Mexican Riviera, and multiple other Caribbean cruises. We would go to Montreal, Canada, every year for one of the winter holidays to be with Paul's parents.

Our first overseas trip together was for Christmas and New Year's. We started in England, then off to Amsterdam, Holland, through Brussels, Belgium, and then a week in Paris, France, visiting Strasburg for a day for a taste of Germany. The trip ended with a week in Ireland, my favorite place to date. This trip was huge for me because these were the places I'd wanted to travel to the most for most of my life. Seeing the Anne Frank house was a childhood dream, but aside from Belgium, the other four countries were a must for some reason. I loved all of them, and the trip was amazing.

We also traveled to Israel with the Kabbalah Center for Rosh Hashanah and Yom Kippur in 2007, which was powerful and amazing. It was while we were crossing the Sea of Galilee, also called "Miriam's Well," that it came to me that Miriam would be my middle name (it was after that realization that I filed for the legal name change). When my parents went to Israel, I was a typical teenager and wanted to stay home with my friends. Clearly the timing of being there and the changing of my name had a lot to do with it. It was on that trip that I had seen how much I had forgiven my parents and really loved them for all the good they had done. I found myself in the Dead Sea, covered in mud, standing and swimming in the same location at the same resort that my parents had been decades before. I found myself floating involuntarily in the sea, with tears of gratitude falling from my eyes, looking to the sky and thanking them for all they had given me.

I more recently traveled to Japan and Thailand as well. Being able to take photos of myself in the places that they had been, in many different places of the world, was wonderful and left me so thankful for them. And they would visit me often from the other side, both at home and while abroad.

After her passing, mom started to visit me right away, and she did so regularly from the other side, and eventually made an agreement to be a full time guide for me. She said she was working with children on the other side to heal her own wounds, and she slowly transformed in front of my eyes. At first she looked as she did when she passed. After a few years passed she started looking like her healthy strong self again, around the age of sixty. She became a really good mom over those years, and after nine years, she told me she was no longer going to be guide, that her work was complete in that capacity, but that she would still be with me. Dad does not visit quite as often, buy he does visit. Oftentimes we would all meet together on the other side. I've experienced three way hugs with them many times, and although they spend little time together there, they always come together for me. If I am struggling in any way, one or both of them show up with messages of support. My mom would always make herself known with her perfume or presenting herself to me visually, dad would just appear. I now have two amazing parents that will stay with me for the duration of my time here. Although they still never divulged any information about my adoption, I feel so blessed by this gift my mother insisted made me crazy!

Being a medium is a gift I never take for granted, as most of my relationships continue with people after they cross over. How many people get to finish what they couldn't while here with their loved ones? I'm humbled that this is the case for me, especially with my mother.

As for my travels, I still hope to see many places including Germany, India, Australia, New Zealand, the Northern Lights, and for my mom, I will take an African safari at some point. But the one place I've not gotten to yet that really pulls me the most is Greece. It's always been on my list, just hasn't felt like the right time. A Mediterranean cruise would suit me just fine!

My marriage had not been good for the last few years of the five we had been together. In fact, it started failing shortly after we said "I do." Paul wound up being one of those guys who married me, and soon after, his true colors had come out. On New Year's Eve 2008, I finally left him after four previous failed attempts. Paul would make promise after promise to honor his vows, to change, but like most, he never did. Fortunately, my friend Sierra (who had introduced me to Landmark Education) had seen some of what was going on, and if it weren't for her waking me up by being courageous and pointing out to me how he would physically push me out of the way and be verbally abusive to me, I may never have allowed myself to see what was actually happening. I was one of many battered wives who just forgave more than she should.

After Paul painfully restrained me on two different occasions, I filed for a restraining order and had him removed from the house. This was two months after I'd left and his multiple false promises of getting out. It wound up being a much greater loss than I'd imagined. Losing my father-in-law was more painful than losing Paul. His dad and I were like true father and daughter, as we had a past life in Wales as father and daughter (likely what drew me there when I visited the U.K.), so our connection was immediate and strong. But the loss would extend far greater than that.

My Kabbalah teacher felt I was going down a very dark path, believed that Paul would never hurt me (in spite of the fact that he already had more than once) and I was banned from the study group. Paul was still welcome. It was more than unjust, as I was the one who volunteered, tithed, hosted events, and more. It was a typical experience in my life. I lost an entire community because of choosing to take care of my safety and well-being. My argument for the risk of being a battered women meant nothing. They felt I was choosing something out of fear, which I certainly was!

Fear of some things is healthy, which is not the same as having faith and trust in God that you will be OK. If you put yourself in front of an abuser again and again and expect God to remove you from any harm, to me, was complete insanity. Once a man physically manhandles a woman, all bets are off as to how far he might go. I wasn't going to find out. Paul had already hurt me well beyond measure. I was absolutely devastated and did the only thing I knew to do; I dug into the next program with Landmark Education.

This six month program included two weekends in Phoenix, Arizona. Sierra and I had found ourselves in a partnership that we agreed to continue to explore in spite of me being newly separated. We both knew the risks. Her family lived in the Phoenix area, and neither of us had been to Sedona before, so this trip would include meeting the family and heading north to one of the most gorgeous places on earth. My parents and I had made it as far as Flagstaff on one of our road trips from Colorado, but Dad and I got ill and had to head home. We got that close, but it wasn't meant to be, until now.

After our weekend program, we headed north, not knowing life was about to change again. We took the exit for Sedona, and as we drove in on Highway 179, I started feeling a vibration in my body. I felt as if I were being lifted out of the car seat. I started tingling and felt my breath change. I felt giddy, almost high, and very happy. My breathing relaxed. I saw a red hill with green evergreens and felt such a sense of peace and joy come over me. And then we came around the first curve with a view of Courthouse Butte, and I gasped. Sierra and I looked at each other and simultaneously said, "Oh my God! I'm home!"

That night we went for a hike at Boynton Canyon to experience the vortex there. My knee wouldn't allow for much of a hike, so we went up the side of the hill and stayed behind on a rock that gave me a view that I can't even attempt to describe. I had a Native American past life come to me, and I felt more strongly that this was home, where I was meant to be. On the way back to the car, we came across a family of javelinas. We were terrified, but after about two minutes of psychically talking to one that was staring directly at me (those kinds of minutes that feel like time has stopped along with your breath), they let us pass, and I felt initiated into Sedona. That was the day I started planning my move. Who knew it would take three years to get there?

The next day we got a call from Sierra's adopted mother ("Mama Floyce") that Sierra's grandfather had suffered a massive heart attack. We cut our time short and headed to Phoenix. I was quite nervous, as Sierra had warned me that Mama had never accepted her being gay and that I should be prepared to be rejected and not allowed in the house. Well, from the first moment, it didn't go that way at all. For some reason, I was the one Mama opened her heart to. Within a few short visits I was naturally calling her Mama, and she soon after began calling me her other daughter. When I asked her, "Why me?" she said, "Because you're special."

To this day, I still don't know what that means for her, but it really doesn't matter. I was the lucky one—I had yet another mother!

During the three years it took us to get to Arizona, I finalized my divorce, which was horrific because of Paul's obsession with greed, and his perceived entitlement to my parent's money. Three weeks after our divorce, I got a call from the local police stating that there were charges against me for murdering my mother. He had convinced many people in my life that I had left him for Sierra, which was as far from the truth as could be. I left Paul because he wasn't a good person, and I knew exactly where these murder charges came from. He knew the guilt I carried about my mother's falling at home and the relationship I'd had with her, so he pushed my deepest wound, a button that would cause me the most pain. He hit below the belt.

Paul owed my parents a lot of money from a loan they'd made to him, so I promptly called another lawyer, who called the police immediately, which stalled them taking further action. I hired another lawyer to deal with the loan and still kept the divorce lawyer on the radar. Three lawyers, one nightmare. They put a stop to all this nonsense immediately, and I never spoke with anyone further about it. I never shared with his parents what he had done, as they already knew who their son was, and whatever lies he'd told them, and all the other people who'd left my life remain in ignorance. Some of those people are in my adopted family and believed this story. I was dumbfounded, but they are convinced that I murdered her under the umbrella of hospice. If I was going to murder her I would have done it when I was 19, or very long ago. Why would I have gone through the trouble of buying a home for her to live in and everything else I did to bring her home with me? Guilt and grief can make thinking clearly difficult, and I have compassion for that. But for my own wellbeing, I could only let go, feeling if they believed him I was better off not having them in my life. When I saw Paul for the first time after the murder charges were filed, I advised him he would be an accessory to the murder if anything actually came of this. His immediate response was, "I didn't make that phone call (to the police)!" I'd never mentioned a call. He may as well have just admitted it, as three weeks later, the charges were dropped. Need I say more?

We had a spec home to finish and sell, which unfortunately didn't close until two weeks after it went into foreclosure. I'd never had bad credit up until that point in my life and had seven years ahead of me now to correct it. I had three properties to let go of. There was just a lot of business to tend to. Welcoming him into my life was the messiest disaster that I'd ever invited in (except for the adoption story). Quite serendipitously, I had found a job doing health education as a nurse, as I needed a steady income again. The divorce had burned up the last of my inheritance. I wound up giving Paul most of what he wanted simply to make him go away. There is no price too high for one's peace of mind, health, and well-being.

After eighteen months at the new job and the visit to Sedona, it was time to put my plan in place to move. I intended to transfer to the Scottsdale office with my current employer, I would find a surgeon to do a cervical disc replacement after twenty-two years of being put off by every doctor I went to in Florida and Colorado (due to the hit and run accident in 1988 that left me with severe nerve pain down both arms and other symptoms), and I would then move to Sedona and work from home. People laughed, asking me how I would survive, as Sedona is so expensive, and saying that my employer would never let me work from home. My response was that I would thrive, not just survive, and that all the employees would have the opportunity to work from home. They thought I was crazy, but I knew what I knew. When I have certainty about something, it simply is what it is. The human resources gal at work said getting a transfer was unlikely since we had just had a big layoff, but she said if anyone could make it happen it was me. A week later, the transfer was approved, and things started rolling!

In September of 2010, I left Denver for my new life in Arizona. A few weeks before departing I reviewed (repeated) the first Landmark program as a way of completing my time in Denver. Paul just "happened" to be volunteering at Landmark that weekend in August. Paul never did anything for free, so I knew God put him there that weekend. It wasn't easy for him with my being there. I offered him a chance to talk, believing this was an opportunity the universe had given us, but he left the building on a break and never returned. I wasn't surprised—he could barely look at me without trembling and turning beet red. Guilt is toxic, and you could see it clearly over there with him. This would be the last time I saw him. Over the next two years, he wrote me a few emails, telling me how I'd ruined his life, that I didn't know what harm I'd done to his parents, and that he forgave me for all the things I had done that "weren't in alignment with Jesus." They were the most laughable communications I'd gotten from him, and I never responded. That part of my story was complete.

There were also four of the main members of the Kabbalah study group there that day. Talk about miracles! I had begged all of them to do this program, warned them all about the study group having no integrity, and I came to find out that most of them had now done it, and the study group disbanded. I received apologies, and I got to complete my time in Denver with everyone I needed to.

Sierra stayed behind in Colorado until the house sold. I lived in Phoenix for seven months, found the surgeon I needed, had my cervical disc replacement in May of 2011, and then moved up to the Verde Valley, not knowing what I was going to do for work but trusting my plan to the fullest. I put my faith to the test. Six weeks into my recovery, my boss called to tell me it had been approved for us all to work from home! On August 10, 2011, I moved to paradise: Sedona, Arizona.

I moved to Sedona on my own, as my relationship with Sierra had been painfully falling apart for a while. Over the next few months, my relationship with Sierra would come to an end, and we broke up in November 2011. She had seen me through the toughest time in my life, but the core of who she was simply wasn't a match for who I was. She was the greatest loss of my love life. It would take me three and a half years to finally release her through a long process of internal work, therapy, and a lot of spiritual work. Soul mate and twin-flame relationships are of another dimension. But there were tremendous benefits to the letting go I learned to do. I learned never to attach myself to another human being again, to never disappear in a relationship again, to never trust anyone more than myself, to never give myself fully someone who was giving less then that of themselves, and I will always love her and be grateful for it all. The love I shared with her was the kind of love that everyone should experience as far as the depths and far reaches it could go. And as they say, better to have loved and lost than to have never loved at all.

The pain of that detachment helped me see a very important thing; I kept marrying my mother. Paul and Sierra were also Libras (Sylvia was a Libra), and in so many ways, they were just like my mother; saying things that put me down and made me the problem, and I was always the person who had to change. They came to me to heal, wanting to learn all that I had spirituality, ultimately saying it was too much work and being abusive in their own ways. Paul and Sierra were also alike in the fact that they both used me. I had little hope that I would ever find a person who truly suited me, but I was ok with me, and that's all that mattered.

I was now deeply involved with my new love: Sedona. I found the local gem club, which fed my rock addiction beautifully with rock-hounding trips. I engaged deeply into nature with hiking and returned to a hobby I loved: photography. I would facilitate full-moon drumming ceremonies every month and had really created a nice life for myself. I attended different churches and meet up groups, and I quickly started making friends and creating a community of my own.

26

In 2012, I met a few amazing women who would become my Sedona family. I have so many friends at this point from all over the world whom I now consider siblings, some closer than others, but each one is dear to my heart; they're my family of choice. My life was full, and I was very happy at this point in my life. I had healed so much. I was content being alone. I was free of my adopted family obligations while still keeping in touch with some of my adopted cousins on Facebook. My adopted cousin Beth and I remain close to this day. I had an awesome job that kept me living where I wanted to live, I was surrounded by amazing people whom I could count on for everything and anything, and most importantly, I was in love with myself and had developed a deep relationship with God through my studies, meditation, and following Amma. She had been the other mother figure in my life who had shown me that all I needed was myself and God, and once I had moved to Sedona, I felt very drawn to Amma in a new and deeper way.

One day in August, I had a thought to search for my childhood friend Miriam. I had thought about her many, many times since taking on her name as my middle name in 2007. I easily found her on Facebook. We reconnected, and it was as if not a day had gone by. She too had become a nurse. We discovered many similarities in our paths, and we enjoyed rekindling our sisterhood. She also seemed more at peace with her adoption after all these years.

Miriam came for a visit in April 2013. We were still the same "sisters" we had been over thirty years ago. We talked a lot about life, loss, and regrets. I was surprised to find that after losing my twin flame, my adopted family, my adopted parents, my inheritance, and my marriages, I was left realizing that none of it mattered. All that did matter was that I was happy, and I no longer had a need for anything, not even the truth. Not to say that it wouldn't be nice to discover it (the truth), find my birth family (most of all my brother), as I would always be open to that, but I was at peace with myself and my life, something my mother's passing offered me. I was whole in a way I had never been before.

In June I went to see Amma again for the annual retreat in Santa Fe, New Mexico. Even though I had found my soul's *E* name, I still wanted Amma to name me because I knew it would come from a completely pure source, and I wanted to know how she (and God) saw me. Considering this was my ninth attempt, and nine was a power number for me (a multiple of three), representing completion, I knew this would be the year I'd get my name.

So I got in the line to find out they had changed how they were doing things. You got in the name line based on how many times you tried already, and this time I made the cut! I was, in fact, going to get my name! After Amma joined us in the hall and started darshan, we all got in line. Amma was truly something to behold, as she had multiple lines of people coming up to her: two lines for darshan, a name line, a question line, and sometimes a mantra line too. She also was constantly discussing with her staff whatever business needed to be attended to. It was fascinating to behold. But most of all, it was pure joy to see her comfort, console, heal, play, and bring joy to so many people for hours on end, sometimes over twenty-four hours at a time, thousands and thousands of people to hug, no eating, minimal drinking, rarely taking breaks. Truly astounding.

When I finally got up to her, I was kneeling on the floor to her right. She was unusually busy this particular morning with so many people around her. The swamis helping her with the name line were just to my left. This was exactly how it went to get one's mantra, and I was having memories of that moment in 2004:

> *Amma is hugging people, one after the other. A swami gives her my intention for my mantra. Amma says something to me in her native language of Malayalam. The swami then pulls a small paper from a box and hands it to me. Amma then looks at me right in the eyes, smiles, and taps my left cheek with her first two fingers and showers me with rose petals. She has such a look of joy in her eyes, and from that moment on, she was my mother.*

So this morning, nine attempts later, as I knelt next to her, I felt hopeful for a similar experience, but it didn't happen. Amma was very busy today. She was unusually serious doing a lot of disciplining with her children while hugging and healing everyone who came to her lap like nothing else was going on. I saw the swami show her a piece of paper that seemed to appear out of nowhere. I didn't see him speak with her at all. She looked at it and said a name out loud and returned to giving darshan. That was it. She never looked at or acknowledged me. The swami directed me to get up.

I was at a loss. I'd waited to so long for this, and that was it? Boy, was Emmy disappointed. I felt cheated. After all this time, and nothing, not even eye contact. (Most of Amma's children hunger for as much contact with her as possible, as each touch, glance, or any connection at all is a major blessing). Even though another part of me knew everything was perfect, and that there are never any accidents around Amma, that all things are purposeful, I still hung my head in defeat and followed the swami, reminding myself to trust what was happening.

Amma's swami pulls me aside, holding a little white slip of paper in his hands, and says to me, "Your name is Kaumudi." (Pronounced Cow-mu-dee.)

My body shakes, then tingles, and then I feel an intense sense of love come through me. I feel giddy, and excited like a child. I shifted simply by hearing my name into a space of light and love!

He grabs my arm and says, "This is a very unusual name, rarely does Amma give this name. It's a special name."

I ask, "What does it mean?"

And he replies, "Light of the moon."

My knees give out, and just as with Esther, I'm stunned, and then I feel such a sense of honor. I laugh inside myself for my disappointment. I then think, "What does that mean, Light of the Moon? It means that I'm the source that lights the moon. What lights up the moon? The sun. And what is a sun? A star. What does Esther mean? Star."

I'm dumbfounded once again. I feel an emptiness inside that instantly fills with the love of God and guru. Amma knows all, and this was another example of that for me. She had no way of knowing, other than her omniscience, that I had changed my name to Esther. My name journey has come to a close in the most beautiful and magical way. Jai Ma! (Victory to the Divine Mother Mata Amritanandamayi!)

The next couple of years were spent enjoying life, settling into Sedona, enjoying visitor after visitor, exploring the area and deepening my spiritual connection. I was able to see the fruits of my labors and of my experiences. I rarely thought about my adoption, but when I did, I did exactly what I had been doing since that DNA test in 2005: turning it over to God, and letting them (God, my parents, and birth mom) know that if it was meant to be, they would have to make it happen because there were no further actions that

I was aware of that I could take. If any were to come up, the commitment would always be there to keep turning over any stone that would cross my path.

PART TWO

The Good Stuff

27

It's April 25, 2015. I'm fifty-one years old, and I have come to a very peaceful, free, and solid place in my life. Miriam called me earlier in the year to let me know that she is coming to Phoenix for her graduation for her master's in nursing. She is visiting with her new husband, Mike, whom I'm anxious to meet and get to know. They have come to Sedona just for the day, so I put on my tour-guide hat, which is one of my favorites to wear, and take them out for a day tour.

Mike is sitting in the passenger's seat next to me; Miriam is in the back seat behind Mike. We're between destinations, chatting it up, when Miriam mentions that Mike has adoption in his family as well. They both share with me that he did a DNA test and was able to connect with birth family. Miriam suggests I look into it, and although I'm extremely skeptical, she offers to send me the information.

I, in keeping to my commitment to leave no stone unturned, say, "Yes, please." I'm already resigned to it not panning out for me, but I'm working at staying open if there is some slim chance for a miracle. I figure, at this point, ten years since the last DNA test, what do I have to lose?

The rest of the day was lovely, and I'm always left feeling joyful and grateful about how much my heart smiles when she and I connect. It had always been that way.

Within a couple of days, Miriam had sent me the information for Family Tree DNA. I took a few minutes break from work and picked up the phone and dialed. The gentleman on the other end of the line explained how it worked: there is a test called Family Finder (the one Miriam and Mike had told me about), the cost was ninety-nine dollars, and there was a 99 percent chance of finding a relative. Once they receive the test back at Family Tree DNA, it would take about six weeks to get the results, and matches would be on the website. I thanked the man, hung up, and thought, "That is impossible." and I got on with my day.

For the next three days, I kept thinking about that call. There was no way it was possible. All I'd ever done was come up against brick walls and closed doors. Every step of this journey thus far had led me nowhere, so why would or should this time be any different? And then I remembered my promise to myself, and this was another stone to turn over. I picked up my cell phone and got a different gentleman on the line and said, "I called a few days ago. I spoke with someone who said that there was a 99 percent chance of finding a relative. Is that true?"

The man replied, "Yes! The only thing we cannot guarantee is how closely related the relative will be. It can be anywhere from a birth parent to fifth cousin."

I replied, "Really?"

He again said, "Yes!"

And I said, "Send me a kit."

That was April 30, 2015.

I hung up the phone and was a nervous wreck. I found it almost impossible to digest this possibility of finding someone, *anyone*, who shared my DNA. Some part of me doesn't believe that there was anyone at this point. But I surrendered. Each time I got nervous, I meditated. In those quiet moments of reflection, I began to realize that since Miriam had returned to my life, the subject of adoption had come up every so often, even more so in the last six months, always being brought up by something or someone else. It was in movies, books, and conversations.

I remembered one particular conversation with a newer friend over lunch at the local Indian restaurant, and I thought, "Why is this coming up again after so many years? I wonder if something is coming?" It was almost as if something was poking at me. But because of the depth of the pain of the past, I just let it go as quickly as it arose, never attaching to it again to avoid any further disappointment. But I couldn't help but ask, "Is this it?"

The test arrived a few days later. I ripped open the package as quickly as possible without damaging the contents. My hands were shaking. I read the instructions feverishly. I spit in the tube, swabbed the cheeks, sealed it up, filled out the form, and got it ready to go in the mail the next day.

I was shaking as I drove to the post office and deposited it into the mailbox (versus using the one at home). I was taking no chances that this test would not find its final destination. I kissed the box, looked up to the sky, reminded them that it's still up to them, that I would continue to do my part, and I let the kit go, knowing it would be six of the longest weeks of my life.

During this waiting period, I had been seeing my friend and chiropractor, Dr. Karen, for a few different health issues. As she was adjusting me, she said, quite out of the blue (but not really because she is also psychic), "Are you searching for your family?"

I was stunned because she didn't know about my sending the DNA kit off. She said my mother was in the room. I got chills. She then said it was my birth mother and that she wanted me to keep going. She couldn't see if there would be any contact with my brother or not, but I should keep going. Dr. Karen also said that there was a sister and something about Ohio. To say that I was left in the land of curiosity would be an understatement. What did this all mean, and why was it coming up now?

That six-week wait somehow, quite miraculously, was cut in half. I sat down at my desk, opened my computer, and to my surprise, I had gotten an email saying my results were in! I immediately started flipping out. I was once again a nervous wreck. I couldn't sit still, and my hands were trembling. I had a tension headache buzzing through my head.

I didn't know what to do with myself. I got up and paced in my office for a few minutes, did a lot of deep breathing, tried to center myself as best I could, and then I sat down.

What do I do? Should I look now? Should I wait? How can I wait? I need to calm down. It came so fast. It's only June 8, 2015. What if there is something in there I don't want to see, like nothing but fourth or fifth cousins? What if there is a parental match, or most importantly, what if my brother is there? I had sworn decades ago never to be a what-if person, and there I was drowning in what-ifs. So I close my eyes, take three deep breaths, open them up and click.

The first and only close match I saw was a man named John Every. Every other match was a distant cousin, so I focused on him. The name was completely unfamiliar to me. There was a photo of a man with buzzed gray hair, gray facial hair, not smiling, sort of a flat affect. We looked nothing alike, and I recalled that my brother and I likely have different fathers.

I look to the right of the screen and see that we share 1,967 centiMorgans in common. What does that mean? Click. Answer: This relationship holds the possibly of grandparent/grandchild, aunt/uncle to niece/nephew, or sibling/half sibling.

There is a note he wrote that he was also adopted. (Deb, the medium in Denver said one of my brothers was adopted out!) Oh my God! I feel an energy rush through my groin to my solar plexus, through my heart, throat, then into my head and eventually my eyes, which start to leak. I'm shaking inside and out; I have goose bumps all over my body. The tears are just falling with no ability to control them.

I put my face into my hands, and I just weep for quite a while. I feel fear, joy, excitement, relief and so much more. I'm not quite sure what is happening right now, but I know that my life has just changed, forever. I've found a blood relative, with the potential of it being the brother I've yearned for information about for the last eighteen years!

I close my eyes, take another three deep breaths while sniffling, and ask myself, "What do I do now?" I'm way too emotional. I will sit on this until tomorrow, hoping for a clearer head. I spend the rest of the evening and most of the night a nervous wreck with very little sleep.

The next morning:

I get up feeling emotionally exhausted and go into the office. I open the computer and sign in to the website and get back to the page where I had been. I again ask myself what I should do. And then I notice there is a link for an email. Click. The email address is an address with a woman's name in it. I don't know what it means, but it's all I have to go on, so I write the following note:

Hello John,

My name is Esther. Today I received results from my Family Finder test, and you're the first one on the list showing as a potential "Full Sibling, Half Sibling, Grandparent/Grandchild, Aunt/Uncle, Niece/Nephew," so I thought I would reach out.

I see that you were adopted. I was adopted as well, but the story and details are mostly unknown to me, thus why I've done the DNA test.

If you're open to communicating, I would love hear from you to see what may be possible here as far as connecting with a birth family member.

I hope this finds you having a wonderful day.

Click. And the waiting begins. Oh my God! What has just happened? I've emailed a birth relative? Not likely a grandparent, he doesn't look old enough, but he could be an uncle. Oh my God! Either way, I've finally found someone!

The day went by uneventfully, then the next. I barely slept, and no reply was received. Another day, no sleep and no reply. I started searching the web for any John Every I could find. I found a link to something from 2001 with a John Every who was searching for anyone who may be family, and I sent a note there as well.

Another day went by, nothing, then another, and another. After a week, on June 16, I sent another note through the DNA test website to him. Nothing. I told myself every day to just keep letting it go. Maybe he didn't get the email, maybe the email address was incorrect, or maybe I just needed to accept that, in spite of doing a DNA test, he didn't really want to find anyone. Maybe he just wanted to know his origins, and that was it. Either way, I didn't know what the situation really was, so with resignation and a heavy heart, after a week, I let go and again told God, "This is still all up to you."

I got myself a new journal on the thirteenth. On the front is the Serenity Prayer, which I'd used many times over the years, having learned it during my time in Overeater's Anonymous:

> *God grant me the serenity to accept the things I cannot change, courage to change the things I can, and the wisdom to know the difference.*

My first entry: "It came to my attention today that I probably should start capturing what's been happening as of late re: DNA test/adoption stuff." The remainder of the entry was getting things caught up to date.

> *It's the morning of June 16, 2015. I sit down at the computer after breakfast to find an email from John Every!*

> Hello Esther, it's time. I was adopted by my father. I think I know who my blood father is, though I don't know much about him and not sure where he lives

(somewhere in Virginia). I would like to hear more about you. And please ask anything of me.

John

It's very short, and he says he is an open book. What a relief! I feel like it's safe to finally give myself permission to get excited. So many people are not open, so this to me is a very positive start.

I wrote him back very quickly with a little bit more information about myself and a few questions, and the next phase of waiting began.

I went for an electrolysis session, and another out-of-the-blue moment happened. My practitioner asked me, "Do you know if you have Viking blood?"

Um, "No," I say. I mentioned to her that I was adopted, and she recommended a DNA test called 23andMe, which can give you that information as well as your haplotypes (a group of genes within an organism that was inherited together from a single parent). I figured I'd check into it when I had some time, again, not ignoring any possible avenues.

After that appointment I headed to my nurse practitioner's office to review some lab work. After going over my results, she suggested I do a test that would give me health information about genetic mutations and health risks, something I've never been privy to. The test is called 23andMe! As I've said many times on this journey, you can't make this stuff up! I ordered the test!

Two days had passed, and it was the evening of June eighteenth, 7:17 p.m. AZ/PST Time.

My phone rings; it's an unknown number. I had given John my number so I answer the phone and say, "Hello."

I hear an unfamiliar voice saying, "This is John Every."

My body shakes. I get chills. I sit down. I nervously say, "Hi!" and our first conversation begins.

Right out of the gate I ask him if he ever lived in New York, he replies, "Yes, I lived in Brooklyn with my mother and grandmother until I was five." And in an instant, I know. If he says nothing else, I know.

My mother told me so little, but the one thing she always was consistent about that lined up with what my aunt Mary had told me was that it was just the three of them (my mother, my mother's mother, and a little boy about three years old). He tells me his birthday is March 2, 1961, he is three years older than me! And our birthdays are only a few days apart, which I feel is important for some reason, but I don't know why.

He shares with me that my mother's name is Helen Parlett, and she was born in Virginia! Helen starts with an H, which is one letter from the I that the pendulum showed me. I read it wrong! And the one thing on my birth certificate that never made sense to me, now makes sense. My parents actually did leave me a hint, and I never knew it! My mother in fact was born in Virginia!

The conversation continues to bring light to so many things, including what the Denver medium had told me and my mom confirmed before she passed: I do in fact have three brothers—two are older, and one younger. Helen's eldest son's name is Mac, and the youngest is Daryle, who grew up with John. Daryle and John are ten years apart in age, and we all have different fathers! He was confirming more and more.

The more he speaks, the more I'm certain that this is my brother that I've been searching for for over thirty years, wishing for forty-three, and knew of for eighteen. He then mentions an older sister named Tina, who lives in Ohio! Come on now! Dr. Karen hit it right.

He shares that he only met Tina once at Helen's funeral (and doesn't know anything more about her), that Mac came and met the family one weekend many years ago but doesn't keep in touch (he was adopted by his birth father). John says he is going to ask Daryle to take a test to see/confirm what our connection is.

John went on to share that Helen raised both Daryle and him, but because they were ten years apart in age, they hadn't spent much time together. Daryle's father, Merle, had adopted John when John was five years old, long before Daryle had been born. John said he was going to talk to Merle to see if Merle recalled Helen mentioning a pregnancy or baby in 1964. John shared that he'd grown up with a lot of lies, not really knowing much about his birth father, that there were two birth certificates for him, and that the one he had said Merle was his birth father, although he was not. John also shared, with some hesitation, that Helen was a swinger, and swinging was a very big focus in her life. For some reason, this didn't come as much of a surprise, as we did all have different fathers.

John told me that Mac was "sold" to his biological father, at our grandfather's demand, and as we know, I was also sold. She was sixteen when Mac was born. Grandpa, Helen's father, William, forced her to marry the father, but when it didn't work out, he forced her to sell the baby. Some of my adoption painting was getting filled in very quickly during this conversation, in which I just discovered I was no longer an orphan or an only child!

Helen had a sister, Pearl, who went by Micki and a brother, Billy, who was mentally impaired. John told me that Helen died in 1990 from lung cancer, which was the chest area and consistent with the heart-attack experience I'd had with her thirteen years' prior at the John Edward gathering. (As a medium, when someone dies of something from the chest, it can be either lung or heart. My gut felt the cancer pushed on her heart and that it likely was a heart attack that caused the death.) Helen was Protestant but for years was studying to convert to Judaism—no one really knew why. John told me she'd sung on the radio with Johnny Cash and Patsy Cline, and at the Grand Ole Opry! And now I know why I was so drawn there, and why my first song I chose to learn when I did vocal training was "Crazy" by Patsy Cline. I was getting chills throughout the entire phone call. A part of me realized that no matter the physical distance, a genetic connection cannot be severed.

John continued on telling me he had just become an RN in 2014. Seriously? He lived in Hollywood, Florida, from 1986–1990, right down the road from Michelle (Micky) and not fifteen minutes from my parents' apartment! He said that he and his wife had been planning on moving to Chinle, Arizona, as he wanted to work on the Navajo Reservation in northern Arizona! I immediately remembered that pendulum swinging over the map of northern Arizona. Wow!

In one phone call, all the things that my birth mother Helen had told me during that visit to John Edward in 2002 had come to pass: he came in June, I was not Jewish, she died of a chest issue, John was headed to northern Arizona, and I was already living there!

We talked about the possibilities of how we were related and agreed with a three-year age difference we weren't grandparent/grandchild. We discussed the possibility of uncle/niece, but uncle Billy (my birth mother's brother) would be the only possibility, and he would have been a teenager, living at home, and was mentally impaired—it just wasn't likely. We agreed to sit on it, but either way, based on how many things lined up, we were both pretty excited and fairly sure that I had found my brother!

I hang up the phone, and instantly the tears are pouring out of me. It's impossible to describe how I'm feeling. I have chills. I'm trembling. I'm excited. I'm terrified. I walk out of my office and fall apart. I can barely breathe, struggling to take in the reality of what has just transpired. What a glorious day it has been. I just found the one thing I had been desperate for all my life and had given up on ever finding. The experience is surreal at minimum.

28

It's been almost a week since I've heard from John. It's June 28, 2015.

I just returned from this year's Amma retreat, and her main message to me was to allow this to come in small increments, be patient, digest one thing at a time. Well, time currently is excruciating for me! I have a hunger so strong to talk more, learn more. It has been a challenge letting in the notion of "I've found my brother."

His last email ended with, "We may be brother and sister." I imagine he is moving through as many emotions and thoughts as I am. Daryle has agreed to do the DNA test, so we will know even more in the next couple of months. And, I sent in my 23andMe test as well.

At the day's end, I got another email from John. He shared about his wife's surgery and recovery. He had read my entire website and bought my book *Celebrating Death*, which took me a bit by surprise. (Neither the website or book are still in publication.)

He said, "I usually am not a big reader, but I'm half way through your book in just a few days. Many of the pages brought tears to my eyes." *Wow!* It was clear he was interested in getting to know me. He sent five photos: two of our mother Helen when she was around thirty years old, and one at fifty-one, which was the year she'd died, and that just happened to be the age I was right now! The other two were of John and Daryle and one of John's birth father and half siblings. He very strongly favored his paternal line.

At first, I was just in shock. I couldn't see any resemblance, but I think I was too afraid to let myself see something, or that I would be making up that I saw something because I wanted it so badly. But the more I looked, the more I saw me from my younger days. Her facial structure was very similar. And when I looked at Daryle, I immediately knew he and I were going to look alike, although I again didn't even let myself go there. It was all just too much. I was anxious to see more photos, but that was all he could find.

He ended the email with "Hope to talk with you again soon." Me too!

I am and have been so anxious, so hungry for more, so I figure since he called me first, let me call him next, so I pick up the phone and dial. It's now June 29. As soon as John answers we dig in more deeply about the possibilities of our connection.

As far as John knows, our uncle Billy currently lives in a group home with his child and wife, who is also mentally impaired. He has another child who is with the mother, and no one knows where they are. We agree he would have been too young, around fifteen, still living at home and mentally impaired. We rule him out and conclude that we're definitely siblings.

Oh my God! Again I'm vibrating with excitement, shaking, have chills all over and my eyes start to leak again. I can't hold it back. I'm accepting this new reality, the one I still cannot believe I've found.

John shared that Helen was a Taurus but wasn't sure of the date. (As ecstatic as I was I was quite surprised that John didn't know his mother's birthday, but I knew someone else would be able to verify it for me at a later time.) He grew up with Daryle until he was seventeen when Helen, Merle, and Daryle moved to Maryland from New Jersey where they'd all been living since John was five. John finished high school in New Jersey, worked to pay the bills, and then enlisted in the air force.

John, Helen, and Grandma had been in New York from when he'd been nine months old (the end of 1961) until he'd been about six (1967). Grandma had died in 1968, and John hadn't been allowed to go to the funeral because he'd been too young, just like I hadn't been allowed to go to Aunt Sylvia's funeral because I had been too young.

The more we talked, the more related we got and felt to each other. Helen's funeral was the only one he'd been to. Helen had made a few records and sang on some radio shows with Aunt Micki. Helen had been a waitress at a high-end hotel in New York City when they'd lived in Brooklyn. She'd married Merle in 1966, and most interestingly, he had been her first cousin, so my brother's adopted father was his first cousin, and the same for Daryle with his birth father. So, that made my baby brother my second cousin as well!

John said Helen had been dating a Jewish man in New York. He remembered a man named Milton, whom she had him call Uncle Milton. We both agreed the likelihood of this being my adopted uncle was very strong, but we of course couldn't be sure. He had done some digging and found out Tina is actually our aunt, he wasn't sure whose sister she actually was, but she is Helen's younger sister and currently lived in Ohio! Dr. Karen got it right, except that she is Helen's sister, not ours. Daryle lived in North Carolina and according to John was a little ambivalent about me but was working through it. Aunt Micki told John that Helen once had told her Helen had had a stillborn baby girl, but that was all Micki knew.

When John had reached out to his birth father, they apparently weren't very receptive, especially the stepmother who he said accused him of just wanting money, and he hadn't had any contact with them since. I asked why he'd done a DNA test since he knew who his parents were. He said he did it mostly to discover his heritage, and to find family. Like me, he'd wondered if he had Native American roots. His house was decorated with many of the same type of Native American decor as I have in mine. He has tattoos of his bear totem. Yet based on the Family Finder test we did, neither of us have any Native American blood. (This was quite disappointing after the 2005 DNA test that said I was twelve percent Native American.)

We talked about him looking for work on the reservation and how amazing it would be to have him living up the road. He'd been having a hard time finding a position, so I told him I'd reach out to a contact of mine who was a nurse there. We discussed how my adopted mother, Sylvia, may have known about Daryle who was seven years younger than me, which had never entered my mind before. There had to be a contact person, someone letting them know what was happening, but who could it have been? It was a wonderful conversation chock full of goodies. And I continued to have to let it sink in. I was speaking to my big brother!

After our call, I reached out to my adopted cousin Faith, Milton's daughter. For years, Faith had promised she would do a DNA test if it ever became available that testing could provide matches. This time something was different, and she said she'd have to think about it, that the thought of her "daddy cheating" was difficult for her. I was frustrated, as she was the one who had told me decades ago that he was a cheater and that she would do anything for me. Now she's not sure she wants to know, but she will think on it and let me know.

29

It's now the last day of June and my dear friend Julie in Colorado had an Ancestry.com membership and she was going to start my first family tree! WOW! Julie and I met working a metaphysical fair together and the she was in a women's healing group that I facilitated for three years. Julie runs a metaphysical shop online, in her home and at fairs. We share a love for crystals and rocks, and in spite of my move to Sedona we have stayed in touch.

Julie was so generous and helpful. She found Helen's marriage certificates; her name was Helen Lougene Parlett. Her date of birth was April 26, 1938. I would have been twenty-six when she passed away, the same age she was when she had me. I found myself feeling a little sadness about not being able to meet her, but truth be told, all I ever really was interested in was finding John. Helen made choices for herself that impacted the whole family. I felt that John and I never had a choice in the matter, so I didn't feel much loss over Helen at this point. I still was just working at taking it all in. I knew my mother's name now. Just being with that took something.

Later in the day, I got a text from Faith's number, but it was her husband telling me she will never do the test and that I'm making baseless accusations about her father. He was a lawyer and was behaving as such versus being my loving supportive cousin as they both always had been. He said, "She wants nothing to do with this nonsense." (Even though she had promised for years to do this.) This reminded me so much of why I never felt a part of my adopted family. I would never have treated any of them this way.

I replied with an apology for the upset, as that wasn't the intention, reminding them that she had agreed to do this for years, and that I wished them well. I thought it likely I would never hear from them again, and I was hurt, but I also figured after so many years, when a door closes, another one will open. For my own sake, after years of doing this, I knew the best thing I could do was just let it go.

I spent the evening with a bubble bath. My inner child was so nervous that John wouldn't like "us." I had to laugh. After all these years, I really didn't care who liked us or not, but this one was big and I could understand the insecurity I felt. To be rejected in any way by my birth family would be excruciating. But my adoptive parents appear as I'm meditating and tell me that all of this will pass, it just needs its own time and not to worry. I could sense Helen in the background, which made me smile. She clearly has been working very hard, at least since 2002 to make this happen. How grateful I was that my mothers both were up at bat for me now. What a change that was, and a very welcome one!

I've not slept at all the last two nights, as I'm totally wound up with excitement. My head is spinning with thoughts and information. I see visions of puzzle pieces flying around from a thousand-piece puzzle, one by one slowly finding their place. I have so many emotions, some of them are impossible to describe, as this is a new experience, one I don't quite know how to integrate. I clearly don't know how to be with the one thing I figured would never be complete and now that possibility is a reality. But I sure am liking the words "I have a brother!"

Julie emailed my first family tree. I have a family tree! My own. My very own! A huge gift to start the month of July off with four generations of Parletts and Everys. Grandma Peg (Helen's mother, my grandmother) is Margaret Mary Parlett—they called her Peg. Grandpa was Alonzo William Parlett—he was called Bill. More pieces of this magnificent puzzle!

Julie also threw together a Shapiro family tree as well. She was a psychic medium as well and said during the building of the tree that Milton accepted me as his daughter. I could feel my body respond. It felt like the truth, yet I still had doubt for some reason. She said that he told her that Faith knew and that the truth could be too traumatic for her. She said the Shapiro line was really calling me into the family. But how would I ever know the truth?

I'm struggling with how slow this reunion is going. I talk to my psychic friend Kim to see what she gets and why there are such long gaps between contact with John. Kim was once a client of mine. At her first reading, I asked when she was going to do readings herself, and now she is one of the most awesome psychic medium's in the Denver area. I trust her explicitly and here is what she has to say:

Today is July 9, 2015. John is adjusting right now. He is distracted with other things. Give it time. Faith is reconsidering, but it may be well over a year before she will do the test. She sees four people around a card table with a kids puzzle that has about twenty-four pieces. She describes the only man at the table—that is clearly my adopted dad. She says he is my biggest fan and that he says he will always be my "real" father (and that he is!).

He says to relax and let it happen—it will all fall into place. He says that he is with me and to be patient, and when I feel alone to remember he is with me and not to worry.

She then describes my adopted mother perfectly. She says that my father only agreed to the adoption for her (which he admitted to when alive). Her arms are still crossed about the adoption. The other two women are my aunt Sylvia, who died when I was eight (Faith's mother), and my grandma Shirley, who was the neighbor next door in Long Beach. Her granddaughter married my cousin, and we really felt like we were family.

Their message was the same: that I'm on the right track with the puzzle. Give it up; let it go to have it all. It will come back in a wave, and everything with John will come together too. They suggested I keep exploring out of the norm, and that this is really more about the process.

But the most important thing I think she shared with me was that the "family hole" I'd had all my life would be filled by self-love only. No more beating myself up now, only self-love. It was a beautiful reading, and it reconfirmed my belief about Uncle Milton (Lary's brother who passed when I was two) being my biological father. But until Faith was willing to do a test, I really didn't have any options that I was aware of. I felt good after the reading, but still a bit down. There was more letting go to do.

It's been a week since my reading with Kim. I got a voice mail from John that started off with "Hi, sis!" I don't think I cared much about anything else he said after that! It had been two and a half weeks since we'd had contact and I was feeling down about not having more. I understood that I have this inner child that is yearning for her big brother, and that all parts of me are excited, anxious and wanting as much of him as I can get. But his wife just had surgery, and I had to remember to allow things in small increments (Remembering the message Amma had given me in June).

It wasn't easy to surrender to the process. It had been forty-three years since I'd found out I was adopted, thirty years of searching, and eighteen years knowing about him.

Over the years, I could feel him out there, spent time wondering, fantasizing, dreaming, singing to him, and now here he was. How the heck was I supposed to stay calm?

I had random questions going through my mind:

- What if one of us were to die now?
- What if this means I have come to the end of this life's journey?
- What if we never speak again?

And then I realized I was what-if-ing again, and the only thing I could do is to stay in the present moment and be grateful for what I've got, which is more than I was told I would ever have, and way more than I ever expected I would! I had such tunnel vision about finding my brother that it never occurred to me that there may be other people that would come along with finding him. Pretty silly in hindsight!

> *It's been two days since my mind was full of all those questions. John and I talk for one and half hours. He gives me details about his current nursing job, about his wife, and what she does, and more family information:*
>
> *Daryle was in the marines. He was in Afghanistan four times and is dealing with a lot of post-traumatic stress because of that. He is curious about me, but that's it right now. Once he and John visit, he will do the DNA test. John said that he himself was in the air force for four years and then moved to Hollywood, Florida.*

It still amazes me that we lived so very close to each other for those years he was there, and we both left within a year of each other. In 1990, he moved to Salisbury, Maryland, to help Mom die. She had divorced Merle quite a few years earlier and married an African American man named Gordy. They were married for over ten years. Gordy was known to be cheating on Helen and was found in a murder-suicide two years after her death. Gordy wasn't willing to take care of Helen when she was dying, and asked John to come. John lost everything in that move, but he was the one who was supposed to be there with her. Mom died in July of 1990.

I ask John if Gordy was abusive to her, and John says yes but doesn't know to what extent. I share with him my vision of seeing a very dark-skinned man yelling at her while she was lying in bed, crying. This validates a connection I've had to my birth mother in spite of our being physically apart for all these years. It amazes me, and it makes sense of this repetitive vision I've had for so many years. I'm speechless and my heart is warm and open.

I respond in kind by sharing more about my history. We then talked about the fact that after the conversations we've had now, we're declaring ourselves siblings! We make it official! What a magnificent moment. I'm flying high!

We finished up the call by setting a tentative date of September 18, 2015 for me to come visit them and set the intention that he will be living in Arizona by January. Could it really be that my big brother was going to live just a few short hours from me? In northern Arizona! There is just so much to take in.

I shared the call with my Facebook community. John made a comment: "Hugs, sis. I'm so glad we got to talk on the phone and can't wait to hug you in person. I just had to smack my forehead that I didn't think of this earlier, but until that day, if you're up for it, we could Skype?"

Of course I said, "Absolutely! Yes!"

I immediately am in action looking at flights for September 18. I also contact a friend who is a nurse and lives on the reservation asking who John could contact about a nursing position there, a place I myself had considered applying for a job at not that long ago!

All I know is that a reunion, the one I've waited for almost my entire life, is only two months away! I have such a nervous stomach right now, along with butterflies, my head is tingling and I'm shivering. At the same time I'm numb, as if I've been stunned or in shock. Could this really be happening?

I called John. Apparently I beat him to the punch. He said he was going to call me tonight (July 22, 2015) then decided to wait until the weekend. I couldn't help but smile at the connection. We talked more about my visit. We had both assumed that I would just be staying with him, so being on the same page also felt really nice. He shared about his dogs and we learned that we share our favorite breed: the Rottweiler, and we both have had one.

He shared about his wife's family and that one of her sons lives with them. I asked how she is feeling about all this and he replied, "She has no choice!" We laughed, and he said she was completely on board. I wanted to jump through the phone with excitement, and I told him so. He too was very excited. John seemed to wear his heart on his sleeve, which I absolutely love in a man. We're very alike, which I find pretty awesome. Getting to know him is like eating your favorite meal for the first time, not knowing it's your favorite just yet, but you savor every delicious bite!

My friend Julie continues to work on my tree and is doing some genealogy work for both me and John. What a gift she is in this process, giving of her time and energy to do this for us. She is an angel in this process, without question, and an angel for whom I have such deep gratitude.

I checked in with John. It was a quick call, but we couldn't help but share a little of our excitement for our meeting. He ended the call with "We also know September will be here before we know it." How cool is that!

I heard from my adopted cousin Beth today (July 28, 2015). She had not seen any of my Facebook posts about what was happening. I had been wondering why she hadn't commented or called, and we spent well over an hour going over every detail of what's happened up until now. It was a surreal experience, sharing the story with someone I grew up with, who had been the only person from my adopted family who truly has been by my side all these years no matter what. I found it a challenge remembering everything, as there were so many details already, and I can only imagine how much more there is to come.

Beth and I talked about my uncle Milton possibly being my birth father, about how logical it seems, and about how I looked like Zelda and Faith, and how they would always say I was like a little sister to them. I texted her the pictures John had sent. The one with Daryle in it as a child again left me thinking he and I would look alike, as I saw a strong resemblance from how I looked as a child. Just the thought of it gave me butterflies. To think that I was on my way to possibly finding someone alive that I looked like was insanely exciting for me. Beth said that I look exactly like Helen when I was heavier. What? Did she really say that? It was something to savor...I looked like Helen! We looked at the photo of Daryle together and she said, “That’s you.” We completely agreed that he and I look alike. Oh my word! I look like someone! I actually look like someone!

Later that day I had posted something on Facebook about the “10 Things You Can’t Buy with Money”:

Manners
Morals
Respect
Character
Common Sense
Trust
Patience
Class
Integrity
Love

John made a Facebook comment that instantly brought tears to my eyes: “Missed one: Family.” Can’t measure the smile that brought to my face. Family, yes—but this is *my* family!

I texted John to see how my sister-in-law (did I just say sister-in-law?) did with her surgery. We got caught up with that, and we found ourselves laughing and sharing a similar sense of humor. It was joyful, light and open. This is just so awesome.

Yesterday (August 2, 2015) John posted a photo of a little girl and boy sitting in a tree looking at the night sky with the caption: "We're in each other's lives for a reason. Thank you for showing up." His comment: "To all my friends and family, including my new found sister."

Instant tears flowed and another huge smile came across my face. So full of emotion. Gratitude swelled through my entire being in that moment. How many years had I wished on the first star to find him while singing "Somewhere Out There"? And this is the post he shares, and mentions me. I had gotten the sheet music shortly after hearing that song for the first time and I would play it on the piano, unsuccessfully every time, because I would just cry with this deep, painful yearning of the unknown. How is it that he picks *this* post? This whole situation is big. So big. Bigger than any words could possibly express.

In the mail came a package from Julie. It was two packets of information, one for John and one for me with the family trees and all the genealogy she was able to find. She has been so generous with her time and support. For the first time, in my own physical hands, I was holding my own family tree! I still can't digest that I have my very own! With names that are accurate, and even a few faces now. How is this even happening? (Strictly by the grace of God.) The gifts abound!

I also got my preliminary 23andMe results in. I have very strong European lineage, British, Dutch, French, and Irish show up most strongly, and Baltic. I can't help but notice that the places I'd traveled to in Europe, where I was called the most to go, are all components of my DNA! The Baltic piece confuses me a little. I thought about the test I did in 2005, and it showed an exact match for northern Portugal. All I could think of at that point was that the family migrated through Portugal at one point, and it's Baltic. Julie and I talked about all the different possibilities, but that still seemed the most logical.

She shared with me that as she was looking over the Shapiro tree my paternal great-grandmother Taube was coming through. Great-grandma Taube passed in 1951, and my father didn't speak much of her or my great grandfather. Julie said Taube wanted to connect with me, and as I stared at both her and my grandfather Abraham's name on the tree, I felt a very strong energetic branding of the Shapiro name in me. It's a little difficult to describe, but I felt as if they were saying, "You are a Shapiro."

I've always felt such a strong connection to my dad and was quite proud of being his daughter. In that moment, it felt like something clicked into place, but I also felt like there was more, so I went into a shamanic meditation.

I ask Great-Grandma Taube to come through. I tell her that I'm open to any messages she may have for me.

Quite suddenly I hear a voice I'm not familiar with, a woman's voice, very distinct. She says, "Esther, you have great change coming. Your life is about to begin. A new chapter. Do not let the circumstances frighten you. You need to be an open vessel right now. Your birth father and Zelda reincarnated, but your adopted father and mother are with you all the time. I will be teaching you. Your real work is about to begin. What's coming next could not have been possible until the pieces of your adoption were resolved and clear to you. You and John share Native American roots that run very deep. You will understand more later."

Wow! I'm a shaman who is going to be trained by her great grandmother! Traditionally the grandmother passes on her gifts to the granddaughter. I felt a very strong excitement for what is coming next. Thank you Great Grandma Taube!

The next morning, I was distracted by a piece of shungite (a black, lustrous stone) I have sitting at my computer. Shungite is a very powerful, ancient healing stone that detoxifies your body by absorbing and eliminating any negative or health hazardous energies. I'm a bit of a rock hound, and I love using crystals and minerals in my own home as well as healing work that I do for others. I leave it by my computer along with a few others. I picked up the phone and called Julie.

The first thing she asked was, "Do you have a piece of shungite?" Really? She wanted to be sure I was keeping it nearby during this time. Julie was clearly on this journey with me.

She said based on more research, the Shapiros came from Lithuania, not Poland as my father had told me. Also likely a migration. While she was searching my grandmother Minnie (Shapiro) came to her. I sent her a photo, and she said that definitely was her. What was even more amazing is that as I looked for that photo I came across the one and only photo of I have of Great-grandma Taube! Next to her is my Great-grandfather Yisrael, who looks very much like my father.

Julie asked some questions, and as we talked, I found myself questioning if this is truly my birth family, but I kept being reminded that they're my family because of my parents. There was nothing at all coming from my adopted mother's side other than the occasional visit from my mom, which I'm always comforted by now. How blessed I am to have been able to not only heal my relationship with her, but to have one now that is based on love, respect and she truly is a supportive energy in my life. What an amazing life I have.

It's August 17:
I text John: "One month!"
His reply: "It's going to be a looooooooong month!" Smile.

31

It's been fairly quiet the last couple of weeks. John and I have exchanged a few text messages about his wife's recovery and that he hopes to get more serious soon about job hunting out here in Arizona. We laugh, we joke, and I'm always left with a sensation inside that I can't describe. The trip is only three weeks away. I feel like I need to be pinched!

> *The big day is finally here. It's September 17, 2015. I currently am sitting on the first flight of the day to Detroit, the next will be to Baltimore and lastly a shuttle to John's. John and I shared a few texts in the last couple of weeks. He did hear back from the hospital on the reservation, and it looks like he's got the job, although there are few delays. I'm just thrilled for him, and I feel so grateful that I was the one able to get him connected there.*
>
> *I remember something my "brother" Mike said. (Mike is a very close and dear friend that I met at*

Landmark Education in 2005. We had an instant knowing of each other because of a wonderful past life we'd shared that I discovered in regression meditation shortly after we met. We have been like siblings since and he is my go-to-guy for everything. He is the brother of brothers and has set a seriously high bar for my birth brothers!) Mike told me when I first found John that there was going to be something John needed from me that only I could bring him. I, of course, hoped it wasn't bone marrow, or a kidney, and here we are: it was a job!

Last night, John sent a text, "Less than 24 hours. Arg. Can't sleep." Then this morning another: "12 hours to get here, sheesh, hurry up! :-p"

I'm laughing, not only because of the messages, but also because he and I use the phrase "hurry up" in the same way. I think I'm getting glimpses of what a DNA connection brings, something I have no context for at all.

It's quite difficult to express how I'm feeling. Everyone is so excited for me, but for me it's so much more than excitement, yet there is no word. This is surreal.

After a long couple of flights, I arrived thirty minutes early into Baltimore. My shuttle wasn't for another two and a half hours. How on earth was I going to sit still for all that time? I wasn't! I looked online, booked a rental car, and off I went. This was one of those moments that being frugal simply wasn't going to apply. I drove like a crazy person, shaking inside the entire time, ran through the toll I was supposed to pay on the bridge (they would bill me later, I had no time for that now!), immersed in the thinking of the reality I was in now. I was driving to my birth brother's house! After more than thirty years of searching, and eighteen years of knowing about him, I was about to look at the man of my dreams. With every toll booth, stop light and turn, I couldn't get myself there quickly enough.

We were texting periodically, me to tell him how far out I was, him to tell me when he was leaving work. He had gotten home and was waiting for about ten minutes. As I drove into Salisbury, I really took a long look around. This was where my birth mother had lived. This was where my family has been. How many times had I been to Washington, DC, and Baltimore, only two hours away? Many! This is crazy! My nerves were amping up, but in the best of ways. I felt an anticipation that I'd never felt before. And finally, at 7:15 p.m., I drove up to my brother's house. I could barely keep myself together.

> *I walk up to the door. The screen door is shut but the inside door is wide open. I knock, as I can't see anyone, and I hear, "Come on in! What are you knocking for?!" Still not seeing anyone, I open the door tentatively, slowly step inside the house, and from the hallway he comes out. There he is, a little shorter than me, buzzed gray hair, sweet soft eyes, big soft lips and well-groomed facial hair. We immediately fall into each other's arms and within seconds we're both in tears. Time stands still. While doing my best to breathe, I'm overflowing*

with emotion. I keep telling myself in my head, "You're hugging your brother! You are hugging your brother! You are hugging your brother!"

After a very long hug, taking a moment to look at each other, we sit down. John starts showing me all the photos he could find. It's indisputable how much I look like my birth mother in her younger years. With each picture I see similar features, or memories that I do not have, and John shares stories about them. I'm in a dream. He then shows me two pendants and a matchbox that were my birth mother's...Helen's. I'm a bit haunted by them, being so close to them and touching things she had touched and worn. It's strange, compelling and certainly overwhelming.

I ask John about the apartment in New York, he says they lived on the second floor of a red brick building with wrought iron railings, and fire escapes. Exactly what I had seen in my visions years ago!

I share with him that every night I'd look for the first star to come out and I would make a wish to find him. I start to cry again and say, "What will I wish for now?" with the realization that something I'd been doing for eighteen years, wishing for for over thirty years and wondering about for forty-three years has been fulfilled. I'm aware of the void that is disappearing slowly and magically being filled with new and amazing things.

I ask John if he knows the song "Somewhere Out There." He says he does not. So I pull it up on the internet, hit play, and am doing my best to sing it to him among very heavy tears. This song has always been for him. I never dreamed I would actually be singing it to him. Never once have I been able to hear it without tears.

He is sobbing in kind. We share and shed a lot of tears, then hold hands and share a very long hug. I can barely breathe. I'm not even sure if this is actually happening. It is so beyond surreal for me.

I then got a tour of his house. I was stunned. The house was full of Native American and Celtic art work, much like my own home. John had smudged his room with sage for me, something I do almost daily. It truly felt like home, and so completely different from what I had been raised with in my adopted family. In one day, I saw a bit of what shared DNA could offer. John and I don't really look alike. He showed me a photo of his birth father and other half siblings, and he clearly resembles them. It mattered not. How on earth would I sleep tonight?

I spent about three hours last night on the phone with a friend back home talking about and processing what had just occurred. It was impossible to sleep. How does one rest after something like this? Reviewing the day only made it more real and exciting. It was already overwhelming and I'd just gotten there. I was experiencing a range of emotions I couldn't have anticipated and cannot possibly describe. But in spite of being tired, I was bright eyed and bushy tailed in the morning. John was taking me on a tour of the area and to see the house where our mother last lived and passed away.

As we drive around, I have thoughts of wondering what my life would have been like had I been with them. When we get to the house, which is set back about a hundred feet from the road, John pulls into the driveway just enough to be out of the road. We sit and talk. He shares with me that this is where Helen and her last husband, Gordy, lived. They had some animals on the property. That left me wondering how much fun Helen and I might have had sharing our love for animals. John then tells me a bit about her last months and her life with Gordy. Suddenly I have a flash of the vision of the dark-skinned man yelling at her. This was the house where that happened!

John was her end-of-life caregiver. He shares with me what some of that was like. My heart sinks, realizing what I missed. I feel the loss of being with Helen at the time of her passing, and so much more. I'm not sure why I'm having these feelings now, possibly because it is right in front of me. I'd never felt that sensation before, and it's tough. He tells me she never said a word about me, not even on her deathbed.

Shortly after getting back to John's house, Miriam arrived. I had asked if she could join us since she was the one who told me about the DNA test. I had to include her in this, and they were all more than welcoming and grateful to her, as I immeasurably will always be.

Around noon, we all headed to the Sage Diner to meet Merle (Helen's ex-husband/first cousin who is John's adopted dad and Daryle's birth dad), his wife, Cora, and her daughter Missy. When Merle got out of the car and turned toward me, he just stopped and stared. After a few moments, we hugged. He pulled back and stared some more, and then we headed into the restaurant. We all sat around the table, and he just continued to stare as if he was haunted.

In that moment, I became aware that I actually do look like someone. They said I was a spitting image of Helen. Merle then said that as far as he was concerned, he was my stepdad. He said that if I had stayed with Helen, then he would have raised me. For him, that superseded us being cousins. I wasn't going to argue—it touched me so deeply. I now have another dad!

While at lunch Merle asked so many questions, most of which just dropped my jaw further and further:

"Do you sing?"

"Yes."

"Did you know your mother and aunt sang with Johnny Cash and Patsy Cline?"

"Yes." John had told me. They were amazed that the first song I chose to learn to sing in vocal training was 'Crazy' by Patsy Cline!

"Do you like horses? Your mom rode horses and motorcycles. Her first bike was a Honda."

"I rode horses avidly as a child and young adult and they're a sacred animal to me. My first motorcycle was a Honda Rebel!"

At this point I was wondering how many more questions and comparisons would continue.

"Can you tell fortunes?"

"Well, not fortunes, but I'm psychic and do readings for people."

He says, "Your mother was psychic, and so was your grandmother Peg. She lived with your mom in Brooklyn and was a well-known psychic medium there."

Wow! So now I know where I get it from. Typical grandmother to granddaughter lineage! Holy cow!

They kept sharing things:

- Helen always kept aloe in the house; I've always had aloe in the house.
- She loved to dance; I love to dance.
- She was an artist; I'm an artist.

On and on and on, this went. It felt as if they already knew me because of this.

After lunch, when saying our farewells, I began to cry. Merle—or Dad, I should say—hugged me so warmly. I could feel his love for me already. He pulled away a bit, still holding my shoulders and told me I look so much like my mother. His eyes welled up as he wiped my eyes and said, "Don't cry baby." He stole my heart in that moment. And then I realized those arms had held her too. I had a strong sense that she was the love of his life.

We went back to the house, and Miriam spent the evening witnessing and enjoying all that she had helped create. John shared more about himself, and more things came up that we share: he wanted to be an astronaut as a kid, loves the night sky and space, went to culinary school, loves to cook, and more. It was absolutely fascinating to me how alike we are on the inside in so many ways. John brought out some of Helen's things (he only had a few), and I had my second moment of heart fluttering. I wondered how she wore these things, how they would have looked on her, and then the little girl in me just ached wishing she could have something that was Helen's.

John then brought out a small child's rocking chair. He said Helen gave it to him as a third-birthday present, but he had always felt suspicious about it, as if it was a gift of distraction, possibly from when she disappeared to have me. I had a strong sense he was right, as I oddly felt like I'd known that chair or seen it before. But for now, we said our good nights.

In the morning we heard from Daryle that he was on his way. In the meantime, Merle apparently was very anxious to spend more time with me, which I didn't expect. I thought it would be the one meeting, but he and Cora came over with Missy for another visit. John said he'd never seen Merle so impatient about anything.

The conversation continued from the night before with many questions and more information. Here is more of what Merle shared:

- Helen was a hostess for a closed/private mafia establishment in New York. (This piqued my curiosity because my parents had told me that Dad [Lary] had been offered a job to run a bowling alley in Hawaii as a front for the mafia when I was an infant. He considered it, but Mom refused, and I always thought that was a strange and very random thing.)
- Helen liked to go fishing.
- Helen did ceramics.

- Helen made her own pickles.
- She worked in the same factory as Merle building electronics and actually helped build the power pack for the space rover.
- She had her gallbladder out. (This left me wondering about my own digestive issues.)

Aside from the pickles (I enjoyed eating them, not making them!) and building electronics, we shared all the other things.

Merle told me he called my aunt Micki, who absolutely refused to believe who I was. He asked her about the name Milton Shapiro, and she clammed up. Everyone felt she knew something and had a fear of being found out. But who really knows why people behave the way they do. I figured, until I meet her, the jury was out.

Micki was my mother Helen's eldest sibling. Her birth name was Pearl. She got the nickname Micki in high school, and it stuck. Helen was next in line, then Billy, and finally Tina who was the youngest. I was told that Billy wound up having mental issues after having rheumatic fever as a teenager. My grandfather had run moonshine. He had apparently not been a very kind man back then. He refused to get Billy treatment because he had a "date." Billy's fever had been 108°F. My grandmother stood in front of the car as my grandfather was leaving for his "date," and he ran over her. She had been hospitalized for almost three weeks, and Billy had permanent brain damage from the fever. Tina had been sold/adopted out to Micki's in-laws, who'd raised her. She, too, had some mental issues and didn't really keep in touch with anyone but Micki from time to time.

And in my generation: my eldest brother Mac apparently loved to cook, and so did John, Daryle and I. Apparently Mom loved to also—she reportedly hadn't been very good at it!

By mid afternoon, everyone left and we were just waiting for Daryle. When he finally pulled up on his Harley, I found myself anxious to look at this man, to see if my suspicions were correct about us looking alike. The thought of looking at anyone who looked like me was still perplexing and exciting. After being told about his deployments, his post-traumatic stress disorder, traumatic brain injury, and attention deficit disorder, I wasn't quite sure how this was going to go.

Daryle removes his coat and shoes as he comes inside. He hugs me as a stranger would: quick, polite, and distant. He is clearly haunted by looking at me. I certainly am haunted too!

I look up at his face: there are my eyes! Whoa! Now I know what everyone sees when they look at mine. They're mesmerizing. Oh! My toes! There are my toes! He's got my Flintstone feet!

And, boy, do we look alike! His hands, his chin, his forehead, chunky upper arms and no butt! (All of us are flat bottomed!)

I could not stop looking him over. I caught myself staring quite a few times, fearing being rude I looked away, but I couldn't help myself. I was in a dream. It was seeing another version of myself, live, right in front of me. I was speechless, fighting back tears, full of words but unable to express much of anything. He was the first person in my entire life that I could look at and see myself in ways I never had before.

Daryle shared with me that he recalled Aunt Micki once telling him about a premature baby. He recalled Aunt Micki telling him that she had gone to watch John when Helen had gone off with one of her men. If the index card I'd found in my adopted parents' papers was correct, I would have been born three weeks early.

Daryle said Mom wore a chai pendant for years (the Hebrew word for "life"), she studied Hebrew and the Jewish faith, but he never knew why. We all were suspect it was her way of keeping me close and doing it for her Jewish boyfriend at the time (possibly my uncle Milton?). He shared his weight issues and that Helen had them as well. Daryle brought tons of photos for me to see. All this was a pleasant surprise after hearing how hesitant he had been about meeting me.

We just finished a lunch of homemade rabbit stew that John made (my first rabbit stew ever), and I ask Daryle for a photo together. We've been visiting about ninety minutes now, most of which I've spent staring at him. He gets up and walks toward me. I stand up. He very unexpectedly throws his arms around me and starts crying. I'm crying too. I have my baby brother in my arms, who looks just like me! This hug is significantly better than the first.

While holding me he says he is struggling with letting all this in, and that it's haunting to look at me, as he feels like he's looking at his (our) mom. In this moment I feel Daryle as the nineteen-year-old young man with a broken heart from losing his mother at such a young age. And, apparently I'm a "Mini Me" of Helen.

I'm so grateful this hug is being caught on camera since my first hug with John wasn't. Some things are left to one's memory, and neither of these hugs will ever be forgotten.

Daryle has a son, Cody, from his first marriage. Cody is twenty-two years old. Daryle's second wife, Carissa, apparently was more of a mom to Cody than his birth mother. Cody has a very young son named Colt, so I have a nephew and grand-nephew! Daryle got Cody on the phone with whom I got to FaceTime with! Very cool. Daryle shared that the time in the Marines took him to Okinawa, Japan so we had stories of Japan to share. It was a long evening of sharing, staring, laughing, and crying. Daryle and I spent the last hour of the night alone talking, bonding, sharing, and creating a relationship that I'd never dared dreamed possible. Being a big sister already felt so good. Being a little sister was equally as magical. I was in bliss.

Daryle posted the following on Facebook: "So today I hugged a sister I didn't know I had. The story is too long and complicated to put in words. But through an unbelievable chain of events, my brother and sister searching DNA, I have another sister. Never been a believer in fate, but I'm starting to believe my wife when she says everything happens for a reason. This feels like a dream. It's like looking at my mom. I can't even sleep. I've been around the world and seen and done many amazing things. This truly tops them all. I'm on top of the world. I'm in the same house and town with three of my siblings. Never take family for granted!"

John, Daryle, my sister in law Joy, and I hung out until mid afternoon on this glorious Sunday. We spent time looking at both John's and my DNA test. Daryle did his swabbing and would mail his test in tomorrow. He voiced a fear that was similar to mine: "What if we aren't a match?" He said he'd be brokenhearted for me, which I found incredibly sweet. This was simply another surreal be-in-the-moment thing, which by this point I'd mastered after forty-three years on this journey. Considering how much we resemble each other and Mom (Helen), it's not likely a concern, and everyone else told us the same.

After reviewing the DNA stuff, which shows no Jewish origins at all (something I didn't realize at the time) I had voiced to them a few times that I was feeling frustrated that Helen had not come through to me. I had such a strong sense that she would, but nothing. We all discussed why that might be, and I suddenly had a vision of Johns little rocking chair in my mind. I asked John to bring it out. I again said how frustrated I was and put my hand on the arm of the little chair. And then what I'd hoped for happened in an instant:

Helen is standing in the living room with us ready to share. She has messages for each of us, and immediately began speaking:

"John, you're looking in the wrong direction for your father's confirmation. There are a lot of Baker family secrets. She shows the #6 (there are five kids that John knows of, so there likely is or was another, or

he is #6) as far as how many kids there are. She walks over to him and gives him a kiss on the forehead and says "Son, I did the best I could in giving you Merle as a father." John is crying like a baby.

Helen then moves over to Daryle: "Continue on the path you're on. Open to your spirituality. Trust in you and who you are. Be gentle with yourself and your son. It's purposeful that he is your mirror. Learn to love yourself and let go of being a soldier." He was sobbing, said that it was like he was talking to her soul. Well, he was.

Helen then says to me, "I made a lot of mistakes and hurt a lot of people. I'm sorry for that." She then tells me she couldn't communicate with me until we all met and were in one room together, a question I've had since seeing her in Kansas all those years ago at John Edward's event of why I haven't seen her.

She then says, "I was with your uncle Milton for two years." She shows me (like a video I'm watching from above) that she and Milton (he was dressed in a suit) were in an antique-type store. Milton picks up a small rocking chair (it's the one John had that I was now touching) and brings it to the register. I continue hovering over them, and can see that Helen is very pregnant at this point even though it doesn't show like most pregnancies do. The register is one of those very large gold registers. She tells me it's mid-February 1964.

The scene then flashes to the apartment that John lived in as a toddler, the one that my aunt Mary went to when my adopted dad took her to give Helen some money. Grandma Peg is holding John in her arms. He is crying. Behind them on the floor is the rocking chair with a little brown teddy bear sitting in it. Helen tells John that she is going away for a little while, she wants him to have the rocker to be comforted and to hug the teddy bear while she is gone. (In the current moment John is now crying his eyes out.) John crawls out of grandma's arms and runs over to Helen and puts his hands on her tummy. (Now I'm sobbing because I always felt that he used to touch me while I was in her belly, talking or singing to me.) He is very upset that he wasn't going to get to see his little sister or brother. Everything fades away.

That was the end of the message. Everyone in the room was crying heavily. John remembered the Teddy bear. I got up and hugged both of my brothers. To say this was overwhelming was an understatement. It validated so much for all of us. We sat together for a while letting this all sink in and recovered enough so we could get ourselves out of the house. I had to go into my room alone for thirty minutes just to catch my breath. I was experiencing so much love that my chest was actually hurting. I just laid there in the quiet, doing a lot of deep breathing, allowing myself to integrate everything that was happening. I was living a dream, my dream, and a dream that was never supposed to come true! It was a lot to take in.

After I recovered we went to Merle and Cora's house for a bit. Their house is adorable, decorated with many country style decorations and tons of items that Merle made, my favorite being small carousel horses, about three feet in height. He also has a Harley Davidson motorcycle, and it came to my awareness that most everyone in the family has tattoos and rides motorcycles, just like me. In my adopted family, no one had tattoos or rode motorcycles but me! He had a couple of ceramic pieces that Helen made and some photos he'd stayed up until 1:00 a.m. to find of her to show me. It was amazing to me how everyone was making all this extra effort to find anything and everything that would be of meaning or helpful to me.

During our visit, I randomly asked Merle if he'd ever heard the name Melanie. He said there was a cousin with that name in the Every family, but that was it. I said nothing further, as my intent was to plant a seed. We discussed dinner and all agreed to go out for Japanese food, and that I would ride with Daryle on the Harley and we'd meet everyone there.

We put on our helmets and Daryle drives us to the restaurant on his bike. I get off the bike and Dad (Merle) calls me over. He says that he remembers something important he needs to share. I brace myself. He apologizes, saying it's not that easy remembering things from fifty years ago. I tell him if I never find out another thing that I'm perfectly OK, as I've gotten everything I'd searched for and more.

But he gets serious for a moment and says, "I remember her telling me once that she'd had a still-born. It was a girl, and she was going to name it Melanie. She never mentioned it again."

I'm numb. I'm in shock. My knees give out. I almost fall to the ground and immediately fall apart emotionally. My body shakes and I collapse in his arms. He says he hates to see my cry, but I tell him these are good tears, the very best kind. I'm letting go of forty-three years of pain.

My gratitude for this man in this moment is exponential. I stand up, turn and walk straight into John's arms and am crying, so many emotions going through me. (Even now while writing I cannot hold back the tears.) This is the most defining moment of this journey thus far. My birth mother named me! The name Melanie instantly lost its darkness.

All the years I knew my soul's name started with an E, that Melanie was nothing but riddled with lies, that what Mom Sylvia had told me about her naming me after the character in *Gone with the Wind* wasn't the truth, that it was Helen who'd named me! Sylvia once told me that if "they" had wanted to find me, they could because they knew my name. I couldn't help but wonder if they kept my name as part of an agreement, and I wonder what it was like for Sylvia not to have been the one to name me. I've always known there was something awry with my name. Maybe Helen loved *Gone with the Wind* too—who knows? I despised the name because of the lies and its meaning. The name itself is beautiful, but it wasn't mine. And now, I can finally be at peace, for the first time, with Melanie.

After a few minutes of gathering myself we go into the restaurant. My eyes are leaking (and continue to do so through the entire meal, involuntarily). We sit at a hibachi table and enjoy a wonderful show, delicious food and many laughs. I realize that I had gone to Benihana's for my birthday for about fifteen years of birthdays, and here I was, as if I was having my first birthday with my birth family, my family, and the one I clearly was a true part of. Incredibly surreal! Never did I feel like this with my adopted family. I was so obviously different from them, always felt uncomfortable, and here I feel like a part of something I'd never felt before.

Merle says he is paying the bill, no arguments allowed, because he is more of a father today than he was three days ago. I weep more. I ask him since he feels that way if it's OK to call him Dad. He smiles, tears well up in his eyes, and he says, "Yes!" I really do have another Dad!

After dinner, Daryle and I get back on the motorcycle, don our helmets, and I put my arms around my baby brother, and my eyes continue leaking. I'm overflowing with gratitude. I cannot believe all of this is happening. He revs up the bike and off we go.

We ride through the neighborhood and get to a stop light. Daryle turns to me and says, "I never imagined having a big sister sitting on the back of my bike with me."

I smile and squeeze him tighter. He isn't the only one in a bit of shock. We get to the highway and he hits the throttle and off we go till the bike reaches about ninety miles an hour. I'm screaming, "Woohoo!" at the top of my lungs, arms stretched out, flying as high as I could possibly be at this point in my life. I could have done that for hours, but he gets off on the next exit, slows down and randomly pulls over.

He is crying. He turns to look at me and says, "I feel Mom is on the bike with us." I felt her as well. We cry together for a moment, and he takes off again. He parks the bike in front of John's house, I get off, then he follows, and we fall into each other's arms for a very long hug.

So many surreal moments. How much can one person possibly take in?!

Merle and Cora came by for one last visit that evening. Most of the conversation was about Daryle and his spiritual struggles. It was awesome to see him open up and everyone support him. Saying goodbye to Dad was rough on us both. He kept shaking his head back and forth, saying that I would never know what this meant to him. I told him I had a pretty good idea. He shared that Helen once told him that she would come back to haunt him, and here I was! He smiled, and then we laughed. Cora deeply touched my heart. She was a purely loving maternal presence and kept saying, "God bless your heart." God has. I don't know if I will get to see them again, but they're forever in my heart.

The rest of the evening I spent cuddling in John's arms on his love seat and visiting with Daryle. My inner child was in bliss. It was his request I cuddle with him, a little sister's dream come true! Once John and Joy went to bed, Daryle and I stayed up and talked for a long while. He showed me a motivational video that he watched daily to keep focused and positive. He shared how much this time has meant to him. He regretted not being closer to Mom, John, and Merle, and he was committed to changing that now. He said I was very easy to talk to, and he wanted me to be an annoying big sister. My pleasure! He shared something he learned in the marines about forming, storming, and mourning (a process to help teams perform better, but has practical applications to help move one along to completion) and encouraged me to stay positive and keep all this alive. And then he gave me a dog tag off of his shoe for a soldier he loved and lost. He couldn't have given me anything more meaningful.

After a restless night's sleep, I said goodbye to Joy and then woke Daryle to say goodbye. John was already off to work. Daryle and I shared more hugs, more tears, and lots of gratitude. Daryle said he would do his best to help John move to Arizona so he could see me again sooner rather than later. I got in my car, drove off, and watched my baby brother waving to me in the rear-view mirror until I turned the corner. I was so full of emotions: sad to leave, ecstatic having been with them for four days, happy to have more answers, anxious to know when I would see them again, sad for the few things I wished I had experience with Helen. There was a smorgasbord of feelings inside of me and I was in a dance with all of them the entire two-hour drive to the airport.

I spent almost the entire first flight writing and capturing all the events of the weekend. So much was formulating and integrating. So many puzzle pieces finding their place and settling in. I was so present to the magic and miracles that have occurred. I was anxious and excited for what is next with my family. I had faith and trust that one day there will be confirmation of the Shapiro/paternal side of things, but for now, I was so at peace with it. All I had wanted was to find my brother (and the truth), and instead I got an entire family—and then some.

Merle has four children from a first marriage: Carol is the oldest, and then three boys: John (called Big John), Michael, and Jim. Then Merle married Helen, adopted John (aka Little John) and then they had Daryle. (Merle married Cora years later after divorcing Helen when Daryle was still a kid.) They're all my cousins and now step siblings too, except for my brother John. Then there is Aunt Micki as well as Grandma Joanne who is my grandfather's second wife. Her presence in his life apparently changed him pretty dramatically for the better, eventually becoming a church-going and loving man and husband. My uncle Billy died in 2014, and who knows what will come about with my aunt Tina and brother Mac? Time will tell more.

I was surprised by how much I already loved them all, especially my brothers. Each of us essentially had grown up as only children, as John had left home when Daryle was only seven years old. I was in awe at how easy it had been to be with them, that I could just be myself, which was a huge gift in itself. No pretending to be something else, just me, and they seemed to have loved me just the way I am. I spent many moments being overwhelmed this weekend. I imagined as time goes by I would see more, find out more, feel more, and experience more about what had transpired. Today's Amma reading was to take life in small increments (again!)—boy, is that the best advice for all of this. The last few weeks were about biting into life with humungous bites, all of which I was embracing. Now it was time to savor and digest.

I thought about everyone who had passed and was on the other side. Helen now said I would be able to talk with her anytime. So now both of my mothers are available to me. Dad was always there—he just remained quieter. I was keenly aware that since at least 2002 when Helen came to me at that John Edward event that she has been working very hard to get us all to this place and time. I know Mom and Dad (Lary and Sylvia) have helped as well. They have made things right. The boys now have some forgiveness work to do, but they're so happy I imagine it won't be too difficult for them. All has somehow turned out well in the end.

I returned home with a grateful and full heart, more open and expansive than ever before. Today I can say I know what it feels like to hug my DNA, to be with family that I look and act like, think like and clearly am a part of. I was so quickly accepted. My haunting looks seem to be a good and healing thing, and my brothers and I immediately, with the first photo together, were teasing, goofing around, giggling and behaving in ways I only imagined siblings to behave.

John is already a space of solace and comfort to me. Daryle has tugged at my heart much as my inner child does. My sister in law Joy told him, "Sometimes guides come in the form of a sister." Wow, did that touch my heart. I hope to be whatever he needs me to be. It was clear this time together impacted him profoundly.

As my final flight descended into Phoenix, it was clear that I was leaving forty-three years of lies, deceit, and immensely indescribable pain and betrayal behind me. John should be moving to Arizona by November. The job I'd set up for him worked out, and he would be three and a half hours away! That pendulum had been accurate all those years ago. These were the moments that require pinching. I was living my dream.

Since returning home, a few amazing things had happened. I spent some time considering how I may confirm whether I was truly a Shapiro or not. My cousin Faith was clearly no longer an option, but it came to my mind that I had my half sisters as a possibility. They could potentially be my cousins. (Not sure why I hadn't thought of them before this! Sheesh!) It had been a long time since we'd had contact, but I missed them and figured I really didn't have anything to lose. So I gathered up some courage and called my adopted sister Gabby. She was the eldest of the two (Sunny was the other). We had a great reconnection, and she agreed to do a DNA test for me without any hesitation! I will finally know if I was a Shapiro or not! And I got my sister back, which was awesome. Another gift in this crazy journey!

It also came to my awareness that Helen died when she was fifty-two, and I was currently in my fifty-second year of life. I remembered all the visions I had of the black man yelling at her while she was in bed crying in a fetal position on her right side, and now I knew that her last husband Gordy was African American and abusive. She and I were connected in more ways than I'd realized, which warmed my heart and soul tremendously, and I was so grateful for all of it.

> *Today (October 26, 2015), John arrived at his new place in Ft. Defiance, Arizona. Daryle did get to help them move, and if they weren't headed this way tomorrow I'd already be in the car!*

My brothers arrived late last night. We had little time to visit, as we were all tired and Daryle's shuttle was at 4:00 a.m. Boo! I'd rather have a few minutes than nothing. After a short few hours' rest, Daryle left, and John and I slept a bit more. He hung out until I had my afternoon break from work, and then we enjoyed Sedona a bit. He was still quite emotional about things. My eighteen years of searching for him clearly put me ahead on that healing curve. I asked what it's been like for him, and he voiced his frustration that Helen hadn't said anything on her deathbed about me. He was amazed at how similar we were. It was a joyful afternoon together. Saying goodbye was much easier knowing we were now up the road from each other. It was all still very surreal.

I went for a float session today (October 29, 2015). (You float in twelve inches of water that contains one thousand pounds of salt, and you're enclosed in a pod that is designed for complete sensory deprivation.) About ten minutes into it, once I finally relaxed, I started to cry, quite hard. I was aware that I was grieving a life and dream I had been creating for myself. I was letting go of the story of my adoption. I had held onto this story for forty-three years, searched for thirty, and yearned and searched specifically for John for the last eighteen of them. I learned to live with a huge gaping hole in my heart, a missing, a sadness, a void that was excruciatingly painful. I cried for at least thirty minutes in that pod.

During those thirty minutes both of my mothers came to me. Helen, looking much like she did in the one portrait I have of her, was standing in front of me. Mom Sylvia was on my left standing behind me. Helen silently opened her arms, offering me a hug and to hold me. I moved into Helen's arms, and as I did Mom Sylvia took my left hand and held it tightly for support. I fell into my birth mother's arms for the first time. I just held her, feeling the wonderment of having both of my mothers' nurturing and supporting me. I was crying so hard I had to sit up in the pod to breathe. I'd never been that present to a mother's love other than being in Amma's arms. I was once again present to the blessing of the gift I had of communing with the other side. I was held, healed, and uplifted by both of my mothers. What a miracle! I thanked them both for all they had done, forgave them, and left that pod more healed than usual.

It is November 4 and Daryle's results are in: we share 1,918 centiMorgans of DNA, and John and I have 1,967 centiMorgans. There is no doubt now that Daryle is my half brother! Although we all "knew," having the confirmation is both comforting and another celebration!

Less questions, more answers, and way more than I ever could have dared wish for or imagined!

Time was moving so quickly. It was already November 12, 2015! Got to text a bit with Daryle today. He said Mom was very buxom (now I know where I got that from!). Her CB handle was "West Virginia Boobie." Ha-ha! Carol, Merle's daughter, was doing some photo digging and investigating for me, as she has a love of genealogy. There was one photo of Helen, Merle, John, and Daryle with a little blond girl in it. Daryle was quite young, and I would have been about the blond girls age. I find myself looking at that photo pretending that I was that little girl, with my own blond curls. I can't help but wonder what would it have that been like?

Today I had a family Thanksgiving at my home (November 21, 2015). My first with blood family! Mama (Sierra's mother with whom she has little to no contact with now) and Grandma came up from Phoenix, I had my closest friends, and John and his wife joined us. It was a first in many ways. We all sang "Somewhere Out There" to John. He bawled like a baby again. I still could not get through it without crying. How different it is to sing it now without that deep yearning inside. It was surreal, and in many ways, it was impossible to describe. We took a group photo, and the memories are with me forever. It was a wonderful miraculous Thanksgiving!

December 10, 2015: Gabby's results were in: I am not a Shapiro. It was a bit baffling and definitely disappointing. Thirty years of this story had been about Milton showing up as such a strong possibility, psychics saying I was definitely a Shapiro. My friend Julie who was a medium said Milton claimed me as his, my psychic medium friend Kim saying my parents say that I already know the truth. If not, then what was his role? And who is my birth father? And, considering spirit has never lied to me, why is this the first and only time?

I'd never really had much caring to know, as all the lies were around my maternal side. I often felt as if there was no birth father at times. But now the hunger was there and growing. So many things had pointed to Milton. I wondered if he thought he was the birthfather? I was sad, disappointed, and aware that I may never know. I now have more grieving to do. All I could do now is what I'd done for so many years: trust, surrender and remain at peace with not knowing. If I was meant to know, I knew my parents and God would make it happen.

It was a week before my fifty-second birthday (which was February 25, 2016). Over the holidays, I had gone to John's. We'd had a fun time. John had surprised me with a bracelet that was a heart pendant that said "Little Sis" on it. More tears for us both. I'd immediately called Daryle and told him about the bracelet and told him that there was a "Big Sis" version, and I'd requested (maybe more demanded!) a belated Christmas present. He'd said it was done! John started calling me Sissy, which I just adore.

A few hours after rising on this beautiful last day of March, Grandma Joanne called to tell me she'd spoken to Aunt Micki again, who'd said she was now open to meeting me! This was after months of her refusing and denying I was who I said I was (and who DNA says I was). I was thrilled! Grandma and I had only spoken on the phone a few times. We'd immediately hit it off. She was a wonderful, warm, positive woman with a deep, strong faith. She had been trying to so hard to get Aunt Micki to shift, but Micki had just refused, saying, "I can't help her." I told Grandma to let her know I didn't want any information from her—I just wanted to meet her. It worked! So I made my reservations to visit her in Ormond Beach, Florida, while Grandma Joanne would be there too. I'd get to meet them both!

I've done well with remaining at peace around finding my birth father's side of the family. Now that some time had passed I'd learned that my brothers were not the best communicators, yet I knew the connection was strong, and I remembered that I was likely a bit needier, considering my history. This past Saturday night, I had a dream that a woman I did not know gave me my birth father's name. A lot of energy going on around this. I couldn't help but wonder if it was just my psyche at work, or was this feeling correct?

Was something about to happen? My friend Julie in Denver had gone to a genealogy seminar. She'd heard a story about a woman who'd found her birth father through DNA matching a first cousin. I knew immediately, with absolute certainty, that this was what was going to happen for me. Now to sit back and wait for things to unfold.

John and Daryle rearranged their lives to join me on the Florida trip. I felt so loved by them and got a sense that Helen had been doing her magic from the other side, as this all fell into place in spite of no probability. John planned to come spend the night before our flight and head out on this journey together. My dream brother, bonus brother, and I were going on a family trip! Whoa! Talk about more amazing gifts. Daryle was able to get a room in the same hotel as us, and his wife was joining him, so I would meet Carissa, my other sister in-law, as well as my aunt and grandmother. Holy cow!

I've been so blessed already, but I've started having more thoughts about my birth father: Does he even know about me? If so does he wonder about me? Would he want to meet me? Do I have siblings? Would they want to know about me? All the natural questions I'd had for so many years were coming to the surface again. I felt so blessed I could not even expect anything more, yet there was and is more. There never was much consistent conversation from my parents about my birth father, only that he was Jewish. Sylvia had said once that he was a doctor, then a businessman, then he wasn't even in the picture. It was another mystery. I had random thoughts about who he was, but my curiosity was piquing.

One thing I wish to make clear was that my Dad: Lawrence Willard Shapiro was my father through and through. I do not even feel comfortable calling my birth father "Dad" or "father." Likely because there has been no connection with whomever he was. For many years I wondered if he even existed, which only makes sense in a lost adoptees head. But Lary was the only one who got that designation, unlike Sylvia, who raised me but rarely occurred as a mother. I did call Helen "Mom" at times now because: a) I shared that with the boys, and b) because she clearly never allowed us to be completely disconnected and had worked so hard from the other side to bring healing to this situation. She had been acting like a mother, for which I'm eternally grateful. I truly believed that if I was meant to find my birth father, I would. That much I knew and trusted!

I reached out to a few matches on GEDmatch today. Seemed like most of them were on Helen's side. I also got a message from Grandma Joanne that Aunt Micki was "over the moon happy" that her "niece and nephews" were coming down to see her. She acknowledged me as her niece! Tears. Things were opening up more and I was ridiculously excited about what's to come! Doesn't feel like April Fool's Day to me!

It's been a few days since I checked GEDmatch, and I started thinking about this issue of being half Jewish. One of my new DNA matches that I contacted had a Jewish name, but he told me he was not Jewish. I was wondering what the likelihood was of me being Jewish at all. I didn't feel it in any way, clear now that my Mom's side was not, but still a mystery. I'd been thinking a lot the last few days about Sylvia telling me, "They know your name, if they want to find you they can." Aside from Helen, who is "they"?

Florida is only three days away. I want to bring something special for Aunt Micki. I paint a wood picture frame for her and place a picture of the boys and me in it and personalize it with our names. I'm feeling very excited, anxious and a little nervous, more with each moment that passes. This is another huge moment coming in my life that I have no idea how it will go, but I'm ready. So, so ready!

34

John and I are on the plane headed to Daytona Beach. We both look at our boarding passes, April 9, 2016, and then gasp when we see his reservation code: HLYEYN. Close enough to Helen for us both! And here I am, sitting next to the brother I searched for for so many years. Surreal! I periodically poke his arm to remind me that this is not a dream, although it most certainly is! I wonder how this motherless child, erased from one family, raised within another family that was never a fit, had gotten to this place of having so much family. My gratitude is immeasurable.

John and I spent both flights laughing, poking each other, crying, and enjoying each other. John shared a lot of stories with me, of course things that I found entertaining but have no way to verify, so I will keep them to myself. But, wow, my family sure had some drama! We got to Daytona just fine. We texted Daryle and asked if he needed anything from the store. He said a rubber ducky:

typical Daryle. Well, big sisters are required to meet certain demands, so I serendipitously found a purple rubber ducky for him! We met up with Daryle and Carissa at the hotel. He cracked up at his purple rubber ducky! We got rooms near each other, which was awesome. Carissa is amazing, I loved her the moment I met her. She is the perfect person for Daryle.

We went out for a disappointing seafood dinner, but driving along the coast, being with each other and the water was so healing and beautiful.

Daryle shared that he had started using medical marijuana after I shared what it had done for me. He had a natural trust in me that was amazing to me and often left me wondering how it would have been if we had been raised together. He had to work through a lot of old beliefs around marijuana, including what had been taught in the military, but he was getting symptom relief now that he never had before. It was amazing watching him move through things.

This morning, after breakfast we head for Aunt Micki's. I nervously walk into her apartment ahead of everyone with prompting from my brothers. The door to her apartment opens. In front of me is a very small and frail woman with beautiful gray hair that looks like it was carefully put up in a large and flattering bun. She is wearing oxygen.

She invites us in and hugs me right off the bat. It feels oddly comforting being in her arms, as if she is not a stranger to me. Grandma Joanne comes quickly over to me and gives me the biggest and warmest of hugs. I know her because of pictures on Facebook. She is filled with excitement and enthusiasm. I'm directed by two women I don't know to sit next to Aunt Micki, so I take my seat on the end of her bright-red couch as she sits in her chair next to me. (I quickly learn she sits there specifically to smoke by the window, which she apparently does a lot of!)

The unknown women are two of Aunt Micki's closest friends: Joyce, her best friend for many years, and Helen, another dear friend with a surprising name, to say the least. They're here to support her, which I find incredibly sweet, reminiscent of my own girlfriends (one being named Joyce!). We all immediately started talking.

Aunt Micki keeps looking at me much as Merle had, a bit hauntingly. (I can't express how it feels to be looked at like that: as a stranger that looks at you as if they've known you forever.) After about fifteen minutes into the visit, and a lot of questions about me and my life, Aunt Micki breaks into tears, excuses herself, and Joyce and Helen assist her into her bedroom for a bit to recover. Apparently for her too, I look very much like Helen. She comes back out about ten minutes later to the living room, and we share many more things. It feels impossible to share fifty-plus years, but we just keep going.

After answering quite a few questions my brothers had, she changes direction and offers us gifts: whatever belongings we want to take with us are ours, and she treats me equally to my brothers as far as what there is to take. I'm feeling a part of a family in a way I never have before. (She had recently been put on hospice and was given eleven months to live, so I'm very grateful she chose to meet me now.)

None of us fight over a thing! In fact, we each are excited for the treasures the other one is taking home. The first thing I ask for is a lion sculpture with the most mesmerizing eyes that I've been looking at since I sat down on her couch. She tells me she was an avid artist with her own pottery studio for many years, and that Helen worked with her too, and the lion was Micki's design and she has had it for years. Perfect!

She then pulls out a collection of butterflies of all sorts. She says to take as many as I desire. There must be five hundred pins in front of me! Carissa and I share them. I've always loved butterflies and am quickly realizing how much my aunt and I are alike.

Aunt Micki shared some of her past: she and Helen were born in Berkeley Springs, West Virginia (again confirming what was on my birth certificate), that they both sang and Grandpa was their manager, and he kept everything for himself so she eventually quit. She was angry with him for many reasons. She recorded singles and had a radio show. Helen and Grandma Peg worked for her at a clothing factory at one point. She shared with me that one of her physical traits was she had a lot of facial hair and shaved to this day, another thing I can blame Helen for! This is the type of stuff that makes me smile because it's familiar, and now familial. She gave us the list of health conditions in the family and shared that our heritage is French, Irish, British, and Dutch! Seriously? All the places I've already been in Europe and wanted to go to most! In spite of not "knowing," some part of me knew this too.

Micki said Helen disappeared when she was twelve years old. By that point, Grandpa's abuse had begun. They found her with a truck driver at a hotel, and ever since then she has always had boyfriends, sometimes many at once. Because of that, Aunt Micki said she really couldn't be sure who my birth father was. She said she never knew Helen was pregnant with me, as Helen was quite overweight at the time. She recalls Helen disappearing for about six weeks but never knew where she went; it seems no one did. (This conflicted with Merle saying she told him she'd heard of a stillborn child, but she seemed very genuine about this in the moment.) This clearly lined up with the vision Helen showed me telling John she was going away for a while and would not be coming back with the baby.

Aunt Micki confirmed the story about Grandpa running over Grandma Peg when Uncle Billy had been sick. Even though that left Uncle Billy with mental disabilities, he'd still wound up marrying twice and having two children, but no one knew where they were at this point. I asked Aunt Micki what her favorite memory of Helen was. She became a bit withdrawn, reflective and nostalgic for a moment, then said, "We got so annoyed with Grandpa at one point we went outside and just started throwing all our records like Frisbees." She paused and then said, "I loved her." She seemed sad.

John asked why Helen and Merle divorced. Aunt Micki said she wasn't 100 percent sure but felt it was because of Helen's swinger lifestyle. Aunt Micki felt Merle would have done anything for Helen, and anything to keep her. She agreed with me that they were the loves of each other's lives. In fact, Aunt Micki had found him very attractive and had a crush on him many moons ago, before he and Helen married. She said he went along with Helen's lifestyle, but it was her thing, not his. Mom had even invited Aunt Micki into the swinging, but she declined. I just can't imagine the hole Helen had in her heart to have such a ferocious need for sex. Sexual abuse is so incredibly destructive, and I imagine what Grandpa had done to her was the source of this emptiness she had. Although my abuse was minimal, I can understand the wounding to some degree. I'm sad that they all had to go through that, and grateful Grandma Joanne was able to help my grandpa become a better man, and that he even wanted to be.

Aunt Micki shared some very private things that day about her own life. Then, during a pause in the conversation, and out of the clear blue, she asked me if I knew the name Sidney Malet. I gasped and said "What!" I was so shocked I almost passed out from dizziness! That was name of the delivering doctor on my birth certificates. How on earth would she know this name, let alone think to bring it up?

Many years ago, my friend Rachel in Colorado (who had successfully helped her sister find her birth family) finally found Dr. Malet alive and living in California. She'd actually spoken with him on the phone once. He'd denied remembering anything about a private adoption, agreed to look at the birth certificate if she faxed it him, so she had. I'd thought I had a real lead, finally! But the next time she'd attempted to call him to follow up on the fax, the number had been disconnected. Another disappointing dead end.

I asked her how she knew the name, and she'd shared that she had been born a hermaphrodite. By the time she'd reached her twenties she had been at a desperate point with it. She'd said she felt like she was turning into a man and despised her body. She had never been comfortable with intimacy and felt broken. One day, she had been seriously considering suicide, and while walking and contemplating it, she saw a sign for a doctor's office, a gynecologist, so she'd gone inside begging for help. She'd described it as her last attempt at reaching out for help. It had been Sidney Malet's office. He'd had to have also been my mother's gynecologist, as one of her more consistent stories had been that the doctor had called her one day, saying someone had wanted to give up their child. Maybe that had actually been the truth!

They'd eventually become lovers. She said he had been the love of her life. She looked for and found a book he had given her with an inscription in it. It was clear by the look on her face how much she had felt for him. He also did her surgeries to correct the physical issues. She then told me that she and Helen once compared breast size and Helen won! Ha-ha! (Thanks again Mom! Ha-ha!) She said I definitely look like Helen except for the lips/mouth and curly hair, but I'm built like her, sound like her at times and laugh like her. She said I also look a lot like herself when she was young. She shared some photos and film negatives, and there was one picture of Helen where I definitely look like her. But I look a lot like Aunt Micki too. She also clarified a lot of historical things for my brothers.

As for Grandma Joanne, she was living in NY when she'd met Aunt Micki, who was twelve years Joanne's senior. Aunt Micki essentially had become like a mother to her. Aunt Micki had always dreamed of having a little girl of her own. It had been a deep yearning that had never been fulfilled (until she'd met me, she said). She'd brought Joanne to Virginia and got her set up in a little apartment. She'd asked Grandpa to check on Joanne now and then, and that had been how Joanne and Grandpa got together. They had been thirty-five years apart in age. They'd become churchgoing people, and it had changed Grandpa forever. Grandma said Grandpa hung the moon. Aunt Micki said she'd never gotten to know the good version of her father and hadn't healed her past nor forgiven him. I prayed she would do so before she passed.

Then there was Aunt Tina. She was the youngest of their generation. Micki was eighteen when Tina was born. Micki was terrified Tina would suffer the abuse the rest of them had (Grandpa was sexually and physically abusive to all the women in the house for many years), so she'd talked Grandma Peg into adopting Tina out to her in-laws. Tina had grown up thinking Micki was her mother because she had been the one who was most present in her life, doing all the negotiations and always visiting, and she still had a hard time believing Peg was her birth mother. Tina and Micki had a very tenuous, on-and-off communication all of their lives because of this. I asked where she lived: Doylestown, Ohio! This again confirmed what Dr. Karen had mentioned, referencing something about a sister and Ohio. Unbelievable!

Aunt Micki accepted that she was dying. She got tearful a lot during this first visit, and her regret and sadness of not being closer to the boys was obvious. She was so grateful and happy to meet me, a "miracle and gift," she called it. I was happy and grateful as well. I came home with about a hundred butterfly pins, the lion, some jewelry and photos, and most importantly, many wonderful memories, answers, and a deep sense of gratitude.

It had been two glorious days so far. Aunt Micki's health rallied after our visit yesterday, and she said it was proof of mind over matter. Today we went to her favorite restaurant, called the River Grill in Ormond Beach, Florida. We sat outside by the river. It was so beautiful there and absolutely delicious food. The boys and I went down to the water. We were all leaning over the railing talking about how, as children they would have thrown me in the water in spite of the sign that says, "Do Not Feed the Alligators." We just laughed and laughed and talked about how they would have picked on me. Strange how much love I felt in all that teasing.

Saying goodbye that evening was tough, very tough. We were all crying. Carissa fell apart, Daryle really struggled and John said he wished he'd stayed closer to Aunt Micki. They had regrets which I hoped they would all work through. I myself wished I had more time. She would be added to my frequent call list. There was Mama Floyce, Dad Merle and Cora, and now Aunt Micki. When my parents were alive, I had a self-imposed rule to call them at least weekly, although it was usually more often. My new parents/family/elders deserved the same, at minimum. I was overwhelmed in wonder and amazement at how much family I now have.

When we got back to the hotel John, Daryle, and I talked more about what it may have been like if we'd grown up together. We agreed, looking more realistically now, that I would have been Daryle's babysitter, John would have had to drive us everywhere, and they again said they would have always thrown me in the water if we were at pools or the beach together. I can only imagine! What a joyful thing it is to have brothers to banter with! Maybe it was time to reach out to Mac?

As for being a step closer to finding my birth father, Aunt Micki may not have been the answer. She didn't quite know how Helen wound up having Sidney Malet as her doctor. She hadn't had contact with him in years, I think she knew more, but she was eighty-two, and I wasn't going to press her. At that point, just having met her was more than enough. I wanted to focus on what I did have now versus what I still didn't. I've learned by now that whatever I'm meant to know will come to me, so I let it go. It was more important that I focused on what little time I had to be with her.

I also thought to look at John's DNA matches and mine and whoever was on mine but not his could be possible leads to my birth father's side. I had a dozen or so people to contact. It was the next step. The good news was that at this point, there was no more pain in my search, only fun and excitement. What a dramatic and unexpected change!

I'd never regret that weekend. I enjoyed some time on the beach and being by the water, but to be with my birth family was almost indescribable. I headed home, anxious to see what would come next. I wondered.

35

After I got home, I wrote letters to both my brother Mac and my aunt Tina. I sent them return receipt so I would be sure they got them, and I already got both receipt acknowledgment cards returned to me. As with this whole journey, I let go and had been waiting patiently for a couple of weeks.

Last night (April 22, 2016) I got my first call from Mac. He was in what he called "happy shock." Said this really wasn't a surprise for him, knowing Helen's history. He was in the air force like John, so all three boys had gone into the military. He said he felt Helen abandoned him. He was sixty-two now; we were ten years apart. He went by Mac, a nickname for his last name, which is his birth father's name. No one really knew what had happened back then, but he said he forgave her. My gut said maybe not fully, as I could still hear something in his voice, but mostly I was so grateful to have talked with him.

Mac dominated the conversation with questions, but I gave him room to do so, knowing he was in a bit of shock. I actually couldn't imagine what it had been like for everyone else, as I knew all these years, and they'd known nothing.

Mac shared some of his history; he also had issues with weight, had gastric bypass. He had two other brothers and another half-sister, as well as a twenty-three year old son. Mac did want to meet, thinks the four of us getting together would be fun at some point. Now that would be something!

Nothing from Aunt Tina.

I had been emailing some fifth and sixth cousins on my birth father's side but no real leads. Aunt Micki had thought hard on the subject, but couldn't come up with any leads either. We have been talking regularly and although at first I felt she knew more, it was probably more my hope, as for now, I think she really was telling me what she remembered.

I wake up and go through my morning routine. It's a beautiful day: April 24, 2016. As most days, I then go to my computer and find a surprise email from 23andMe. It's from "A Relative." All it says is "We share a lot of DNA." When I click on the link I see a name that is completely new: Josie, maiden name is Frangopoulos and she is a first cousin. What? I wonder: Could this be the first cousin I knew would bring me my final answers? I respond immediately. With further investigation I see she is from Coney Island. Aunt Micki had told me that is where she, Helen, Grandma Peg, and John were living when I was born! Coney Island, the forbidden city! Hmmmm.

Josie and I started writing back and forth. We realized we would have to have the same grandparents. She said she did the DNA test just for fun for her fiftieth birthday, as her parents are gone and she was just curious. Her father's family name is Frangopoulos. Her grandfather helped build the carousel at Coney Island in the early 1900s. They came from Greece through Boston, some family is still there, and the rest landed in Coney Island. The family ran a lot of business there in the 1960s. She has six uncles: Nick, Spiro, George, Frank and Jack who are twins, Peter and Harry. One of these men would be my father! Whoa!

Today starts very early, as I'm awakened by a hot flash. I see my cousin Josie sent a text at 2:43 a.m., April 28, 2016. In 2004, I received a Vedic astrology reading at an Amma retreat. Per the astrologer 2:43 a.m. is the time that I would have been born, not 2:50 a.m. as on my birth certificate. He said 2:43 was the only time that showed any possible separation from family. I found this timing rather interesting. I had never felt my birth time was correct. Jo says a cousin in Boston, Harriet, was willing to help and will do a test. She is Spiro's daughter. I cannot get back to sleep after that, and am perfectly OK with it!

So much has occurred in the last four days I can barely keep up with it all. Josie (Jo for short) and I spoke on the twenty-fifth at about 9:00 a.m. PST. She is also a nurse (emergency room), a Pisces like me, married with two sons, and also was raised as an only child but has a half sister and half brother. She was raised in Brooklyn and now is in Staten Island.

She shared that one of the uncles owned the Metro on Surf Avenue in Coney Island. They had food, gifts and souvenirs. The uncles would have all been in their forties in the 1960s. All the brothers are passed. The last one lived just a few hours from me in Kingman, Arizona. That was Jack, Frank's twin, who'd recently passed. Frank's wife, Sheila, is the only wife still alive. She is ninety-two and lives in Staten Island with her son, Gil. She has two daughters: Rae and Harriet (Harriet is a popular family name apparently).

She said she would love to help me find my answers. We talked for about thirty minutes. It was a lot to take in to say the least. I had very similar feelings to June 9 of last year when I found John: numb, excited, overwhelmed. This is the first real concrete thing I know about my paternal family. That means I'm not Jewish at all, but I am half Greek! (One really must trust their intuition, as this blew me away!) Now I know why I have olive skin, and even more so, why I've never been allowed to go to Coney Island, and why, for some unknown reason I've put off my trip to Greece. Holy smokes!

I shared this experience on the Facebook page "DNA Detectives" and immediately got a response from someone to contact a woman named Anna, the Greek expert, so I did. Within ninety minutes of posting, Anna and I were on the phone talking. She was wonderful, said today was her birthday, so she would work on this over the next week. Yet for some reason she got on it right away. I was loving this pattern of things taking less time than predicted after so many years of waiting and wondering. My original DNA test was to be six to eight weeks, and it had been three. Now she couldn't help but get to work on this right away. It's truly seemed that everything that at first seemed like it would take time occurred so quickly on this part of the journey. It had taken decades to get to this point, and now things were just coming at me. It was a wonder to witness and experience.

Anna is half Greek, lived in Greece most of her life, and had been in the United States for eight years now and had sort of fallen into doing these searches for people. She immediately found an article from 1960 about a little boy who had been born in February and then had been adopted. His name was Michael. At six months old, the birth mother had changed her mind and the child had been returned to the birth mother, whose name was Patricia Frangopoulos. He had been born out of wedlock but had been raised by her new husband, Constantin Frangopoulos. She had looked them up, and they'd lived in Deltona Beach, forty miles from Aunt Micki! Constantin was a cousin, son of the brother George, of the seven brothers. This Michael was a cousin! Crazy!

Anna started sending me screen shots from all these different photos from anyone on Facebook with the name of Frangopoulos. One was of five of the brothers, an adorable photo. She sent me a side-by-side of Frank and me saying she felt there was a strong resemblance and felt it was him or Peter, as Peter had a son he had given up for adoption. According to Josie, no one knew the son's whereabouts, but Peter had spent time in Virginia. So, just as a guessing game, she narrowed it to Frank or Peter. She ended the day with "More to come."

Tuesday the twenty-sixth was Helen's birthday. I could feel her all day and was so present to her assistance in all this. I spent time looking again at the photos Anna had sent me; it was a pretty big family. I look similar to one young girl in an older photo: Rae, Frank's youngest daughter, but still, so hard for me to tell.

Josie talked to Rae who isn't willing to share at this point. Jo is disappointed but by this point in the journey I knew better than to think anything is final. Jo and Anna also talked that day. There was a possibility that Jo's father could have had a son who may have been my father, making Jo a half aunt instead of first cousin. We would likely never know unless that possible son were to do a test, just like Peter's son who had been given up for adoption.

Anna sent me a chart on percentages of connections and explained it all to me. She put a tree together as well, which was such fun to see. My friend Julie also kept working on my tree on Ancestry. She said that while she was putting it together, a hawk flew by, which was her personal symbol that someone had been found. Now she knew who. Chills.

On Wednesday the twenty-seventh (yesterday), I spoke with Aunt Micki. Gosh, I just love her so much already. I don't really know why, but she was already deep in my heart. She said she'd put up the photo of John, Daryle, and me in her apartment and she was going to send me some photos. I shared that we were getting closer to finding my birth father. It was the only time she got quiet on the call. She said nothing when I mentioned Coney Island and Astroland, the Metro, or that they're Greek. Not sure what was there for her, but I didn't care. I had an aunt who loved me. I was tired of focusing on feeling lied to, as it served nothing, and I had such a gift in this relationship with her. We missed each other terribly.

The day ended yesterday at a standstill with Jo: aunt or cousin? Unless another cousin tests, we may never know. I was so grateful I'd been on this road so long that any disappointment was so momentary and fleeting. I knew how things could shift and opened up in unimaginable ways. My gut told me Jo is a cousin. We shall see. So far, most of what my gut had said had panned out (except the Uncle Milton piece, which I still deeply feel there was more to reveal about). Anna called later in the morning and said she was looking into the X match between Jo and me, and we're 100 percent cousins! Yay! Jo was equally as happy as I was about it.

Sheila, Rae's mother, fell and was in the ICU. Jo felt this was a sign of some sort. Rae's main concern was Sheila finding out that her husband may have cheated on her. My intuition said that Sheila knew, but why bring it up at that point anyway? I had no interest in causing any further harm to anyone because of this story of mine, and we didn't know for sure.

Jo had been a godsend in so many ways. I was so anxious to meet her, and how much fun would it be to go home to New York to my *other* family! Wow! I thought once we got Harriet's test results and knew more there would be a better possibility of that, but until Rae tested, there seemed no point. I knew she would do it, it was just a matter of when. This was so overwhelming, and so awesome!

I also got a short message from my eldest brother, Mac, on Facebook. He didn't really engage, but it was cool that he reached out. Still no word from Tina. Overall, I was finding I was much more peaceful with this piece of the puzzle. John was the first, he was the only one I knew for certain about, but this was certainly another unexpected surprise. Sometimes I felt as if I couldn't keep up with it all, and it was absolutely wonderful being swept away by one's "impossible dream"!

Today (April 29, 2016), my friend Joyce visited. She was also from New York, was also raised Jewish, but didn't consider herself Jewish. When I told her I was Greek, she said there was no wonder now why I liked dolmas so much. We giggled. Then she said, "And you're a goy!" (In yiddish goy is a non-Jewish person, usually said in a derogatory way, but not this time!) Hysterical laughter ensued. What would Sylvia have thought!? Ha-ha!

On Facebook this morning (April 30, 2016), a memory came up from a year ago, it was the day I ordered my Family Tree DNA test with the caption, "Do I dare get my hopes up?" I'd say that would be a resounding "Yes!" And what a year it's been!

Josie had been talking up a storm with everyone in the family. She'd talked to her half sister, a second cousin, another relative, and had been making some progress. Harriet, Spiros's eldest, had ordered a test from 23andMe!

Not only exciting, but so appreciative of an apparent stranger doing something to help me.

My project the last couple of days had been ordering a kit from Ancestry so I had all three of the main tests covered and have an Ancestry account for at least the next six months. I'd waited on it until I'd found my birth father's family, which was pretty cool. Creating my own family tree was pretty surreal. I just looked at it in wonder. I remembered as a teenager in Florida I had done my parents' family tree on a poster board. It took quite a while, and although they'd appreciated it, it had seemed way more important to me. People seemed to take family for granted when they didn't know what it was like not to have one they felt a part of. It was quite a game looking through old records, finding photos, headstones, grave markers of your family members. I found I even have an aunt Jemima! Carol, through her investigations, said we're also seventh cousins seven times removed from Jack Daniels. We're famous! Ha-ha!

I spoke with Aunt Micki again. I cry every time. I just love her so. She told me again that she shares a very deep love for me. I feel so blessed.

Jo had spoken with Rae the other day, and Rae had told her that Jo had a half brother. Jo had suspected this when she'd told me but hadn't been sure. Rae had found him on a Facebook page. They had messaged him and were awaiting a reply. Jo said that I was her angel. If she wasn't helping me, this likely would not have happened. Just love how this works, but truly, she is my angel! Crazy wonderful!

It was mid-May, and Jo hadn't heard back from her possible half brother. She was disappointed, which I understood all too well after so many years of brick walls, dead ends, and closed doors. We were grateful to have each other. Harriet, Spiro's daughter, had sent in her test. I'd sent in my Ancestry kit, and again, we waited.

Aunt Micki and I were talking every few days. I felt a sense of urgency, like I needed to make the most of the time we had left. She shared another story about Sidney Malet: As I mentioned, she had always wanted a little girl. Dr. Malet had given her a baby girl at one point, but then the birth mother changed her mind. It had been devastating to her. She said, considering he did this kind of thing, that he also built and owned the hospital, he could have done a lot of illegal things where babies were involved. That made a lot of sense to me. She said she looked at the photo I gave her every night and said good night to us kids. She also shared that she felt more of a motherly bond with me than an aunt/niece bond, and I told her I feel it too. How blessed can one person be?

Yesterday, May 14, 2016, Merle's eldest son, John (Big John), got married in Sedona. What are the chances! Although I wasn't invited, which was fine and wasn't expected, I did have a chance to meet Carol, my cousin and stepsister through Merle (his daughter), and my cousin Kathy, who was married to Michael, one of Merle's other son's from his first marriage. We met at a local restaurant for lunch. It was so joyful, so easy and comfortable.

Afterward I gave them a quick driving tour of Sedona. We laughed so much. I was so liking this family it was astounding to me. I told them that if I'd talked the way I did with them with my adopted family, especially my mother (Sylvia), they would have said I was nuts. We had been talking about spiritual and metaphysical things, forbidden subjects in my childhood home. They both said, "You are our kind of nut!" I shared about my near-death experience, being a psychic medium, visits from Helen, and none of it was a big deal. Carol told me she did remember Helen once mentioning a stillborn baby girl. I wondered how hard that must have been for Helen. To keep such a secret like that for decades had to be very difficult. My heart ached for her.

I talked with Dad (Merle) today, who was very glad Carol and I had met. I posted photos of my time with Carol, and so many people say we look alike as well. It's still amazing to me to even hear things like that. In talking to Daryle recently, he said, "You never know with this family. Most of us have two titles, some three! Me, I'm my own uncle, Dad is my dad and cousin. Hell, Carol could be my mom! When I get my Ancestry account, and Esther works on hers the website will crash from confusion!" We were laughing so hard!

I hadn't talked with my adopted cousin Beth in quite a while, so I filled her in, and she said, "I thought our family was mixed up!"

I replied, "I used to think that too, and well, we are, but not like this!"

She said, "I feel normal now!" More laughter. It really was crazy. Merle would have been my stepfather, so I called him

Dad, but he was my first cousin once removed. Goodness, it was all too much! Glad we could all laugh at it!

Last Sunday night (June 5, 2016), I spoke with my newest cousin, Harriet for about thirty minutes. Her DNA test confirmed we're first cousins. She voiced a lot of empathy toward what I had gone through to get here. Sometimes I was unsure how I did get here other than sheer perseverance and, honestly, having no choice. She was about ten years older than me, was a bit of a family elder from what Jo said. She did live in Coney Island as a teen, but returned to and now lives in Boston, which was where the family originally arrived when they'd come to the United States. She worked at a hospital, so also was in the medical field. She also remembered a Milton Shapiro but cannot quite place him. That part of the story clearly was incomplete.

Harriet said she was going to pray that Rae does a test to confirm that she was either a sibling or cousin. Oddly, I wasn't so attached, which I was grateful for, but I was definitely hopeful. She sent a photo of her parent's wedding, which was beautiful to see. I looked at Frank and felt a feeling in my gut again that he was my birth father, but I'd been misguided before, so I let it go.

Harriet kept saying, "You're Greek!" repeatedly, and I told her to keep it up because it didn't feel real to me yet. I shared my friend Joyce's comment about the dolmas, and we laughed, and then she said, "Esther! You're Greek!" We laughed more and agreed to stay in touch.

Over the prior week, I reached out to Anna again for some suggestions on Greek resources. She sent me to a Facebook page: Hellenic Genealogy Geek, which has paid off. I have a book to research and someone else also suggested finding some Greek churches or festivals. I searched some of the foods I love. My friend Joyce then reminded me that "everything is bettah with feta." Now isn't that the truth! She also said my eyes reminded her of the Grecian waters. I just love that! I love being half Greek as much as I love the Dutch/French/British/Irish part of me! What a welcome switch to being able to joke and laugh about the most painful part of my life thus far.

Jo told me that we're from a small village near Sparta, but that was all she knew. I was grateful for that in ways that were tough to express. Mom's side certainly affirmed my love for the UK, Ireland, France, and Holland. The more I looked at my DNA origins, the more I understood the Baltic side of me. I loved Greek food, always have, I'd always appreciated my olive skin, and I was very fond of the Greek people and thought they were the most handsome men on earth. Silly things, but fun to observe. More would be revealed of course, but I was certainly loving getting to know who I was as a human being in a completely new way.

I sit in reflection with all that has happened to date. It's a funny thing though, I laugh, yet I also have tears of sadness. I have a whole story to let go of around being half Jewish now, about Uncle Milton, about being a Shapiro. I'm a Frangopoulos, yet that will never change me being a Shapiro. Dad said I truly was a Shapiro through and through, and now I know it's because of who he raised me to be, who I am, and that is someone I've come to love, honor, be proud of and cherish through all this. I sit here crying now, struck with gratitude.

I sit back, wipe the tears to see the red rocks of Sedona in my view. I feel as if the universe, God, and my parents have blessed me in every way imaginable. I've taken on my wellbeing which improves daily, I have a wonderful job and a fantastic life. I have so many relatives it overwhelms me to think of what things will look like when I know where Rae and her sister Harriet and brother Gil fall in to all of this. I've rekindled my relationship with my adopted sisters Gabby and Sunny and hold a special place in my heart for my cousin Beth for continuing to be the only person from my adopted family who has truly gone through it all with me. The more I write and reflect, the more my heart swells, the more the tears flow. In awareness of repeating myself: how blessed am I!?!?

Today (June 15, 2016) I started reading a book called The Greek Way by Edith Hamilton. I'm so excited about it. I posted it on Facebook as well as posting a video of two strangers who'd found each other through DNA. Rae is the first to "Like" them both. This is the first contact we have had other than accepting Friend requests. Harriet posted the picture with the five brothers. Everyone is making comments about their laughter and the food, and I comment "More things to research Rae!"

Rae and I have some back and forth conversation about Sheila's soup and meatballs and that I hope one day to try the Frangopoulos version of avgolemono soup when I visit. She says, "Would love to be in on the family get together." Yay yay yay! Her sister Harriet comments to Rae she has the recipes, but she does not mention me. One miracle at a time I guess. Rae and I chat for a bit longer and end it with heart emoticons. I have a huge smile on my face. It's just a matter of time.

It was just a year ago today (June 16, 2015) that I got my initial DNA results and sent the first communication to John. Amazing what can happen in a year. I remember how ecstatic I was that he was open to communicating. So much has happened since then.

Yesterday (June 20, 2016) while traveling on my annual Amma trip to Santa Fe, I was visiting the Jemez Mountains and hot springs in New Mexico. Rae messaged me to tell me she had unfriended me. I had put a Father's Day post on Facebook that addressed my dad and my birth father, "Mr. Frangopoulos." She said it freaked her out, and she was over protective of Sheila. She wasn't aware my page was private and only my friends could see it. It aggravated me slightly, but I also understand how shocking something like this can be to some people, and we all have different beliefs and different ways of dealing with things.

I quickly found compassion and understanding for her. I also did not wish to rock Sheila's world, for there was no good that could come of her knowing. Rae was still thinking about the test, but I would continue to give her all the room she needed. She did send another friend request and asked me to forgive her panic attack. Nothing to forgive, I told her it was all good.

This evening at the retreat Amma blessed me with such a sweet darshan (a gift or blessing from a holy person), which, as previously mentioned was in the form of a hug with Amma. Her hugs were always different based on where the devotee was at in his or her life. She imparted energy based on what one needed. How it was that she knew only proved the mystery of her omniscience.

> *It's the full moon, the strawberry moon. After my hug, I come out to the rental car to view the full moon. Tears well up in my eyes. I put my hand over my heart and take some deep breaths. I'm feeling so full of gratitude. I take a moment to check my phone and there is a message from my cousin/stepsister Carol: "Somewhere out there beneath the pale moonlight. Thought of you when I saw the full moon tonight. XO." I'm now sobbing and in awe of how happy I am and how blessed I feel.*

I went to sleep with the joy of God inside me.

While having lunch at the retreat, I talked with another devotee about my experience of life right now. Part of me feels quite emotionless other than the gratitude. She helped me see that I was grieving, and what better place to do it than with Amma? I was grieving the loss of a life with my birth family, not growing up with my siblings, cousins, or knowing my heritage and that part of who I was. I was grieving the loss of my adopted family with whom I had no deep connection, other than Beth. I was grieving not being a Shapiro, not knowing the Frangopoulos side or knowing my Greek heritage and roots, and that there were still things I did not know. The good news was it was a fantastic problem to have!

> *Since returning home from the retreat (which was amazing as always!), the grief has hit me like a sledgehammer. I post something on Facebook about it, and Josie comments saying, "I'm grieving with you, but we have each other now and I love you." How awesome is that!?*
>
> *My heart remains heavy, but less so. I realize now that I'm angry with my birth father. I'm frustrated that Rae is still thinking about the test. My parents' lies weren't all theirs, and I'm sad for that. I'm ready for the whole story to reveal itself and to put it all behind me.*

I got a message from Daryle today (June 27, 2016) that he wanted Big Sis time. More tears. I knew with all my heart that

I was where I chose to be, where I needed to be, and where I was meant to be, yet I still grieved not knowing my brothers as kids. I still remained in wonder who the contact person was who'd told my adopted mom I had a younger brother.

It was the last day of June already. Over the last few weeks Facebook had been popping memories up about all that transpired last year at this time. One particular photo of Helen looks so much like me from my heavier days. And then another one that I would bet my life on that it was me in the photo where Helen was kneeling down to feed a deer. So much to still take in even after all this time. I felt as if life this last year had been one long stretch of "pinch-me" moments.

> *This morning I check Facebook, and a message pops up from my friend Pat. She says, "Esther, I had a vision this morning as I was waking up. You were standing in a ray of sunshine in full color and two people, a man and a woman in grayish color, were reaching out to you with arms wide open. (I somehow know immediately it was my birth parents.) Everyone was very happy. They were your biological parents, and they were so happy to see you and so very proud of*

you. So much love for you! They were smaller figures but coming toward you."

I thank her for the message, and then she says, "OMG! The pic of your birth mother is the vision I'd had of your mother! I'm always in awe when things like this happen. So grateful!" She hadn't seen the picture I posted until after the vision! And she thinks she is grateful?

I share with her that I've been so burdened by grief this last week, and this is how they had to get through to me, by going through her. I know they're working so hard for me, and I'm thankful they picked Pat to be the messenger. I'm still a mixed bag of emotions today: sad, happy, grateful, and so on. And still praying Rae will do the test soon.

I have often been in awe of how many people have had a place in this story and how when spirit wants to get a message across, they will find a way. I'd still been pretty heavily entrenched in the grief, and it was July 3, 2016. I felt both of my mothers around me as of late. I was thinking about how different they were. Sylvia was so shut down, so closed off in so many ways, had a very hard time expressing herself. She had gone through her entire life not being made love to because of her issues. I couldn't fathom the impact that had had on my father other than the obvious emptiness I'd seen in him. Then there was Helen, who'd expressed herself that way a lot, swinging, multiple partners, four marriages, and so on. I don't know how they could be more opposite.

As for my paternal side of things, I was still praying for Rae to do the test. This was the last step within my reach, and I had no control over it. The final lesson.

Today I celebrated nine years with my name Esther. Amazing. I was blessed with the name on 7/7/7! I've continued reading *The Greek Way* by Edith Hamilton. So far it was a great read. She shared how playful and upbeat Greeks are, that they laid down all their differences to play games, and that was what brought about the Olympics. It reminded me of myself, always wanting to play.

> *I'm in another huge wave of grief. It's been ten days since my last entry, and it's still so strong. Within that grief is some intense anger, and I find myself impatient and frustrated with Rae not doing the test. I'm angry that I've gotten this far and only this far. Her testing is the last possible action, and it's out of my reach and out of my hands. In meditation yesterday, both moms said it's coming. I feel as if I made it to the finish line, but I can't cross it. Ugh! Being human is so challenging, but very understandable at this point. To be so close and at a standstill. More lessons in patience, surrender, and forgiving all of it, especially my own humanity.*

Aunt Micki was declining. Her best friend, Joyce, was in contact with me and confirmed my suspicions. She may not come out of this one. My heart ached to be with her. Yet every time I approached going and making a reservation, everything in me said, “No!” I tried very hard to live with no regrets. Mama Floyce suggested that maybe God wanted me to remember her the way she was. Of course that was possible. I wasn’t peaceful about this, but I trusted that if I was meant to go, things would open up.

I was doing a three-day juice cleanse, and it was bringing up so much emotion. I called Aunt Micki, and my heart just broke. So much letting go was needed here. And in two weeks I was going to Denver to say goodbye to my dear friend Ann, who had aggressive cancer. So much grief.

Yesterday (July 17, 2016) I had dinner with my friend Dr. Karen. She was the person who told me that there was a sister in Ohio who turned out to be my birth mom’s sister, Tina. I shared with her what had been happening. Karen said without a doubt Rae was a sister and it was going to take some time, but she would eventually do the test. She looked at the side-by-side photo of Frank (Rae’s father) and me and said, “Without a doubt, he was your birth father.”

We both felt his presence immediately when I showed her the older picture of him with Sheila (Frank’s wife and Rae’s mother). I had such a huge wave of emotions it brought tears to my eyes. Karen says what I need to do now is let it go. OK, sure—*ha!* She also said that Helen wasn’t Frank’s only extramarital affair and that Sheila would not be at all surprised about me. Interesting and affirming to all the things I felt as well.

> *Still very engulfed in the grief and it's now July 21, 2016. This is really quite a process and taking much longer than I would have anticipated. Yet it is what it is. If anyone knows about the dance of grief, I do. It takes however long it takes and looks however it looks, for each of us. I feel like something is coming that is going to throw this over the edge and I will be able to let it all go.*
>
> *Aunt Micki calls just to tell me she was thinking of me and loves me. In light of repeating myself: how blessed am I? I can see this is a time of surrender, letting go, acceptance and self-love.*

Jo has been dealing with some health issues. It's been weeks since we really connected. I've been concerned, so it was good to hear from her. She told me that she was feeling better and that on 8/1/16 she had a dream with uncles Pete and Jack. They were standing by a mailbox pointing across the street where Frank was standing. They were telling her something that she couldn't quite recall, and then she woke up. She felt this clearly was them "pointing" to Frank. I could feel he has been around me a lot lately. I see him with Helen at times in my mind's eye. I get emotional and teary when I look at this photo. I didn't feel emotionally attached but I did feel a familial connection. More prayers that Rae takes action.

I'm on the phone with Daryle. It's August 21, 2016. He is so my brother and completely awesome. He tells me he talks to people about me all the time. When I tell him I love him he says what Aunt Micki always says: "I love you more." Melting, knees buckling, brings me to tears. Never have I felt that kind of love from anyone in my adopted family except my Dad. Daryle says I changed him, that when I enter a room people just get happy. My heart is so full. He says we need to talk more and I say I'd love that. It's still so surreal for me. We're hoping to visit Aunt Micki in October. I pray. Daryle says it meant so much to him to have all of us together like that. I can't wait!

Helen comes through to me today in meditation (September 23, 2016). She says she was with my birth father for two years. I have an insight that she may have been with Uncle Milton as well as "Mr. Frangopoulos." My body shakes, reacting in a positive way to this.

I was processing a lot today (September 26, 2016). It was clear my current romantic relationship was over. She has been a character in my life to portray the final lessons around my wounding with Sylvia. She would say things just like Sylvia would say, as if she were channeling her. She would say things like "What is wrong with you!?" or state,

"That is not normal." It came to a head today for me. Like my mother, she was shut down emotionally, her heart is closed off, and she projects her deep wounds onto others. I have great compassion for that, but I knew it was time to no longer live with it.

I dug in and did a lot of soul work. I went back to so many moments where I felt this same pain: being carried away from Helen, the toddler who saw dead people and was told she was crazy and never to talk like that again, to the child who was terrified of the monster, the kid who couldn't eat like everyone else, the teenager who was rejected at camp. All these aspects were acknowledged, given compassion and then I felt my body and energy all merging into wholeness and being complete on another level. The final healing around my mother issues was complete! I felt so at peace. Another miracle.

I asked Aunt Micki yesterday if she and Mom had struggled with physical issues through their lives, and she said absolutely "Yes!" They would get physically ill in times of stress and grief and processed through their bodies, just like me. So much deep healing happening here.

It is only a week away from Halloween. The last few weeks have been tough. Dad (Merle) has been in and out of the hospital and rehab. Hurricane Matthew made it a bit tough for Daryle to get there. I'd been so focused on Aunt Micki, and I felt badly that I couldn't be there to see them as well. It has been hard. But yesterday I made it to Daytona Beach again.

The boys couldn't join me since Daryle was with Dad, and John, well, we weren't really sure what was up with him, as he would not speak to me for reasons unknown. I'd emailed and texted asking if I'd done something, but he replied in short that it wasn't personal, he'd been working a lot, and one day maybe he'd have some time. What a bunch of crap. Sometimes it was a bittersweet gift to be able to "see" the way that I do. But if he wasn't willing to share, all I could do was accept it, but it was hurtful. I'd seen John do this with another family member, so I knew it was who he was and came from his own woundings. But it still hurt.

As for Mac, he pretty much just watched me on Facebook and occasionally reached out, but that was all.

Aunt Micki's best friend, Joyce, was hosting me while visiting Aunt Micki. She was so generous and had been such a good friend to Aunt Micki for many years. She asked if I wanted to be there when they placed the ashes. I said I didn't, but how kind of her to ask. She had considered me since the very start of this, which meant the world to me.

Seeing Aunt Micki today was amazing. We fell into each other's arms and cried, holding each other so close. We spent the day at Joyce's, so we didn't touch on the past very much, although she did share something very interesting with me about herself; it was between the ages of twenty-seven and thirty-three when she had her surgeries to correct being a hermaphrodite. Her clitoris had been a few inches long, she'd had a prostate, and she'd grown dark, curly hair on her legs and some facial hair, and again she talked of how she could see herself turning into a man. It had impacted her life and relationships greatly. She'd shed many tears, said it had been terribly painful, and to this day had to shave her chin every day. This explained much of my own issues with growing facial hair as I had. When I had been at my highest weight of 333 pounds, I'd had a full beard. Even after years of laser and electrolysis treatments, I had a few stubborn hairs that wouldn't go away. What an odd gift to understand more of my genetics and journey this way.

She shared her anger with Helen for not giving me to her to raise. I shared my theory that my birth father may have given her no choice, encouraged her to consider there was still much we don't know, like why it had cost $10,000, why I needed to disappear, and so on. It weighed heavily on her, and our time was so bittersweet. I prayed she found peace with all of this before she passed.

When we dropped her off at home, while walking her into her building, she turned to me and said, "Thank you for giving me a reason to live." Oh my God! Speechless. I thanked her for living long enough that we could see each other again. I couldn't wait for tomorrow!

Today Aunt Micki and I have the day alone (October 24, 2016). We discover how similar we are, like hating the feeling of wet sand on our feet and between our toes, that we love romance novels, nuts, salt and lots of it. Silly things, but wonderful things. She gives me some more butterflies, but handpicks these.

I ask her, "What shall I do with them all!" and I see in my mind a big shadow box to hang on the wall.

She says, "I was always thinking of putting them in a big black velvet box and hanging it on the wall." Smiles. We laugh.

She shared more about her surgeries. She found the book from 1968 that Dr. Malet signed and gave to her. She had Stein-Leventhal syndrome, which today we call polycystic ovarian syndrome, which I had too! That is what caused the facial hair! Wow! We cried and laughed over all these silly body things that somehow connected us and allowed us to feel closer to each other. She was more and more like another mother. I had fallen in love with her deeply by this point.

She again told me that Dr. Malet had actually built Interboro General Hospital, the hospital where I had been born, that he'd run it, and if there had been illegal adoptions and things of that nature, it would have been easy for him to do it there. She was still unable to figure out how Helen had wound up going to him; they'd had different last names so he likely hadn't known they were sisters.

We had a wonderful Thanksgiving meal at Joyce's, in spite of it being a month early. We took a couple of wonderful photos together. You could clearly see the resemblance, not just of the physical attributes, but the light and joy in our souls to be together. Memories to treasure for a lifetime, as I didn't know if we'd get to make any more.

I left her on that trip with a deep heaviness in my heart not knowing what the future would bring. This was likely the last time I would see her. It was now, like most things, in God's hands.

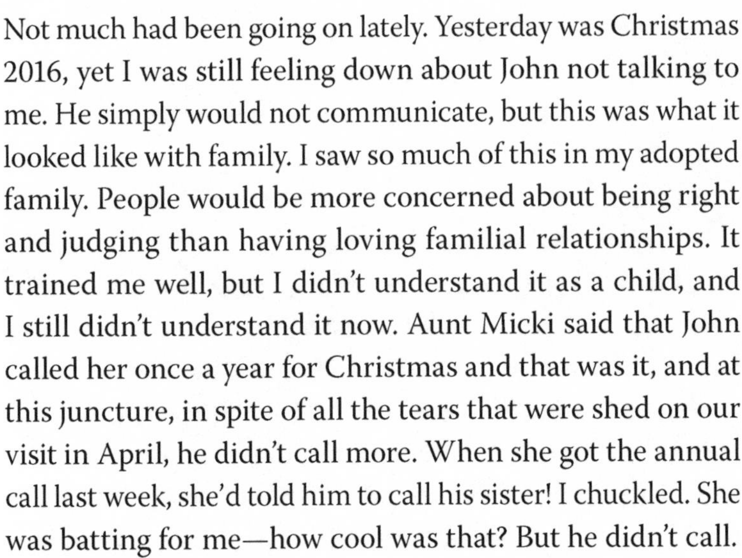

Not much had been going on lately. Yesterday was Christmas 2016, yet I was still feeling down about John not talking to me. He simply would not communicate, but this was what it looked like with family. I saw so much of this in my adopted family. People would be more concerned about being right and judging than having loving familial relationships. It trained me well, but I didn't understand it as a child, and I still didn't understand it now. Aunt Micki said that John called her once a year for Christmas and that was it, and at this juncture, in spite of all the tears that were shed on our visit in April, he didn't call more. When she got the annual call last week, she'd told him to call his sister! I chuckled. She was batting for me—how cool was that? But he didn't call.

About two weeks ago, Aunt Micki and I talked for well over an hour. She continued to tell me I was the reason she was still living and that she loved me *more,* and that I was her little girl. Those moments were embedded in my heart and touched me so deeply. We talked more about things we liked, with almost all of it being a match. The conversations were so much fun and so meaningful. I savored every moment with her.

She had been doing well up until the last couple of days. However, my intuition said she was starting the dying process. I selfishly wanted her to stick around. I would love one more visit, but I didn't know how that would be possible since I now was free of an unhealthy relationship and buying a house, which was looking like it would be a bit of a project. I could only turn it all over to God.

38

Dad Merle finally came home from the hospital after thirty-seven days, and although he was better, he was severely depressed, which wasn't new, but tough to deal with.

> *I sit in observation on how different this holiday season is and that it's a first. Last year, I was in Japan with my "brother" Mike. I hadn't met Carol, Aunt Micki, or Grandma Joanne, nor had I found Jo and my Greek family. Celebrating Christmas has changed in some way now, knowing that I was right and am not Jewish at all. It's all just so amazing.*
>
> *Rae still shows no signs of being ready to do the test. I rarely hear from cousin Harriet. I reached out to Rae's older sister Harriet but no reply and Jo has still been dealing with her health. For now, there is not much connection going on with that side of the family. I feel disappointment only because I have a desire to be close with them. So, I focus on the good*

that's here, I celebrate Aunt Micki every day and remember how blessed I am, how close we are, and what a wonderful problem this is to have: my family.

Tonight I write with a very heavy heart. Aunt Micki is starting her final decline and exit from her body. New Year's Eve is tomorrow night, and it's a bittersweet time to say the least. She went into hospice for general inpatient symptom support. She has been sleeping but eating very little. Her heart is weak, lungs are full and she didn't want to talk on the phone today. That tells me a lot. I'm incredibly sad. The anticipatory grief has begun. What a gift I've had in her: calling me her little girl, always saying. "I love you more." She has filled a hole in my heart. I pray for an easy transition for her, and if it's meant to be, one last visit.

Happy 2017! It's New Year's Day. Grateful Aunt Micki is doing better today. John calls me and is upset because "nobody told me she was in hospice." At first I feel badly, but then I realized who "nobody" is; Me! He's had his aunt all his life, never calls her, yet expects me to be the messenger?

When I tell her he was upset, she says, "Esther, why would you call someone who never calls you or puts any effort into it?"

And she is right, why would I, or should I? She agrees that I'm not the family informant. He has been a huge disappointment to her, and now to me as well. I remember that no matter who it is, I get to choose who is in my life. He couldn't even say it directly to me that he was mad that I didn't tell him, just covertly danced around it a few times. I'm simply done with this kind of drama in my life.

I'm grateful I found him, he was my dream come true, and I still get a say of what and who I want in my life. Jo has also not been in touch, which adds to my sadness. But this is human beings, being human. I want to have people in my life who want me in theirs. How we're connected matters not now. What a huge leap from the codependent girl who attached to everyone and everything because of her desperate need for love and acceptance.

I suspect that all of this drama needed to occur before the book could come to its conclusion. The story was not over yet.

A lot has happened in the last couple of months. It is March 2, 2017. Since I last wrote, Daryle confirmed what I expected; John had an issue with me. He doesn't understand why I call Aunt Micki all the time, or why I call Dad Merle every week. He thinks I have an angle. Argh. What angle could I possibly have? No one in this family is wealthy financially, but they sure are a wealth of love, connection, joy, healing. I want my family. It's that simple. My gut tells me it's deeper than that, but it's for him to tell, not for me to guess.

I asked Daryle what he thought, and he agreed that I had an angle: "To know your family." Thank God, he got it! Yet I could understand where John was coming from; this was what his birth father's family had done to him, and it was what he felt Mac had been doing when he'd visited them back in the seventies. It was his history and story, and he was projecting it onto everyone else. So sad.

The one thing he wanted most he pushed away. It was so disappointing. But it was what it was. On my birthday, I got a Facebook message, "Happy birthday, Sis," and that was it. Last year, there were presents, phone calls, cards. But this was his choice, and it was out of my control. I once heard that a person should be grateful when someone abandons your life— as it spares you from their own personal war. This hit home, yet I was still hurt, angry, and grieving, but I knew I needed to let him go for my own sanity. I had so much else to focus on right now, which was a blessing, but what an irony: *he* was the prize.

Aunt Micki continued to decline. I think she was trying to hang in there for one last visit, which was her birthday on April 3. I made reservations for 4/1–4/4. We would see what God had in store. Joyce agreed she was waiting, but I was not confident she would make it. Although she'd been home since January, the writing was on the wall. My heart was breaking. The time was coming.

Finally heard from Jo after months of silence. She had had a lot of health challenges. I was reminded of my genetics:

diabetes, blood pressure, heart issues, cancer, emphysema. It was easier in some ways not knowing, but at the same time, after decades of realizing I could worry about nothing or everything, I chose to worry about nothing and do the best I could to take care of myself. This body would have to find its way out of here when it was time, so my attitude was always about focusing on what worked.

Yesterday, Jo told me Rae was thinking about doing the test. I'd let it go so much now that I really had no reaction to it. She would do it when she was ready, and I would not pressure her in any way. I was a little cynical about it—how could I not be while standing here at the finish line waiting? But I embraced my humanity, forgave myself, as I'd waited a long time and never thought I'd even be this close to the end of this search, so I found peace over and over again about it.

I sent Rae a message on Facebook today about a coffee post. She loves coffee, told her I'm a Dunkin Donuts' coffee fan, said I looked forward to sharing a cup with her one of these days. She said, "Me too." She then sent a private message saying she was not heartless. She'd been ready to do it, and then Sheila had a stroke, then a brain bleed, but she did look forward to knowing our connection. She would be meeting with Jo today. She said she is at peace and ready. Did I dare get excited?

I wake up (it's March 18, 2017) and routinely look at my phone to find a text message from Joyce: "A star has been born a few minutes ago. Its name is Micki." My heart sinks, my eyes begin to weep involuntarily, and I suddenly am blasted into a reality I knew only a year ago; life once again is to be lived without my beloved aunt Micki.

On the tenth, Micki reluctantly went back into the inpatient hospice. We had our last real conversation that day. I told her to rest and that I would always be with her and that I would always be her little girl. I held back my tears, but she began to cry. My heart broke. I knew it would be our last conversation.

On the eleventh, Joyce put me on speakerphone, but Aunt Micki wasn't able to understand me at that point. I'd been calling daily to talk with the nurses, wondering what she was waiting for. Me. But she couldn't hold out, and I knew it. I'd be going to Florida for the placing of her ashes after all. Joyce and I talked for forty-five minutes. There was crying, reminiscing, and celebrating my aunt who I fell so in love with so fast. She kept telling me that I was Aunt Micki's wish come true and that her only regret was that we didn't have more time together. I cried my eyes out, feeling much the same.

Since then I'd been more at peace, but I still went to pick up the phone only to remember she wasn't there to answer.

Back on the thirteenth, I had bought two roses, one for her and one for myself. I told myself when the first rose wilts, that would be the day she passes. On the evening on the sixteenth, I was in bed saying my prayers, and it felt as if someone came and sat on the edge of my bed. I had to open my eyes, saw no one, but knew it was her.

The first rose wilted yesterday, the seventeenth, and she passed on the seventeenth PST (my time zone), the eighteenth

EST. I was peaceful, but terribly sad. I had let the boys know when she went into the hospice. John just texted, "Thanks." Daryle texted that he wished he was there. I was grateful to have Grandma Joanne and Joyce by my side.

Yesterday (March 22, 2017) brought more healing. I had my star-mural artist who had done the night scape on my bedroom ceiling come back, and I had him add a star for Aunt Micki. She shines right over my bed now. Then I got a card from my friend Joyce, and it was a card with a little crystal that represented a new star in the sky and the card said: "A new star lights the night sky." My favorite quote from the Native Americans is "From the stars we come, to the stars we shall return." What serendipity!

It was an emotional and difficult day, yet so filled with love. I miss her terribly. I still have to stop myself from going to the phone. Joyce scheduled the laying of her ashes on her birthday: April 3. It would have been her eighty-third birthday. I was going to celebrate her either way, so I made my plans to go.

I made it safely to Daytona without any obnoxious April Fools happenings. Spent a lot of time in meditation on the plane and reading Paul Ferrini's *Love without Conditions.* Made it about halfway through the book. It got my mind and heart ready for what was to come, which if someone had told me how the next few days would go, I would not have believed it.

My hotel was across the street from a tattoo parlor. I wondered. I'd been wanting two specific tattoos for almost two years and hadn't found the right artist. I was so anxious to be at the beach and let the water, sun, and sand help me heal, but this piqued my curiosity. While checking in, I asked the gal at the desk about her ink, and she said the guys across the street were awesome. So I moseyed on over, and within five minutes of speaking with the owner, I knew this was the place. I gave a deposit, and we agreed that both he and I would go to work on designing something and I would come back tomorrow, review the designs, and then get the tattoos done.

Yesterday was so amazing that it left me very excited about today. I spent the day enjoying the beach, the pier, the touristy areas. I found a pencil at a local souvenir shop and spent the evening at work designing the tattoos. My aunt was on my mind constantly. In the morning I had a walk on the beach, which was really good for helping my back heal from a serious fall I'd taken at the new house on February 4, 2017. I then headed over to the tattoo parlor for a long and amazing eight-hour day with Michael, my tattoo artist. The owner passed me onto him and, boy, was he the right artist! Finally!

I showed him what I'd designed. He was impressed. He said he was not used to people coming in ready with their piece, and we went to work—talking, connecting, laughing. For a twenty-two-year-old, he was quite evolved and experienced. The tattoos were gorgeous! We put henna designs around the word 'Shaman" on my left wrist and the word "Star" on my right one to bring a bit more feminine power to them, and as a final touch, he added a little butterfly to represent Aunt Micki. It was a serendipitous time.

I wasn't sure what I would do with the rest of my time here aside from tomorrow's celebration. I had considered going to Epcot while I was in Florida, but I wasn't up for all the extra travel, and I didn't know if I could handle all the walking with my injuries, so having the tattoo come together was an amazing gift! And I trusted the rest would unfold perfectly!

Today was a tough day (it was April 3rd, Aunt Micki's birthday), but it was also filled with incredible magic. I met Joyce at the cemetery and a couple of other women who were close to Aunt Micki. Micki's photo was there with a lovely little urn. Joyce read a couple of things that brought us all to tears, but it was good. She said that this had to be hardest on me. I'm not so sure about that, but her sensitivity around it always has been appreciated. We watched the placement of her urn in the space next to her husband Joe, and to his left is Grandma Peg. It was good to see where she is interred. We headed to the River Grill (Aunt Micki's favorite restaurant), and I ordered her fried shrimp in honor of her. It was awful! I just laughed, but ate it anyway. We all talked and reminisced, laughed, cried, and celebrated my beloved aunt.

On the way back to my hotel, I stopped by the hospice. The social worker had been so good to me and said I could come by to see the place if I'd like. She gave me the tour. It couldn't have been a more beautiful place, nicer than any hospice I'd worked at. There was a labyrinth in the peace garden, so I took a stroll in and out of it. When I was finished, a butterfly flew by. She was with me!

The social worker said that if I like labyrinths, there was another at the Ormond Beach Memorial Gardens that was lovely. I took note. I then went back to the cemetery. I needed time with her by myself. It was hard, but good. I could still feel her near me. I got the completion I needed and spent the rest of the evening taking a good long walk on the beach. It was so windy. I felt it was a clearing energy and took full advantage of it. By the time I got back to my room for the night, I was completely at peace, although still heavy hearted.

On the fourth, I spent my last day at the beach walking again until I had to check out of the hotel. The wind was very intense that morning, and it was a chore to quiet my mind with the wind ripping through my ears. I chased a ball for quite a while and felt my inner child start to have some peace around everything that had happened. By the time I got back to the hotel to check out someone else had "found" the lost ball, and I just laughed at how life can be. That ball was my companion during that walk and now had found a new person to entertain. I was headed to Joyce's for a couple of days. On the way there, I found the memorial gardens the social worker had told me about.

It's a sweet little area with ponds, waterfalls, fish, turtles, birds, bamboo, and gorgeous gardens. I walk the grounds until finally I find the labyrinth. It's hand painted on concrete encased by a gazebo. There are a few folks walking around, but they're respectful when they see me walking the labyrinth. I take my time, with each step keeping Aunt Micki in my mind. So many memories come back of our visits, our phone calls, of her calling me her little girl. My heart feels warmer and warmer as I approach the center.

I enter the center. I close my eyes, take a few deep breaths, and in an instant there she is standing right beside me. I gasp and put my hands on my chest and start to cry.

She begins speaking immediately, "I'm all right now, and I will always be with you now. Please let John go. Stop putting energy and hope into something that will not be fruitful for you. Embrace Daryle. He is trying so hard and let the rest go. You are going to be so happy. There is so much joy ahead of you. I love you. You will always be my little girl."

And in an instant, she is gone.

I just stood there weeping for a while, thanking her for coming. It was the moment I really needed to be here for, to have my moment of connection and healing with her from the other side. I was again so present to how thankful I was (and am) for this ability. Now it was off to Joyce's.

We had all of Aunt Micki's belongings to go through. So many butterflies, two big jewelry boxes full of things, books, photos, papers. It was such a roller-coaster ride. We did more laughing, crying, and bonding. Joyce and I really got to know each other better. It was good, and I could feel Aunt Micki smiling that we were deepening our relationship. We spent hours talking, sharing, reminiscing. My aunt could not have had a better friend, whom she left me with as a gift.

On Thursday morning, I headed to the airport with a heavy but grateful heart. It was a very healing time, and I was so grateful. I was a little disappointed that Epcot didn't happen, but I felt at peace and ready to go home to whatever was next. Little did I know what was about to transpire.

I get up to the airline counter to check in, and I'm hearing rumors that the flight may be canceled. As the attendant is getting me checked in, the flight in fact is canceled. I'm the first in line to be taken care of. Seriously? The only flight they can get me on is out of Orlando on Saturday, which is two days away. I guess I'm going to Epcot! I look up and smile with tears in my eyes.

I had a private taxi to my hotel in Orlando. I got there, settled in, had some dinner, and set my plans up for an unexpected but very welcome day of play.

When I got to the park, I got a locker, put my things in it, and began a day that I couldn't have anticipated in any way. I started walking past the silver sphere of Spaceship Earth, closed my eyes and said a prayer, asking Aunt Micki to share the day of fun and healing with me. I opened my eyes, looked to my right in complete disbelief.

In front of me is a huge butterfly along the rim of the lake that is made of flowers. It has to be five feet wide, four feet tall. Right next to it is a temporary butterfly pavilion with larvae, chrysalis, and hundreds of butterflies flying around. As I look out at the lake, it's lined with more bushes shaped like butterflies. I start laughing and sobbing at the same time. I think, "Man, you can't make this stuff up!"

As I walk toward World Showcase (where all the different countries are), there are gardens everywhere with these butterfly designs. Every shopping venue has butterflies and garden items for sale. Unbeknownst to me, Epcot is having their International Flower & Garden Festival. Everywhere I look there are butterflies. I can't help but smile among the tears. I'm overwhelmed by the magic and serendipity of what was happening. And I can't help but feel like Aunt Micki set this whole thing up.

People working at the park voiced their surprise that I'd gone there alone, but I clearly wasn't alone. I got to see, eat, ride, and experience everything I wanted to and more. I knew the park well, so I planned my day, and Aunt Micki was with me the entire time. So much healing happened for me there and when the day was over I knew that when I saw butterflies in the future, I'd better pay attention because they were from my sweet Aunt Micki.

We were more than halfway through April, and there had been little contact with the Frangopoulos side of the family. I'd reached out to Jo a few times, and she'd said she'd call but then she hadn't. No news from Rae. I was struggling with being a bit cynical about the whole thing. And I knew when I started to get that way the only thing I could do was let go more, surrender, and give it to God. I knew this would happen, but it was clearly not going to be by my timetable. None of this had! Ha!

It was May 3, 2017, and I was at the Philadelphia airport, waiting for my last flight back home. I'd spent the last five days in Maryland with Dad and Cora. I got to see Daryle and Carissa for one short day. I was not sure there would ever be enough time to be with these people. I loved them all so much. Much of what occurred was about dealing with the fact that Dad was aging and Cora had health issues that made her sicker than Dad was, in spite of being twenty years younger.

At one point, I told Daryle and Carol that I did not want to overstep my bounds, but I shared my thoughts from a nurse's perspective about what I was seeing, and I made a few suggestions. The next day after Daryle and Carissa departed, he called me and said he paid more attention than I realized and caught the subtlety of what I had said. He said, "You *are* family! There is no overstepping bounds." He called me out!

This was so not what I was used to. I could see the old values from my adopted family running me—more to let go of. I actually had a place to claim in this family. I wanted to claim it and would, with joy. I was completely in love with my baby brother. He had a passion for the women in his life, and although I felt he spread himself too thin, made too many promises, his heart was in the right place. He told me repeatedly that I'd changed him and that because of me, he wanted to be a better man. The more I watched, the more I saw him rising to that. What an inspiration!

Moving forward Daryle, Carissa, Carol, Missy, and I would conference together and be a team in Dad and Cora's care. What an amazing thing to have siblings and family show up to help. Definitely not what I'd experienced with my adopted parents. If anything, my adopted family, for the most part, were filled with opposition and judgment. This was another surreal and wonderful experience for me. I felt like I was getting a do-over, especially with Dad.

Last night he held my hand, just like my Dad Lary would. It even felt like his energy. Merle said, "Do you really have to go?" My father wasn't needy of me like that, but he was in other ways. Merle hadn't had me for the years my dad had, so I understood, and my heart just opened up realizing how he felt about me. He asked when I'd be back. How I wished I'd had an answer. My life was so uncertain at that juncture between having fallen in February at my new home, dealing with a severe injury (I wasn't able to sit down for most of this visit), and financial depletion from having to remodel the house. But it felt so good to have a father again. Cora had become "Mom" on this visit because that was just who she was. I was so blessed in so many ways.

I left with photos and many precious memories. John seemed to have pulled back from everyone. He rarely spoke with anyone now. Although my inner child was heartbroken, we detached and moved on as Aunt Micki said. Dad Merle told me John did this; he may or may not come out of it. None of them understood it.

Leaving was bittersweet, to say the least. Miriam did join us for dinner one night. What a treasure she was. I loved that she celebrated this with me and the family, considering she had a very big part in things coming together. I went home, merging further into this person of many names and origins, with a family of all sorts. I wonder if/when the Frangopoulos piece would ever come to pass.

39

It was the last day of August 2017. Not much had been happening the last few months. I finally had found a place of peace and surrender about Rae not doing the test. I'd given up reaching out: it had become too hard. I wanted to connect, but it had to be there for her as well. I sent a text to John: "Hi, big bro, miss and love you." No reply. It seemed futile. So I moved on, forgave, and let go some more.

I had a wonderful surprise yesterday; out of the blue, my adopted sister Sunny friended me on Facebook. She had connected with the mother of a hospice patient of mine whom I'd lost back in the nineties. (What a small world we live in!) When I posted this, Jo saw it and thought the sister was Rae. Alas, but no. I clarified it was my adopted sister. Not even ten minutes later, Rae messaged me that she had ordered her test from Ancestry! What! God and the parents have been at work! The end of this story just may be on its way! Sister? Cousin? *Completion!*

I'm browsing through Facebook, and Rae messages me, she says she sent her test in today (September 7, 2017)! Now we wait. Ancestry tells her there are extended wait periods, which means at least eight weeks or more. Been there. We'll see!

Talk about anxiety, excitement, fear, wonderful, anticipation. So many emotions are right back to the surface now. This is a repeat of two years ago. It's hard to wrap my head around the fact that very soon I could have the last piece of this story. It may not be my last piece if Rae is a cousin, but I'm pretty sure she is my sister. Another surreal time of my life. Wow, wow, wow!

I wake up this morning (September 30, 2017) to a message from Rae saying that we're cousins. She says she is sorry that it isn't the news I was looking for, and she is clearly relieved and says all the other brothers are good men. I'm OK with it, although a little disappointed but happy to know the results are in. I take a look at the results myself. I see that our shared centiMorgans are 2,036! More than Daryle or John! She is mistaken! She is my half sister! We're sisters!

I'm in shock. I feel tightness in my stomach. My head is spinning, and I'm at work and unable to focus. Tears are pouring out of my eyes. She texts me again saying that she talked with Jo about the numbers and realized she was mistaken. She is also in shock. For the first time, I feel a connection with her, as if we're on the same train track in that moment. I continue working, but it's so tough to focus on anything else. I feel like there is a tornado going on in my head. I just kept deep breathing and allowing for it all to flow.

I'm anxious, excited, nervous, so many things that I can't describe, mostly feeling how surreal this moment is. My search is over! My search is over. MY SEARCH IS OVER!!! Four words I never thought I would get to say. My life is forever changed. My gratitude is immeasurable. The hole in my history that ran so much of my life has been filled. How can this be? I remain in a state of shock and disbelief.

I took the afternoon to go be outside and get a change of scenery. I headed to a local event with a new friend, Joani, and a couple of other gals. I needed to be distracted. Rae and I kept texting, seemed like we were going through all the same emotions but for different reasons. She said she had tons of questions. I was anxious to hear her voice for the first time. I was still in some sort of hyper shock yet utterly exhausted. I just wanted to close my eyes and rest. Forty-five years had come to a close almost to the day! It was late September 1972 when I found out I was adopted. In numerology 4 + 5 = 9, and nine is the number of completion. This was crazy!

I'm thinking about the fact that I now not only have Michelle and Mike (who have been the truest of siblings and have seen me through all of this), but I have nine more siblings: six birth siblings, two adopted siblings and Carol who is much more a sister (technically stepsister) than a cousin to me. Eleven siblings! What! How can that be? I'm an only child no more.

Today is October 1, 2017, and I just finished my family tree on Ancestry. It's so surreal to see it complete. I have butterflies in my stomach, I put my hand to my cheek and sigh out loud with a huge smile on my face, then tears. I'm in disbelief to some degree, numb in a way, yet my eyes continue to leak. This is, without question, the most unbelievable time of my life!

It was October 2, 2017, and Rae and I just had our first conversation. It was two hours of joy. Her voice felt familiar. She shared many details about the family. She told her/our oldest nephew last night about me (my sister Harriet's son), and she laughed and said his jaw was on the floor. He apparently is gay, so there was no issue about who I was for her and the family.

And then she filled me in on others in our family. Our brother Gil has been living at home for thirty-five years and takes care of Sheila, their mother. All the brothers of Frank's generation loved to play cards and go to the track. I recalled the photo of the five of them and how much joy you could see in it. She shared all of who was who, and I took notes in hopes of ever being able to remember any of this! My uncle Jack, Frank's twin, in fact, was the sibling who'd died recently in Kingman, Arizona, just hours from me! Another near miss. My birth father Frank was eighty-seven when he passed in 2004 from COPD. And now I know where my smile and curly hair come from!

I gave Rae my theories about the mafia, that Frank and Helen either had an affair or one-night stand, and that my adopted uncle Milton somehow fit in, and that someone had been communicating with my adopted parents, but we didn't know who. When I mentioned Milton Shapiro, she too knew the name! She wanted to ask Gil but was afraid he would slip to Sheila, so we would hold off, which was fine at this point. She asked when I would visit, likely next year, but it seemed that once the results were in, something in her just switched, and she was right there, connected, open, excited. How I wondered what the future would be for us.

I called my sister Harriet for the first time as well. She wasn't up to talking but gave me a very warm welcome to the family and blew kisses and hugs at me on the phone. Hopefully we would connect again soon.

It had been two days since Rae and I talked. We'd touched base, and she'd said talking the other day had been like talking with an old friend. I felt much the same. It was so amazing to have Daryle, Carol, all the family (minus John, of course) and all my friends celebrating with me. All along this journey I'd been sharing with people what had occurred. Everyone who heard the story asked if I was writing all this down, if I would write a book. Well, here it is!

I'm currently in Puerto Peñasco, or Rocky Point, Mexico, for a week's vacation with my Sedona friends/soul sisters, Joyce and Vicky. Today is November 2, 2017. Three weeks ago, my new friend Joani became my partner, one who promisingly looks like "the one" I've searched for all my life. Things could not be better in my world! I have so much love in my life it's overwhelming.

Today is Día de los Muertos in Mexico, or the Day of the Dead: the celebration of the lives of those who have crossed is such an upbeat, joyful, colorful and beautiful thing here. So different from what I was raised with in Judaism, and so much more aligned with who I am.

I'm keenly aware today of how much all of my parents have been around me, especially the last few days. I've set up an altar for them in the Mexican tradition and have all four of their photos as well as Aunt Micki's on it with all the beauty that the Mexicans add to their altars: sweets, water, candles, vibrant decorations. I was to work on the book while here, celebrating those who I've lost, who loved me to the best of their ability, and who have done so much to right the pain they caused (from the other side) and to heal all that they took away from myself and many others. They made the best choices they could have made almost 54 years ago. I'm celebrating all of it!

It is July 29, 2018. In June I had two surgeries related to my fall last year, so my time of recovery had allowed me to really focus on this story. Each pass of editing brought more tears, more healing, and more celebrating.

As I was doing my second pass through of editing, I review the chapter about my name. I google the meaning of Melanie for the umpteenth time, and notice for the very first time that the origin of Melanie is Greek (Melania)! What? I've always thought it was French, but the actual origin is Greek. I was given a Greek name by my birth mother! Which now poses more questions beyond the last two remaining: If Helen knew Frank was my birth father, did they choose the name together? Did she just choose the name randomly? Did she even know it was a Greek name? And what role did Frank play, if any? Or maybe this is just another magical little tidbit of this very crazy story of mine?

I still anticipated the other three remaining questions being answered at some point:

1. What was my uncle Milton's role in all of this?
2. Who was the informant between my adopted parents and the birth family that allowed for Sylvia to know I had a younger brother?
3. Why did Helen give me up?

Maybe I would get to know, maybe not, but truth be told, at this point, it mattered not.

I'd been planning a trip to New York to meet the Frangopouloses next month (September 2018). I had wondered if this was part of why the editing had taken so long on the book. But something wasn't flowing well, yet I forged ahead and looked at flights today (August 24, 2018). They were ridiculously cheap, so I reached out and let everyone know the tentative plan. Rae responded in a private Facebook message that she was not ready yet, that it was not personal to me, but she was still having trouble working through her father's actions.

As much as I wish for something different, I trusted she would move through this just as she had with taking the DNA test. Although I was frustrated and anxious to meet everyone, I told her it was worth the wait for the test, and I know it would be worth the wait for our meeting. But a part of me knew that it was likely I would not get to meet my sister Harriet. She had been undergoing treatment for lung cancer in a nursing home. My gut said she would pass by January 2019. I hadn't fully recovered from the two surgeries I'd had in June, so for now I accept what is so, as traveling would be a bit hard on me. Yet if Rae was ready, I would have gone anyway.

I got a huge gift today (September 3, 2018) around meeting my paternal birth family. My cousin Harriet, who lived in Boston (the rest of the family was in New York), called, and we talked for an hour. It was only our second conversation (the last was the fall of 2016, and it was a great conversation then too). She gave me some great insight on the family dynamics, which helped me understand what I'd experienced up until now. She reminded me that a family was a family. She said she was so looking forward to getting everyone together and meeting me. We exchanged open invitations, and when the time was right, we would meet each other. As for the rest of the family, that was up to them now. The conversation helped me let go more, and I was peaceful about it now. Another blessing among so many.

It was the first week of 2019. So much had happened in the last few months. After my conversation with cousin Harriet, I really let go peacefully. I sent my sister Harriet a few cards to the nursing home. Her cell phone didn't work well there, so it was very difficult to communicate with her. I was only able to speak with her one more time, as she passed away suddenly on December 22, 2018. I do not always like being right, but I knew it was coming. It took more of a toll than I expected. Grief often compounds other grief. Losing her was a reminder of how much I hadn't gotten to experience, and all those I hadn't gotten to meet.

Rae had been wonderful; she'd texted me right away to tell me about Harriet. Then we spoken on the phone that evening. She felt awful about the fact that I would not get to meet Harriet, but I asked her not to feel guilty, as I also made a choice not to come visit in September, so it was on me as well.

A few weeks before Harriet's passing, Rae even mentioned us talking in January about meeting this year. She posted a video they played at Harriet's funeral of her life on Facebook, and after watching it and seeing Frank and them all in the video, it would be nice. It was odd to me that I still did not experience feeling as if I had missed something back then, but I did feel that way about the people I would never get to meet, and what was possible in the present, as it was all we had.

My brother Gil still did not know about me, and I would venture a guess that he wouldn't until their mother, Sheila, had passed, which I completely understood. There remained opportunity for Rae and me to develop a relationship, but I still left that up to her. I was grateful for the peace I had around it now. I had no idea what the future held with my paternal birth family, but I remained open and looked forward to meeting my cousin Harriet this year, and with hope, Rae and the rest as well.

As for my maternal birth family, I was blessed to be able to spend two days with my step sister Carol in October while on a road trip. Our connection is deeply rooted, and that time together only made it more solid. We moved forward as a team where Merle and Cora were concerned, doing what daughters do. Merle turned ninety this month, so I celebrate him every day, as it is hard to predict how long he would still be with us.

I still do not have any communication with John, which has become easier over time. As Aunt Micki said, why put effort into something that didn't put any effort in return? His silence spoke for itself, and my door remains open if he ever chooses to walk through it. Mac touches base on

Facebook just to say hello every few months. After almost ten months of almost no contact, Daryle just reached out again after doing some deep inner healing of his own. It means the world to me that my baby brother chooses and values our relationship as I do.

I finally received a couple of letters from Aunt Tina, which helped me understand more about my aunt Micki's relationship with her, as she does seem to struggle with her past. But after my last letter sharing that her brother Billy (my uncle) had passed away in 2014, I sensed I wouldn't hear from her again. To my surprise, she contacted me on Facebook recently, but she still considered herself a cousin, not an aunt, meaning she still thinks Aunt Micki was her mother. I feel for her, yet I laugh: she has the truth and cannot accept it. I'd spent forty-three years looking for the truth as I couldn't accept the lies. How funny life and being human is. Hopefully, one day she will find the same peace I have around all this family drama.

It was beyond ironic, and such a lesson in remembering that family is a choice, not a default or obligatory thing. I remain in the space of "if someone chooses me, I choose as well." No more insecure child, desperately needing family and to be accepted, but simply embracing all those who embrace me, no matter how close or far their genetic connection. My friend Kim correctly said it would be self-love that heals this wound. How far I'd come!

Epilogue

Every day since finding my family, they are on my mind. I speak to Dad and Mom (Merle and Cora) at least once a week, and the siblings and cousins as often as possible. I am in touch with Joyce, who is such a great support and blessing that Aunt Micki left me with. My grandma Joanne is nothing but a source of joy. My Facebook page is full of family now. There is an elation that comes over me anytime I have contact with them. Daryle has become one of the great loves of my life. Carol is a surprise gift I couldn't have imagined. I feel complete with my adopted family, grateful my adopted sisters are in my life again, even if distant, and the fact that my cousin Beth remains in my life is a lifelong blessing. My door is always open to John if he ever chooses to knock. As for my aunt Micki, I say good night to her star every night, and the butterflies never fail to remind me of her presence with me. I feel so loved by Helen and am forever grateful for all she's done since our first "meeting" in 2002.

In hindsight, I am keenly aware of all the work all of my parents have done from the other side. Every day I celebrate all the completion I have had to this point. I am so clear that no matter the earthly connection, I want only healthy, loving relationships in my life. Both of my birth families are still families, and behave much like many families do. Even that I can celebrate, as there is nothing wrong with it, and now I know and understand things that only DNA can explain. Even the few questions I still have are to be celebrated, as they mean there is still more that can come, which is exciting. The once desperate, angry, and needy adopted child is healed, and I am thankful for all that I have and let the rest go peacefully. No matter who is or is not in my life, I am free. That in itself is a miracle!

Every day I celebrate the success of this journey. I'm happy with it all! How could I not be? I was never supposed to know anything, and now I know almost everything!

I still can't fully integrate the idea that my search is over. The adoption wound can be a very difficult one to heal. Even after more than three years, each time I speak with any of my birth family I hang up and feel deep disbelief, often still crying with gratitude. I recently spoke with Dad Merle and told him he now has a new three-year-old daughter in his life (since it's been three years since I found them). He laughed and said that this was the greatest surprise of his life, that Helen kept her word when she said she would come back to haunt him, that she did it in the best way, he just wishes it happened sooner. In a way I do as well, but in another way, how can I wish for anything else? It's all been perfect, even with the things I would like to have been or wish would be different. This story of gut-wrenching pain, sorrow, grief, anger, and betrayal has turned itself into an ongoing miracle, a healing I was never supposed to have, knowing things I was never supposed to know, having my birth family in my life and all that goes along with it, and most of all, having the truth (most of it anyway), which was the only thing I'd ever really felt I needed, and deserved.

I now have the two most important things I've ever wished for: the truth about my adoption and my person (Joani). And, I got so much more along with it!

As trite as it may sound, if I were to express what the message is in sharing my story, it is twofold; one is to *never give up*, and the other is to never doubt anything you see, think, dream, hear or experience, even if it isn't logical. All of the memories, dreams and visions I had that I was told were my imagination all eventually were verified as things that actually happened. The spirit world had been guiding me all along, unbeknownst to me.

And, most of all, trust yourself, trust your journey, trust God (or whatever it is you believe in). There are reasons for everything, sometimes we are blessed to find out what those reasons are, and as in my case, sometimes we don't. Knowing why doesn't necessarily make any difference. I have learned to trust that whatever happens, it's for my best and highest good. And by far, if I am meant to know something, it will come to me, in God's time. But I do believe that each and every piece of all of our journeys are meant to be celebrated.

Messages come to us in so many ways. You never know what is around the next bend just waiting to be discovered. If I had not taken action on everything put in front of me, I may not have gotten here, and I have no regrets about any of it. Whatever came to me after knowing the truth has been bonus, and there is a lot of it! I couldn't see past finding my brother John, it was all I wanted because finding him would lead me to the truth, but what I got is immeasurable.

People have asked if I would change things now that I know most of the truth, and the answer is a resounding 'No'. I believe we pick the life we have, the main characters we play it out with, that we are responsible for everything that happens in our lives and that no matter what there is always good in everything, if we are willing to look for it. If I changed any of this, it would not be nearly as sweet in the end, nor would it really be my story. I spent my entire life looking for the truth, to understand who I am, to feel as if I belong and am connected to others the way most people take for granted. There will be no greater winning in my life. But most importantly for me: what once was lost has finally been found!

Three weeks after this manuscript was completed my sister Carol sent me a large envelope of family photos, one of Helen that was taken shortly before she passed away. I'd seen it before, and her eyes always drew me in. This photo set in motion a whole new chapter to this story.

In that moment it occurred to me how much I resembled her in that photo, and made a side-by-side photo with one I just took as a selfie. This was different than times past when I looked at her photo and could see myself in it. I can't exactly explain the difference, but it hit me differently. I posted it on the DNA Detectives Social page on Facebook. Out of almost a thousand likes and almost a hundred comments (most simply stating "Twins!"), one person commented that she, Rebecca, is married to my cousin Steve, my maternal grandfather's nephew. These are relatives I knew nothing about! The connection between Rebecca and I was immediate, she extended an invitation right off, and I will meet them in April of 2019. She already has shared amazing family history, some magical surprises, and I look forward to our week together to unite, share, laugh, cry and heal even more. And I will get to see the family farm, burial grounds, meet other cousins, see dad (Merle), grandma Joanne and meet my eldest brother Mac for the first time! There clearly is more to come!

PHOTOGRAPHS

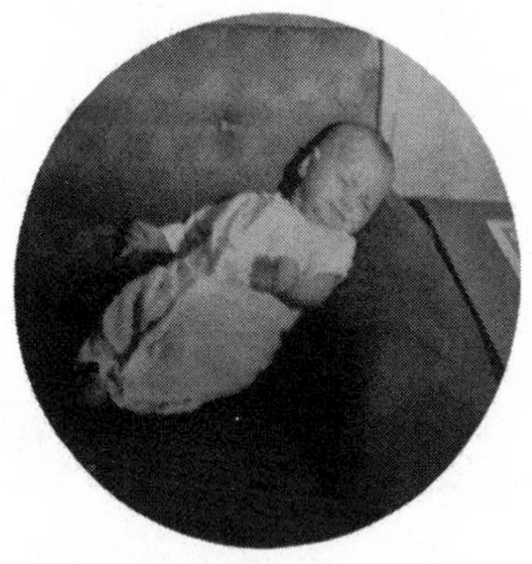

First photo taken of me at 1 month of age, 1964.

Me with my adopted parents, summer 1965.

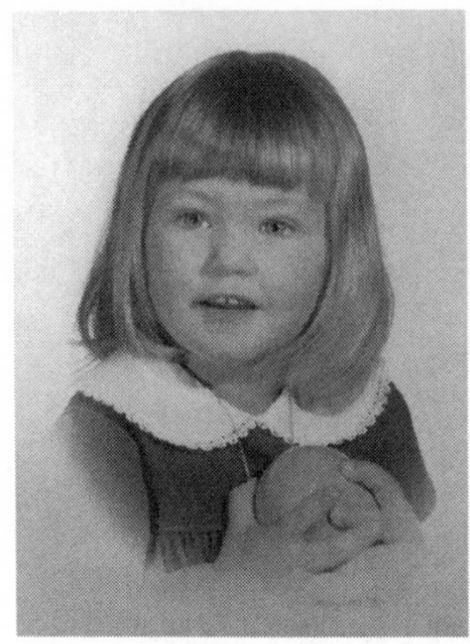

Me at 3 years of age, 1967.

Me with my adopted parents in our back yard, 1976.

Me with my adopted parents on our first Colorado trip, 1992.

My adopted parents on my wedding day with Paul, 2003.

My last visit with my adopted father
a few weeks before he passed, 2005

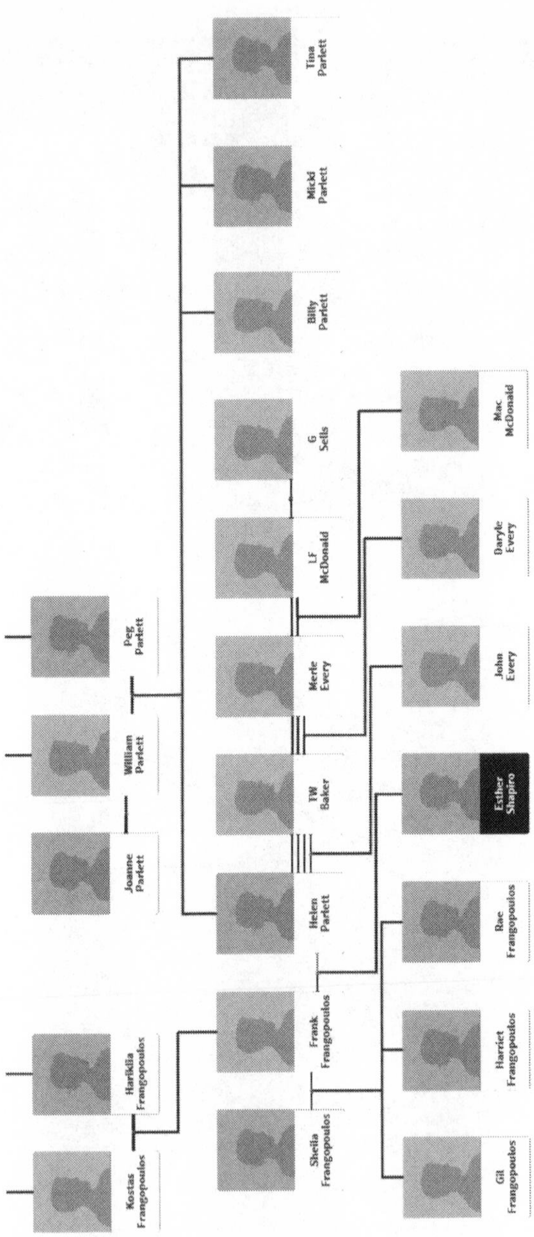

My very own family tree!

Side by side with my birth mother

Side by side with my birth father.

The Every family photo with the mystery blonde girl that I imagine may have been me, approximately 1973.

Joani and I, engagement photo, 2018.

ACKNOWLEDGMENTS

In spite of finding my birth family, I remain aware and grateful for all the "family" I have. My spiritual beliefs have led me down a road upon which I believe we are all truly related. DNA testing is proving this more and more every day, along with the evidence of those who choose to remain in my life and by my side. My appreciation and love for my adopted parents only has grown through all of this. I truly believe now that that they both hated having to lie to me, never foresaw the consequences of the promises that they made, and without a doubt did the best they could. Mom and Dad, thank you.... I love and miss you every day.

Helen clearly has been working very hard to help me find my way through all of this, from predicting my finding John in June, telling me I was not Jewish, to saying that I should use a pendulum which ultimately told me northern Arizona, which is where John and I both live now! I feel her with me often, and now know that she truly lives on through me. I cannot imagine what it was like for her to keep the secret of her only daughter all of her life. Thank you mom, for being a mom in spite of us being apart.

For everyone on earth who had a hand in making this all happen, I am so thankful.

To my sister-in-law, Joy, for giving John a DNA test in 2013.

To my brother John for opening his heart to me and welcoming me with open arms. And, in spite of your choice not to stay in my life, I love and thank you.

To my cousin Josie who did her DNA test in 2016, helping me find my Greek ancestry, thank you for bringing me my Greek roots.

To my baby brother Daryle who chose me as his sister, I love you to the moon and back.

To my sister Carol, thank you for choosing me as your sibling. I treasure our relationship dearly.

To Dad (Merle) who did not hesitate in claiming me for a stepdaughter instead of a cousin, thank you for giving me another father.

To my aunt Micki, who had to give up a lot to open her heart, let me in, and then held on so tightly to her "little girl", thank you for loving me like a mother.

To my cousin Beth, thank you for duping mom and I all those years ago. Thank you for your commitment to our relationship and being the one person from my adopted family that knows this story and stuck with me anyway. I love you.

And especially for Rae, who brought the final piece of this story to me in spite of her own fear of the truth. Thanking you isn't enough.

And for the many other people who are family to me:

Amma you are my spiritual mother, who likely has more to do with all of this than I am aware. You have changed my life so dramatically and have given me a wellspring of unconditional love, a place to call home where I may go to for comfort and guidance forever.

Mama, thank you for being a supportive maternal presence in my life for whom I am eternally grateful.

Joani, for proving me wrong and showing me that God really did make a person just for me, for agreeing to be my wife, being an amazing partner and bringing along even more relations.

And to the two who choose me as their sibling:

Michelle (Micky), you have been an invaluable and unwavering presence in my life for over thirty years. You have stepped up for me when I couldn't be present for my parents. You have shared your ups and down with me, given me a nephew and a space I can always come to for support. Most of all, you have celebrated all of this with me, and I love you beyond measure.

Mike, you have been my rock and my go-to since 2005. You never leave my side no matter how many miles are between us. Thank you for setting a very high bar for my other brothers to meet. You are amazing!

You both have shown me what having a solid sibling can look like.

And to my endless list of friends; thank you all for cheering me on, for witnessing this journey, some for a short while and some since childhood. Having you all mirror back to me the magic, shock, joy, frustration, aggravation, and magic of this journey has made it so much richer for me. I love and thank each of you.

To my editor Gin and publisher Kimberly, thank you both for helping me get this story put together as best as it can be, and to get it out into the world.

And most importantly, I acknowledge myself for having the strength, awareness, stubbornness, and wherewithal to never quit even though all the odds were stacked against me. I am very proud of myself and am still brought to tears knowing that I have brought myself this far.

I can't express my gratitude enough and I remain curious as to what the future holds.

ABOUT THE AUTHOR

Esther is a Registered Nurse, Doctor of Metaphysics, Reflexologist, Psychic Medium, Author, Artist, and Spiritual Coach. When not at work as a nurse, she spends her time writing, creating art, gathering people in celebration of life, hiking, traveling, providing readings (spiritual coaching) and healing work to those who inquire.

Esther honors her guru Amma as major part of her life, enriching her spiritual path as an ongoing practice. Much of her time is spent staying connected with her newfound family as well as her family of choice. Her greatest wish in life is to see a world of peace and unity, taking action consistent with that by being of service and supporting others in having the life they desire.

Esther lives in Sedona, Arizona, with her fiancée and two adorable puppies.

RESOURCES

Websites:

- Family Tree DNA - www.familytreedna.com
- 23andMe - www.23andme.com
- Ancestry - www.ancestry.com
- Alma Society - almasociety.org
- International Soundex Reunion Registry - www.isrr.net
- GEDmatch - www.gedmatch.com
- My Heritage DNA - www.myheritage.com

Facebook Pages:

- DNA Detectives
- DD Social (DNA Detectives Social)

Adoption Books:

- *My Secret Sister,* Helen Edwards and Jenny Lee Smith
- *Finding Family: My Search for Roots and the Secrets in My DNA*, Richard Hill
- *The Primal Wound: Understanding the Adopted Child,* Nancy Newton Verrier

Support/Self Help Books:

- *You Can Heal Your Life,* Louise Hay
- *Feel the Fear and Do It Anyway,* Susan Jeffers, Ph.D.
- *Healing the Child Within,* Charles L. Whitfield
- *The Dance of Anger,* Harriet Lerner